The Cardinal & The Secretary

The Cardinal

The Secretary

Neville Williams

Weidenfeld and Nicolson
London

To J.H.C.

Printed and bound in Great Britain by
Morrison & Gibb Ltd., London and Edinburgh

Contents

List of Illustrations		vii
Author's Note		ix
	Introduction	1
1	The King's Almoner	5
2	The Quest for Peace	23
3	The Power and the Glory	53
4	The Sinews of Power	79
5	Fall from Grace	115
6	Fortune's Wheel	142
7	Master Secretary	160
8	The Logic of Statecraft	189
9	The Road to Wittenberg	211
10	The Pillar Perished	241
	Select Bibliography	265
	Index	271

Illustrations

BETWEEN PAGES 118 AND 119

Cardinal Wolsey, by an unknown artist (National Portrait Gallery)

Wolsey leaving York Place, from Cavendish's *Life* (*Bodleian Library, Oxford*)

Wolsey's seals are taken away, from Cavendish's *Life* (*Bodleian Library, Oxford*)

Wolsey's arms at Hampton Court Palace (*By gracious permission of HM the Queen; photograph by A. C. Cooper Ltd*)

Painting of the Field of Cloth of Gold at Hampton Court Palace (*Department of the Environment, Crown Copyright*)

View of Whitehall, by Wyngaerde (*Ashmolean Museum, Oxford*)

Sir Thomas More, after Holbein (*National Portrait Gallery*)

Henry viii, by an unknown artist (*National Portrait Gallery*)

Catherine of Aragon, by an unknown artist (*National Portrait Gallery*)

Anne Boleyn, by an unknown artist (*National Portrait Gallery*)

Thomas Cromwell, by Holbein (*Frick Collection, New York*)

Archbishop Cranmer, by Gerlach Flicke (*National Portrait Gallery*)

Jane Seymour, by Holbein (*Kunsthistorisches Museum, Vienna*)

Anne of Cleves, by Holbein (*Louvre, Paris; Giraudon*)

Title-page of the Coverdale Bible (*British Museum*)

Title-page of *Valor Ecclesiasticus* (*Public Record Office, London*)

Author's Note

I am indebted to Christopher Falkus for his helpful suggestions on the scope of this study, which originated during my days at the Public Record Office. It owes much to the labours of J. S. Brewer and James Gairdner in a past age and to the fruitful scholarship of Professors A. G. Dickens and G. R. Elton during the last quarter of a century. It is a pleasure to thank in turn Annabel Clover, for typing my manuscript, Alison Elgar, my eldest daughter, for compiling the index, and Jenny Ashby for help in the final stages of production. My wife and family have, as always, been a great encouragement.

N.W.

10 April 1975

Introduction

Cardinal Wolsey and Secretary Cromwell were successively the two chief ministers of Henry VIII; one was the last ecclesiastical statesman in the medieval tradition, who ruled England for fifteen years, the other was the layman who broke the power of the Church to shape the modern English state. Between Wolsey's fall and Cromwell's accession to authority there was no single servant of the crown directing policy, and again in the final years of the reign, following Cromwell's execution, the King dominated affairs to such an extent that he was to all intents 'his own chief minister'. A generation ago Sir Charles Oman considered that 'both Wolsey and Cromwell have been made to bulk too large in the history of Henry's reign',[1] as if both were rather ordinary men, playing comparatively minor roles in what was the most momentous episode in England's development.

Such a verdict has not been borne out by the wealth of detailed research that has been achieved since Professor Oman wrote. Though the King was, indeed, supreme, so that neither the Cardinal nor the Secretary could hope to survive once he had lost the full confidence of his sovereign, Henry was nevertheless content to leave the direction of policy largely to each minister in turn. Fundamentally lazy, compared with his father, and lacking sustained application to deal with the drudgery of routine paperwork – which he loathed – he was delighted to be able to delegate the formation, as well as the execution, of policy successively to Wolsey or to Cromwell for months on end, intervening only when some great personal interest was at stake, such as the divorce from Queen Catherine, or his reputation for Catholic orthodoxy. Both

[1] C. W. Oman, *The Sixteenth Century* (London, 1936), p. 103.

Wolsey and Cromwell were happiest when their partnerships with the Crown were one sided, so that the King was firmly anchored in connubial bliss, had time to enjoy the chase and the tiltyard and the opportunity of developing his interests in music, theology or building. Each minister in his turn took alarm when King Henry showed political initiative or questioned decisions already reached, when the matter seemed straightforward. Henry's interventions, often made behind the backs of his servants, were in general disastrous, for they were brought with an imperfect appreciation of the political situation; they amounted to the flair of an amateur prone to mistakes, compared with the views and actions of professional men whose everyday work developed a sense of continuity and equipped them with the means of tackling the contingent and the unforeseen.

This dual biography, accordingly, affords new insights into the political reformation. The contrasts between the two Thomases are indeed striking. Wolsey, the proud prelate, tenacious of clerical privilege and always looking over his shoulder towards Rome, endeavoured through his mastery of diplomacy to make himself the 'arbiter of Europe'. Although he built up a very considerable legal expertise in the Court of Chancery, he neglected domestic affairs proper and ruled so far as possible without Parliament. The Cardinal was ever anxious to maintain the status quo, whereas the Secretary squarely faced the future and was ambitious to reform the commonwealth, forcing it to come to terms with the modern age. Cromwell, the layman who – unlike Wolsey – had visited Rome, rose sufficiently high in the Cardinal's service for his future to seem jeopardized by his master's fall from power; but he proved to be the real innovator, directing the complicated moves in the breach with Rome to establish a national state, with an Erastian Church, through the legislative authority of the King in Parliament. Domestic affairs, the complete overhaul of the medieval administrative machine (which had sufficed for Wolsey) and the furthering of measures designed to remedy defects in the state and society were to be his principal concerns; the very opposite of the Cardinal, he remained unsure of himself in the realms of diplomacy.

The similarities between the two men are no less remarkable than the contrasts. Each came from humble origins: Wolsey, earmarked as an exceptionally clever boy, passed through the *cursus honorum* of traditional university life, while Cromwell succeeded in bypassing formal education to serve an apprenticeship with the merchant communities in Italy and the Netherlands before embarking on a study of law. Both developed an inexhaustible appetite for work, undertaking the mass of detailed drafting, annotating and finalizing state papers, instructions and statutes largely unaided. Both accumulated offices, the Cardinal being unwilling to part with minor benefices as he acquired higher preferment, the Secretary clinging no less pertinaciously to the junior posts, which were his footholds for capturing the most senior appointment in the government. Accordingly, the one dominated the Church as Cardinal, legate and Archbishop, buttressed by successive bishoprics and the Abbey of St Alban's – the wealthiest monastery in the land – while the other was Secretary of State, Master of the Rolls, Chancellor of the Exchequer and Lord Privy Seal, to name only the chief posts that he held.

Wolsey's omnipotence was in its way no greater than Cromwell's. Both individuals fell suddenly from the King's favour for failure to find the required solution to a difficult marital problem that had been troubling their master's conscience and finally undermined his patience. The two of them by their manner of conducting business provoked resentment from fellow-councillors; neither had built up a party of followers in Council or at court, so each was vulnerable to the intrigues of opponents who pounced as soon as they felt able to convince the King that he was being badly served. Both men were unpopular among ordinary folk, as well as among courtiers and peers of the realm, who regarded each as an upstart, and both have had a bad press from contemporaries onwards – Wolsey enduring the jibes of Skelton, Barclay and others, with his reputation soon at the mercy of the vituperative Polydore Vergil, while Cromwell long lay under the castigations of Cardinal Pole, who identified him as 'the messenger of Satan'.

The flaws in their respective characters have been exposed by historians far more than their achievements have been rehearsed. Both have suffered almost equally from the partisan approaches of the subjective interpretations of the age of the Reformation. The Catholic historian blames Wolsey for failing to reform the Church as legate, and for provoking such unprecedented anticlericalism that the Reformation was inevitable, while the Protestant sees him as the embodiment of a worldly, exclusive, uncaring priesthood. Cromwell is for the Catholic the architect of the English schism, the man who hounded Fisher, More and the Carthusians to their deaths, and the plunderer of the monasteries; while for the Protestant he is the man who betrayed true religion by failing to base the doctrine of the English Church on the sound confessionals of the continental reformers. General writers, too, without the excuse of religious partisanship, have often given scant justice to the two statesmen. For instance the one reference to Wolsey in H. G. Wells's *History of the World* concerns the acceptance of a bribe, and the reader is left unaware of the glories of Hampton Court, the grandeur of Cardinal College and the vision of European peace. A reassessment is overdue, allowing both men to be seen in proportion and establishing their personal relationships with Henry viii. Both Thomas Wolsey and Thomas Cromwell have left indelible marks on the history of England and, combined, their personalities and careers counted for far more than the life and character of the monarch they loyally served until each was overthrown.

I
The King's Almoner

To hand down to posterity a precise date of birth was in fifteenth-century England a prerogative of the royal family and higher nobility. Thomas Wolsey, the future prince of the Church, was not born in the purple and for him, as for the great majority of his countrymen, even the year of his birth is uncertain. It cannot be more exactly dated than between the end of 1472 and the middle of 1474. The strong presumption is, however, that he was born in the earlier half of this span, making him a contemporary of Lucas Cranach, Copernicus, the Chevalier Bayard, Cesare Borgia and his clerical adversary, Cardinal Lorenzo Campeggio. Wolsey was destined to achieve the highest offices in church and state by about his fortieth year and to die in his bed at around the relatively advanced age, for those times, of fifty-seven.

He was the son of Robert and Joan Wolsey of Ipswich, who were by no means as poor or as lowly as either the Cardinal's detractors or George Cavendish, his earliest biographer, determined to answer their charges, made out. Not a few 'Wulseys' can be traced in manorial documents for west Suffolk from the late twelfth century, though definite information about the branch of the family that had settled in east Suffolk comes much later. Throughout the fifteenth century we find Wulseys in each generation carrying on the trade of butcher, which they combined with that of innkeeper at Dunwich, Blythburgh and Ipswich. Robert Wolsey, the Cardinal's father, seems to have moved from St Mary Elms to the neighbouring parish of St Nicholas in Ipswich not long before the birth of Thomas, his eldest child. In his last years he gave up practising as a butcher and though never a free burgess of the borough of Ipswich he served his turn for three years as a churchwarden of St Nicholas's. On his death in 1496 his widow Joan married William Patent. She was probably by birth a Daundy, a member of a well-connected family in East Anglia. (In 1510 Edmund Daundy of Ipswich was licensed to found a chantry in the Church of St Laurence the Martyr, where a priest was to pray for the good estate of the King and Queen, the benefactor and Thomas Wolsey, then Dean of Lincoln, and for the souls of various relatives, including Wolsey's own parents.)

As an unusually intelligent boy, with a strong academic bent, Thomas succeeded in entering Magdalen College, Oxford, at a very early age. He justified the promise his schoolmaster had in him, for he developed his talents for scholarship so remarkably that (as he later told Cavendish) he was known in Oxford as 'the boy bachelor, forasmuch as he was made Bachelor of Art at fifteen years of age, which was a rare thing and seldom seen'. This was the Oxford on the eve of the seminal departure of Colet and Linacre to drink at the fountainhead of Renaissance scholarship in Italy.

The next few years of Wolsey's life cannot be accounted for. There is no suggestion of his returning to Ipswich, no record of his going abroad to continue his studies in Paris, Padua or at another European university in the tradition of the wandering scholar, no hint that he was taken on as a member of a great household, lay or ecclesiastical. The most likely explanation for his activity in those hidden years is that he remained in Oxford to pursue his studies in greater depth. Perhaps it was at this time that he seriously tackled the writings of Thomas Aquinas and the other scholastic philosophers whose books he later suggested Henry VIII might read. The phrase of Cavendish, 'thus prospering and increasing in learning', is the only hint of evidence for the impressionable years from fifteen to twenty-four, and a prolonged, if informal, residence at Oxford would be well within the meaning of his biographer's indefinite statement. Certainly by 1497, when John Colet began his series of public lectures on the New Testament, Thomas Wolsey was a Fellow of Madgalen College. The fact that in the following autumn he also became Master of Magdalen College School suggests earlier teaching experience, though he was to hold the mastership for only a few terms. Wolsey's father did not live quite long enough to see his son firmly established. A vacancy occurred in a college office, that of third bursar. This post seemed more attractive than continuing as an usher, so Wolsey became closely involved with the administration of the property of William of Wayneflete's great college, now forty years old.

That same year Wolsey was ordained priest by the Bishop of Salisbury. Perhaps it is significant for a great ecclesiastic that the date of his ordination, 10 March 1498, is the earliest precise date for any event in his career. This was the very time when in Italy Savonarola was burnt and Cesare Borgia renounced the priesthood. Wolsey was obviously a success as junior bursar, displaying promise of that administrative skill which brought him to power in the state, and in 1499 he became first bursar, a position of great responsibility. Magdalen College was engaged in extensive building operations and the tower went steadily forward under the direction of William Orchard, the great Oxford mason. Tradition has it that Thomas Wolsey was forced to resign his bursarship for having appropriated funds for the work on the tower without proper authority. Though the tower was not to be completed until after Orchard's death, by William Reynolds, there is a ring of truth in the story, for in 1500 Wolsey exchanged the bursarship for the post of dean of divinity. Building was to become one of his principal passions.

His earliest preferment outside the college, in January 1499, was a modest rural deanery in the diocese of Norwich, which gave him the opportunity of visiting his native Suffolk. Next year he was presented to the living of Limington, Somerset, and soon his preferment came thick and fast. This rectory, near Ilchester, was in the gift of Thomas Grey, first Marquess of Dorset, three of whose sons had been Wolsey's pupils at the college school. The boys had secured an invitation for him to spend Christmas 1499 at their home and on this occasion he so impressed their father that the Marquess, 'in reward for his diligence', presented him to the vacant rectory of Limington. After his institution, he had some *contretemps* with an influential neighbour, Sir Amyas Paulet of Hinton St George, who had him put in the stocks. Cavendish's narrative is discreet about the business; it is possible that Wolsey had become drunk and disorderly at a country fair, though this particular tale was first set down three generations later by Sir John Harington. What is certain is that when Wolsey became Lord Chancellor he took his revenge on Sir Amyas by ordering him to be confined to the precincts of the Middle Temple, of which he was Treasurer, for a number of years. Wolsey nominally held the living of Limington until 1509.

Next he acquired the vicarage of Lydd in Kent and obtained a papal dispensation to hold this as an additional benefice. He was vicar of Redgrave, Suffolk, in the gift of the Abbot of Bury St Edmunds, for a bare nine months, but Lydd remained in his hands for some years, during which he increased the height of the church tower. For the last few months of Henry VII's reign he also enjoyed a canonry of Hereford. There was nothing unusual at that time in holding several benefices, providing that when the factor of 'incompatibility' was recognized the individual received due authority from Rome. Absentee rectors, no less than absentee bishops, were a commonplace before the Lateran Council enjoined stricter regulations. There was no shortage in England of unbeneficed clerks eager for an appointment as curate, to see to the cure of souls in parishes where the incumbent was non-resident. Certain dioceses had imposed on them an Italian bishop who never set foot in England; other bishoprics were used to support senior officials in the royal administration, at home or on embassies. What was remarkable in Wolsey's case was that when he achieved the highest summits in the Church, far from divesting himself of his other benefices he clung to them and continued to engross further appointments.

The first appointment to take him away from Oxford and country parishes was when, in 1501, he was selected by Archbishop Henry Deane to be one of his domestic chaplains. This was a post of much influence and was regarded as a stepping-stone for a man of promise. Deane had been Prior of Llanthony Abbey near Gloucester until Henry VII had sent him to Ireland as deputy governor, providing him with the modest revenues of the see of Bangor. In the last year of the century he had been translated to the diocese of Salisbury, yet almost at once was appointed Archbishop of Canterbury as Cardinal Morton's successor – an unusual choice. He also succeeded to Morton's key post in the administration, though whereas the Cardinal had been Lord High Chancellor, Deane ranked as Lord Keeper of the Great Seal. As domestic chaplain at Lambeth Palace, so splendidly refurbished by Morton, Wolsey would have been brought in touch with the greatest in the land and given opportunities of showing his flair as an administrator. It seems in retrospect incredible that only twelve years after Deane's death, in 1503, Wolsey should have himself come to the Woolsack, as well as the cardinalate.

His next appointment seems rather a retrograde step, for Deane had recommended him to Sir Richard Nonfan, deputy governor of Calais, and before the end of 1503 he took up a post as Nonfan's chaplain. Periodic residence in Calais, England's remaining continental strong-hold, widened Wolsey's horizons, for it made him properly aware of European affairs, in which he was destined to play so dominant a role. Envoys from England passed through the town and those returning for Westminster might be forced to stay several days if gales made a crossing impossible. Wolsey could never have grasped the details necessary for planning the 1513 campaign without the background of his experience in Calais. Nonfan, a Cornishman, whose loyalty to Henry Tudor had never wavered, had been richly rewarded. He trusted Wolsey with his financial affairs and here, too, the judgement and attention to detail of the former college bursar was impressive. Before Sir Richard died in 1507 he had recommended his chaplain to King Henry as an able servant.

A royal chaplaincy enabled Wolsey to 'cast anchor in the port of promotion', compared with which all earlier patronage seemed slight. Henry VII, always a devoted son of the Church, seemed at times in his later years more of a pilgrim seeking a crown of glory in the next world than a Renaissance prince bent on expanding his personal rule. One of his greatest cares was the foundation and endowment of the chapel in Westminster Abbey that bears his name. In this quest for spiritual peace Henry, like his saintly mother, attended divine service with great regularity and it would often be Wolsey who celebrated the daily mass either in the Privy Chamber, where an altar stood, or in the chapel. Prince Henry, the heir to the throne, would often have seen the tall, dignified priest at Richmond, Greenwich or Eltham.

The duties of a chaplain in course were not specifically confined to the chapel royal. Any cleric worth his salt would find himself involved in all kinds of extra-official tasks, for the household of Henry VII, like those of his medieval predecessors, was still of fundamental importance in the government of the realm as a whole and was the normal source from which trained officials could be found for all kinds of adminis-trative duties. Herein lay Thomas Wolsey's opportunities. Initially he impressed Richard Foxe, Bishop of Winchester and, by now, Lord Privy Seal, the doyen of England's diplomatists. If Henry VII was his own prime minister, Foxe was his foreign secretary. Among laymen at court who were quick to recognize Wolsey's worth was Sir Thomas Lovell, who had fought for Henry at Bosworth Field and remained very close to him. 'These ancient and grave councillors' came to appreciate the chaplain's prudence and good judgement, and from the wisdom 'packed in his head thought him a meet and apt person to be preferred to witty affairs'. As a result Wolsey found himself used for minor diplomatic missions to Scotland and also to the Netherlands.

He was specially chosen by the King to undertake a secret mission to the Emperor Maximilian I, then in Flanders, in 1508, in connection with the widowed Henry's proposal to seek marriage with Margaret of Savoy. Cavendish's delightful, and very full, story about Wolsey returning from the Netherlands in three days, his task accomplished, only to earn the King's displeasure when he saw him at mass the next morning (since he thought he had not yet left Richmond Palace for the continent), has been discredited because the documents do not confirm the details of time and place given by the biographer. The purple patch in *The Life and Death of Cardinal Wolsey*, however, extends to some 1,200 words – little less than the entire narrative to that point – and Cavendish specifically tells his readers that he heard the story from the Cardinal himself 'after his fall, lying at that time in the great park of Richmond'. It is unlikely that the fallen minister would have bothered to invent the tale and Master Cavendish is more likely to have misheard certain particulars than to have intentionally embroidered the Cardinal's verbal account. It is too good a story and has too authentic a ring to it to be entirely disregarded as one of the myths of history. It is fair to say that Wolsey himself saw his diplomatic endeavours as special envoy to the Emperor as the real springboard in his career. Henry was clearly impressed with his energetic discharge of his instructions and there is little doubt that with Lovell's encouragement he felt it appropriate to reward the chaplain with a post of some consequence. It was on 2 February 1509, the last feast of Candlemas that Henry would witness, that he appointed Wolsey Dean of the cathedral church of Lincoln. This was the moment for which he had been hoping ever since Archbishop Deane's death. The news must have cheered Wolsey's mother in the last few months of her life.

The reward came only just in time, for Henry was seriously ill by Holy Week and a fortnight after Easter, when Wolsey had assisted in the chapel services at Richmond Palace, he died, prematurely worn out at the age of fifty-two. Wolsey, now approaching his thirty-seventh year, looked hopefully to the new reign.

The demise of the crown halted Wolsey's rise, for he was not automatically reappointed a royal chaplain, even though he had become Dean of Lincoln. For many at court the young King's accession seemed to herald a golden age, for he was such a contrast to his father. Wolsey, who was very hopeful of further preferment, was at the outset disappointed. It seems likely that the King's grandmother, the Lady Margaret Beaufort, Countess of Richmond, whose influence was paramount in royal appointments until her death ten weeks after the accession, had reservations about Wolsey's character or ability. He appeared to have missed the boat of key appointments at court when he failed to secure the post of royal almoner, unexpectedly vacant.[1] Royal favour was not, however, withheld for long. In that first summer of the reign Richard Empson and Edmund Dudley, the hated ministers of the late King, were both thrown to the wolves and found guilty of constructive treason. Bowing to popular demand, the young King made no attempt to save them from attainder when Parliament should meet, so both were to be beheaded in August of the following year. While Empson was languishing in the Tower the King granted to the new Dean of Lincoln in October 1509 a house of his in St Bride's parish, Fleet Street. Wolsey made the small house into 'a shrine of all the pleasures' and found it highly convenient when the King was at his nearby residence of the Bridewell. While he would have preferred the more splendid city residence at London Stone in Walbrook, where Empson had lived next door to Dudley, at least the grant was unmistakable evidence of his sovereign's favour. He now 'daily attended upon the King in court, being in his especial grace'. Within the month the recently appointed almoner, whose promotion had so distressed Wolsey, died suddenly and the latter now achieved his ambition of securing the post without apparent opposition. He was soon granted a grace to proceed to the degree of doctor of divinity in his old

1 Wolsey did not become Dean of Hereford until 1512, not, as has sometimes been thought, in the summer of 1509.

university – an essential preliminary qualification for ecclesiastical advance.

The almonership afforded him the opportunity of personal contact with his sovereign, which would normally have been denied to a chaplain in ordinary. Moreover, on the same date Wolsey was appointed a Privy Councillor. From the first he impressed his colleagues – and not only his colleagues – by his zest for work and his outstanding ability as an administrator. King Henry soon conceived for him 'a loving fantasy, especially for that he was most earnest and readiest among all the Council to advance the King's will'. There was nothing coarse about his speech, and his manners were polished. 'He had a special gift of natural eloquence,' wrote Cavendish, 'with a filed tongue to pronounce the same.' This made an immediately favourable impression on the King. The lord almoner had swiftly won his sovereign's confidence, assuring him that he need not bother to devote his time to unpalatable details of policy, in and out of Council, while his interests were so closely watched, provided that he gave his devoted servant sufficient authority to act. There is a hint here that Wolsey quickly came to fill a special role, unknown to the constitution, as an independent, confidential agent of the crown when the great officers of state were deliberating; if so, Wolsey exploited the unusual position in which he found himself to increase his own personal power. The magnates on the Council, lay and ecclesiastical, were liable to be distracted as a result of their other interests; but at this time Wolsey was free from the problems of estate management, building and the cares of diocesan duties, so he could appear to be single-minded and give individual attention to the King's affairs.

In all likelihood it was Richard Foxe, Bishop of Winchester and Lord Privy Seal, who saw in the almoner a most useful ally against Thomas Howard, Earl of Surrey, the Lord Treasurer. As visitor of Magdalen College, Foxe would have known not a little about Wolsey. There is a significant letter from Wolsey to Foxe (30 September 1511) in which he relates with obvious relish that Surrey was not at all well received at court and had gone home to Norfolk the next day, much put out. Could not, the young councillor suggested, the Earl of Surrey be utterly excluded from power? Were such a feat achieved, this would in Wolsey's 'poor judgement' have remarkably good effects. In this same confidential note Wolsey informed Foxe a little nervously that he had gone over his head to King Henry in submitting independent views on diplomatic affairs and hoped that he would not reap the Bishop's displeasure for failing to write to him for some little while. There is other evidence that Wolsey, now at the heart of affairs, was making the most of his superiors' absences from court to assume fresh responsibilities and to operate, so far as possible, outside the normal bureaucratic framework. The almoner's subsequent rise to power could not possibly have been so meteoric without his first having convinced the King of his utter devotion and impressed him with his extraordinary ability and judgement. His real chance of proving himself was to come with the French war.

Henry was in no mind to confine his displays of courage and military prowess indefinitely to the tiltyard at Greenwich, nor could he remain satisfied with the purely personal glory of overcoming an opponent in the lists for the chivalric love of a lady. He had an overriding ambition to cut a figure in European politics, breaking his lance for a righteous cause and, even more, striving to extend England's continental possessions beyond the tenuous bridgehead of Calais. In short he became determined to renew the Hundred Years' War. All this Wolsey divined, and much as he hated the waste and horror that warfare brought, he would not dare go against the King's wishes. A few weeks before Henry's accession the French King, Louis XII, had won a remarkable victory over the Republic of Venice at the battle of Agnadello, to become the master of northern Italy. The following year Pope Julius II had detached himself from the League of Cambrai to make his own terms with Venice and turn against the French aggressor. Soon Louis was besieging the Pope in Bologna and attempting to weaken papal authority by summoning a schismatic general council of the Church to Pisa. In October 1511 Julius II retaliated by forming the Holy League with Spain and Venice to defend the Church's unity, initially by undertaking to expel the French from Italy. Next month Henry VIII abandoned England's isolation by joining the League. By all accounts Wolsey was one of the two chief instruments in weaning Henry from peace – not on the grounds of renewing age-hold hostilities with France, but of rallying to the Pope's side. He succeeded in persuading the King that Rome was for kings, no less than for ecclesiastics, the fountain of honour, though undoubtedly he was preaching to the converted. The other major influence came from Catherine of Aragon, who was determined to make England the ally of her native Spain.

Those last days of 1511 were truly a watershed and they formed the turning-point in Thomas Wolsey's career. He could so easily have been thrown overboard as a scapegoat had operations continued as disastrously as they began, with the ill-fated expedition under the second Marquess of Dorset (whose father had been Wolsey's patron) to the coast of Guipuzcoa, to mount an invasion of Guienne with Spanish aid. In May 1512 a stout army had embarked at Southampton – the finest troops, Henry told his ambassadors in Europe, he had ever seen. But already by August dysentery was taking a heavy toll of the ten thousand English archers encamped at San Sebastian, and while Dorset waited in vain for the Duke of Alva's promised force of cavalry and artillery, his men drank the heady wine of the country with a freedom that cost many lives. Ferdinand of Spain had deserted England to occupy Spanish Navarre and much of the odium for this treachery stuck to Wolsey. Dorset complained about the morale of his officers, his inadequate supplies and general mismanagement, which would make it a fool's errand to attempt the invasion of south-western France. A herald was sent out from England with instructions that the army must winter in Spain, but he was shouted down by mutinous men who had had more than enough of campaigning. Against orders Dorset embarked the survivors of his army.

The fiasco was humiliating for King Henry and grievous for Queen Catherine, but for Wolsey it could spell the end of a political career. He was vulnerable because he had carried on much of the correspondence with Ferdinand himself. In Council the peace party headed by Archbishop Warham gained strength and won over various of the more experienced members. Henry saw the division in Council as being largely between clerics and laymen, for Shrewsbury and Herbert, like his boon companion Charles Brandon, encouraged him in his desire to fight a continental campaign, while the Archbishop had no illusions about the Holy League. It was touch and go. Apart from conflicting attitudes at court, there was the fresh uncertainty in the wider diplomatic sphere caused by the death of Pope Julius II. King Henry was not, however, going to surrender his cherished ambition of leading an invasion of France without a struggle, and he took pride in the fact that before his death Julius had assigned to him the title 'Most

Christian King of France' in anticipation of his conquests. Perhaps his appointment of Wolsey as Dean of York in mid-February was as much a warning to the peace party of his intentions as a further mark of favour towards a junior councillor whose position needed strengthening. The week after Giovanni de' Medici was elected Pope as Leo x, the King of France renewed his alliance with Venice to aid his recovery of Milan and this turned the Emperor Maximilian towards the Holy League. Wolsey had no little share in smoothing matters, so that by the Treaty of Mechlin, signed in April, the Kings of England and Spain joined the Emperor for a joint invasion of France, though the foxy Ferdinand had made his own secret terms with Louis xii.

Wolsey was determined to grasp the opportunity presented him of organizing the 1513 land campaign in such a way that he might not merely retrieve his reputation from the tarnish brought by Dorset's ill success in Guienne but gain undisputed recognition as an indispensable minister of the crown. The smoothness of the war preparations owed a very great deal to the almoner, who was active in arranging for supplies, troops and transports for France and for the defence of the Scottish border. Perhaps it was his noted impatience with the creaking bureaucratic ways of a bygone age that helped him to cut corners and ensure that decisions were taken and implemented in a manner that suited a modern nation at war. In France he himself commanded two hundred men, while Bishop Foxe directed only a hundred. His genius for organization was apparent: he left nothing to chance, worked incredibly long hours and could inspire subordinates. Foxe wrote to him: 'I pray God send us with speed, and soon deliver you out of your outrageous charge and labour, else ye shall have a cold stomach, little sleep, pale visage and a thin belly, *cum pari egestione.*' The almoner thrived on it all. He did not care a jot about his lack of sleep or the interminable paperwork, provided his exertions were recognized by King and Council. He infected Queen Catherine with his own enthusiasm for an all-out effort to bring the King of France to his knees. When Henry was away she arranged that she and Wolsey should exchange weekly letters – an indication of his unusual position at court – and when he had crossed with the army she wrote telling him that she was 'horribly busy with making standards, banners and badges' in those hectic weeks of 1513; when James iv of Scotland was killed at Flodden she proudly sewed a part of his coat to a new banner for Henry. It was Wolsey's thoroughness in the careful preparations for the expedition of thirty thousand men in France no less than the advantageous peace which he subsequently secured from Louis XII that ensured his swift ascent to become Henry VIII's chief minister. Effectively the war had made him.

King Henry, setting out from Calais, began the siege of the small town of Thérouanne and in August beat off a French relieving force in the battle of the Spurs, where the prisoners taken included the Chevalier de Bayard and the Duc de Longueville. Thérouanne's surrender was the first English success on French soil since 1453. Next month Tournai, 'the wealthiest city in all Flanders and the most populous of any of this side of Paris', fell to the English and as the King prepared to return home in triumph, well satisfied that the ignominy of Guienne had been more than eradicated, came news that on 7 September Surrey had annihilated the Scots at Flodden. Some were anxious lest the King's well-publicized successes in Hainault should appear by comparison with the northern victory to be a mere sideshow. Henry had tasted enough military glory to plan more ambitious campaigns for the spring and had hired a contingent of Swiss mercenaries – still reckoned the picked troops of Europe – out of the £160,000 Parliament had voted. At Candlemas there was an investiture in the great hall of Lambeth Palace to honour the chief commanders of the previous year. Lord Treasurer Surrey, just seventy, regained the family dukedom of Norfolk, which he had lost for fighting with his father against Henry Tudor at Bosworth; Lord Herbert, the Lord Chamberlain, even more advanced in years, was created Earl of Worcester, while Charles Brandon, almost Wolsey's age, became Duke of Suffolk. The almoner, surveying the scene in the hall where he had supped so often with Archbishop Deane, knew his own reward would come with the next vacant English bishopric. In the event he did not have to wait very long.

When Tournai had surrendered Henry had given Wolsey the bishopric on the spot, but this was only an earnest of preferment to come that would match his extraordinary services to the crown. Indeed the title of bishop elect of Tournai was to prove an empty honour, causing Wolsey's agent, Sampson, many weary negotiations to counter the efforts of the rival French bishop elect, Louis Guillard. Sampson was soundly reproved by his master for dilatoriness and lack of drive. 'Ye need not doubt thereof,' Wolsey wrote to him in grand style, 'the Pope would not offend me for one thousand such as the [French bishop] elect is . . . I would not have you muse upon the moon, but to go straightly and wisely to my matters.' He never succeeded in taking possession of the see, but long before this was self-evident Wolsey had secured much more tangible rewards.

The coalition against France was not to be renewed. Already Maximilian and Ferdinand were separately negotiating with Louis to extend the truce; all three were past-masters of statecraft, so Henry was in danger of being left high and dry. Moreover the new Pope, Leo x, was as anxious for peace as Julius had been for war, and Henry was reluctant to disregard his initiative, for he awaited from Rome the cap of maintenance and a papal title that meant much to him, while Wolsey was even more certain that he must in conscience act as the Pope required. King and almoner were both aware of the intentions of perfidious allies, for the ambassadors in Spain and the Netherlands sent home disturbing reports of backstage intrigue. There were idle tales that Henry was so incensed with Ferdinand that he was contemplating divorcing Queen Catherine for being her father's daughter, but all this was insubstantial gossip. In this strange world of Renaissance diplomacy, where so much depended on a ruler's personal whim, there was nothing surprising about Henry's *volte-face*. Matrimonial diplomacy played a major part with him as with his rivals. While Ferdinand of Aragon was planning for a grandson to marry Renée, Louis xii's second daughter, who might be invested with the Duchy of Milan, Henry turned his thoughts to the head of the house of Valois. Louis xii had been widowed when Queen Anne died in January 1514 and there lay a marvellous opportunity of interesting him in Henry's younger sister, Mary, as his third bride – 'the most attractive woman ever seen', ran the courtly reports. The fact that she had been affianced to Charles of Ghent, heir to both the Spanish and Habsburg dominions, made the *bouleversement* even more attractive, for this would be a splendid snub to England's allies, who had done their best to double-cross Henry. Through the Duc de Longueville, a prisoner-of-war at the English court, Wolsey and Foxe opened negotiations for the French marriage as part of the bargaining for a treaty of peace. Wolsey bore the brunt of the diplomatic exchanges and held out for hard terms. After much haggling Henry was to retain his prized conquest of

Tournai, to receive from Louis XII an annual pension and also the prompt payment of the arrears of the pension due under the terms of the Treaty of Étaples.

By a separate treaty this *entente cordiale* was sealed by Princess Mary undertaking to marry the French King. Henry announced that her long-arranged betrothal to Charles, so often postponed without reasonable excuse, must be dissolved. So at the royal manor of Wanstead on 30 July, in the presence of Wolsey and the Dukes of Norfolk and Suffolk, the Princess formally renounced her marriage contract with the Habsburg heir. Her proxy marriage took place a fortnight later at Greenwich and plans were hastened forward for her removal to France, as the bridegroom, weaker and less active than his fifty-two years would suggest, anxiously awaited his seventeen-year-old 'nymph from heaven'.

The successful conclusion of this diplomatic revolution redounded to Wolsey's credit. Henry later assured the Pope that Wolsey had 'laboured and sweated' for the peace treaty more than any one. Nor was the almoner backward in speaking about his achievement. 'I was the author of the peace, so I will exert myself to confirm and maintain it,' he told the Venetian ambassador. Twelve months before it would have been out of the question for the royal almoner to have assumed the direction of England's diplomacy, and this would have represented rather a slight on the other sovereigns who negotiated through high-ranking dignitaries. Such was Wolsey's sudden eminence that no one now questioned his role. By July 1514 he was not a *coming* man, tipped for high office in the medium term; he had arrived. At home his support was sought by people who shrewdly calculated the weight of influence he already commanded. Cambridge University wanted to elect him its Chancellor, though he stood down in favour of the most distinguished of Cambridge alumni, John Fisher, Bishop of Rochester. That great Plantagenet figure, Lady Margaret Pole, soon to be restored to the family title as Countess of Salisbury, granted him an annuity of 100 marks for his counsel and aid. Even now he was regarded as the best channel of communication with the King.

While the question of the bishopric of Tournai remained unanswered the Dean of Lincoln had added the precentorship of St Paul's Cathedral and the deanery of St Stephen's Westminster to the already long list of benefices and prebends. These were but an *hors d'œuvre*, for in the first week of 1514 occurred the death of William Smith, Bishop of Lincoln for the last eighteen years. He had been a *protégé* of the Lady Margaret Beaufort and, though intermittently employed on embassies, had effectively dropped out of public life soon after the turn of the century, to devote his energies and his considerable wealth to sundry benefactions. The vacant bishopric was immediately bestowed on Wolsey, since Erasmus heard of his promotion on 4 January and the confirmatory papal letter was dated 6 February, four days after the investiture of Norfolk and Suffolk at Lambeth. Notwithstanding the decree of the Lateran Council of 1512 about pluralities, Wolsey was permitted to hold Tournai *in commendam* with his English see, though he was unable to retain the post of almoner. He was consecrated a bishop in the chapel of Lambeth Palace on 26 March by Archbishop Warham, assisted by Foxe of Winchester, on whom he had modelled his career, Fitzjames of London, who had been the scourge of Colet, and three others. Lincoln was the largest diocese in England and one of the richest so far as the Bishop's temporalities were concerned. Since the see of Lincoln included Oxford, the Bishop had a special role to play with the university. But before Wolsey could be enthroned, he had at his feet the much greater post of Archbishop of York.

As absentee Dean of York since February 1513 he had been content to leave the administration of the cathedral church to Thomas Dalby, the Archdeacon of Richmond, yet he had approached the Bishop of Worcester, the Italian Silvester de Gigli, to serve as his agent in Rome to deal both with the Cardinal Archbishop of York, Christopher Bainbridge, who was English ambassador in Rome, and also with the papal curia at large. Bainbridge, a close friend of Pope Julius II, did not long survive him. Once news of his death arrived in England in the summer of 1514, Wolsey succeeded in securing the archbishopric for himself. Thanks to Bishop Silvester's shrewdness and speed of action he borrowed, on the security of his predecessor's estate, some £3,400 from Italian bankers to meet the heavy expenses in Rome connected with his promotion. Bainbridge had died in suspicious circumstances, perhaps being poisoned by his chaplain, Rinaldo di Modena, and Bishop Silvester was believed by some to be implicated in the affair. The late Archbishop had called him a traitor and had written to King Henry that fellow cardinals were amazed that 'such an infamed person' was employed in matters of state. Rumours were now current in Rome that Bainbridge had been put out of the way by an assassin hired at the instance of an English prelate. An investigation was mounted by the curia which showed Silvester's innocence, for Bainbridge's putative poisoner Rinaldo died from self-inflicted wounds, having confessed to the crime, but refusing to name those at whose instance he had committed it. This unsavoury business caused Wolsey much trouble. Renaissance Rome, exemplified by Borgia methods and morals, was for him unknown territory. Though the papal bull consenting to his appointment to York was speedily made on 15 September 1514, the innuendoes associated with Cardinal Bainbridge's death took time to live down. Wolsey had already been angling for a cardinal's hat through Bishop Silvester and coveted widespread legatine powers, such as Bainbridge had enjoyed. In the circumstances Leo x was in no mood to be hurried into endorsing such distant claims on papal preferment and the new Archbishop of York was to find his patience severely strained.

Christopher Bainbridge had been the only English cardinal at the time of his death and Henry VIII, as a devoted son of the Church, felt it would be a notable slight if England were not at once assured of representation in the College of Cardinals. When news – false as it happened – reached England in 1511 that Pope Julius was *in extremis*, Wolsey talked earnestly to his master at mass and 'shewed unto his Grace how much honour and also furtherance of all his affairs in time to come should ensue to him if that by *his* commendation some Cardinal might attain to be Pope'. But a cardinal's hat was a vital preliminary to a papal crown and Wolsey mused on this in similar terms to Henry's romantic dreams of becoming Holy Roman Emperor. Not so long after his conversation with the King at mass and well before the vacancy at York occurred, he had secretly despatched the papal collector and historian, Polydore Vergil, to Rome to convey his greetings to Leo x on his election and also to broach with Cardinal Hadrian the delicate subject of his own election to the cardinalate. It seems remarkable nerve, yet Wolsey delighted in intrigues of this kind when the stakes were so high. Even before his translation to York, he used Bishop Silvester of Worcester's offices with Leo to try to obtain legatine powers, preferably for life, and the Pope agreed to sanction this, provided Wolsey would give him some credit in the marriage treaty between Mary Tudor and Louis XII for having supported their union. Effectively Bainbridge's death strengthened Wolsey's case, though the manner of it nullified this advantage. The King of France added his voice to Henry's special pleading. Wolsey himself drafted an appropriate letter for the royal signature urging Leo to bestow a cardinal's hat on him, since 'his merits are such that the King can do nothing of the least importance without him and esteems him among the dearest friends'. 'Our most secret councillor', forced to wait for what he regarded as an overdue honour, himself wrote to Pope Leo in July 1515. Personally, he said, he wanted the cardinalate as a means of binding the King to the Pope, though Henry desired the appointment for him much more than he wanted it himself. Since the King of England, he said, had consistently proved himself to be a friend of the papacy, his request should not be refused, for if he were to forsake the Pope, Leo would be 'in great danger on this day two year than ever was Pope Julius'. There were further letters in the same threatening tone.

Any final reservations Leo may have had were overcome when during the summer Francis I, the new King of France, set out to cross the Alps with a massive army, intending to regain Milan. Just before his decisive victory over the Venetian army and the hitherto undefeated Swiss mercenaries at the battle of Marignano, Leo had withdrawn his final objections. The title chosen for his cardinalate was 'St Cecilia trans Tiberin'. The Bishop of Worcester, who had not found the selection of a title an easy matter, wrote to Wolsey to say that St Cecilia was a fortunate choice, 'as many Popes had proceeded from it'.

The red hat with its heavy tassels arrived at Dover early in November and was given a symbolic welcome by the gentlemen of Kent. Wolsey had planned an elaborate ceremonial and it was conveyed to London 'with such triumph as though the greatest prince of Christendom had come into the realm'. The papal prothonotary who had travelled from Rome with the hat 'seemed to all men to be but a person of slight estimation'. To make a better show, on landing he was presented with a sumptuous change of apparel, adding to the pageantry of the procession through the garden of England to Blackheath, where a deputation of temporal and spiritual peers paid reverence. By good fortune Westminster was full of the greatest in the land for the meetings of Parliament and Convocation, which enabled the Cardinal to impress all with the height of his authority. The great hat was taken through the City of London to allow the lord mayor, sheriffs and aldermen and the members of the livery companies and guilds to make their obeisance, and was then placed with equal pomp on the high altar of Westminster Abbey as if it were the crown imperial. On the Saturday following an unusually elaborate high mass was celebrated by Archbishop Warham, assisted by the two Irish archbishops (Armagh and Dublin), the senior bishops and mitred abbots, during which he consecrated Wolsey cardinal – it was more like 'the coronation of a mighty prince or King', thought Cavendish, than any other ceremony. The sermon of John Colet of St Paul's struck a less adulatory note. In all the panoply of his glory, said the Dean, Wolsey must remember that a cardinal, like his heavenly Master, came not to be ministered unto, but to minister.

Humility was in truth a virtue that escaped Wolsey throughout his rule. Even now his presence inflicted Warham with a painful sense of his sudden inferiority, for as My Lord of Canterbury proceeded down the nave men noted that no cross was carried in front of him, while Wolsey had two, one as Cardinal, the other as Archbishop of York. After the service of consecration the Cardinal in his scarlet habit was escorted back to York House by eighteen temporal peers, headed by the Dukes of Norfolk and Suffolk, who would prove his bitterest and most determined enemies.

It was almost an apostil to those splendid proceedings in the abbey church that on Christmas Eve Wolsey became Lord Chancellor in succession to Archbishop Warham, now totally eclipsed, and took his oath of office privately before the Master of the Rolls. In the preceding March Erasmus, with caustic exaggeration, had reckoned he was omnipotent; now it indeed seemed to be so, for in church and state he was undisputed second-in-command under the King. 'In point of fact,' commented the Venetian envoy Sebastian Giustinian, who had an audience of Wolsey within the week, 'for authority he may be styled *ipse rex*'.

2
The Quest for Peace

Ever since the peace with France Wolsey had overshadowed other councillors, despite his lack of high office. Archbishop Warham, although the friend of the Oxford Reformers Colet and Linacre, was essentially a conservative in politics, looking back to the stable years of the old King's reign and uncertain of himself with the young Henry. His advocacy of peace had not endeared him to the King and once Wolsey achieved a cardinal's hat the Archbishop realized that it would be difficult to play second fiddle to him in Council. Some have accused Wolsey of interfering in the departmental business of the Chancery to force Warham's hand. Undoubtedly the latter resigned from the Chancellorship of his own will, and was not dismissed, for it seems unlikely that the King felt it necessary to drop him a broad hint about the wisdom of laying down the great seal. As far as possible Warham would retire from secular administration and concentrate on ecclesiastical affairs, though at many turns he would find the shadow of the Cardinal, especially when the latter received his legatine powers from Rome. In 1515 William Warham seemed older than his sixty-five years and few would have anticipated that he would outlive Wolsey (as well as Foxe and Ruthall).

Richard Foxe was not a contender for supreme power. In many ways Wolsey had been his *protégé* and if he distrusted the new direction of his foreign policy, he was personally relieved at last to be able to lay down after many years the burden of diplomatic negotiations. Within five months Foxe had resigned as Keeper of the Privy Seal, to be succeeded by Bishop Ruthall of Durham. My Lord of Winchester intended devoting his time to diocesan affairs and to his new foundation

at Oxford, Corpus Christi College, which he had at first envisaged as
a house where the monks of St Swithin's, Winchester, could be
trained. He soon decided that the chief need was for a college in which
secular clergy could be taught humanist studies. The reputation of
'Foxe's beehive' of industrious scholars, who mastered classical
Greek, grew rapidly and soon Erasmus reckoned the college to be
'one of the chief glories' of the realm. This new society helped to fire
Wolsey with the grand idea of founding Cardinal College.

There remained a good *rapport* between the two men. When
Wolsey soon afterwards tried to persuade Foxe to return to court for
some particular discussions, the old man pleaded his diocesan cares,
which had been neglected for so long. Had he not so valid an excuse
to offer, he said, the Cardinal might think him ungrateful or forgetful
of his past kindness. He was not wasting his time in hunting or
hawking; nor was he seeking a retreat from the world, for his peace
of mind was troubled night and day by men's iniquities, more than he
dared to write about – of the same sort which Wolsey had told him
were troubling him when he was Bishop of Lincoln. Foxe already
recognized in Wolsey's discharge of his duties as Lord Chancellor
'more diligence and labour for the King's rights . . . than ever I see in
times past in any other', and he warned him against the perils of over-
work, urging that he put aside public affairs after 6 pm each day. The
younger man disregarded this advice. The same letter ends with the
warning that Wolsey, when law term was over, should endeavour 'to
keep the Council with the King, wherever he be'. This, too, he
deliberately neglected, preferring that the great nobles should go
home to their estates and leave him as undisputed master of policy.
Richard Foxe, for so long in the royal service, found it harder to put
state affairs out of his mind than he imagined. A year after retirement
he wrote to Wolsey saying he had renounced 'meddling with worldly
matters', though the waging of wars he had been instrumental in
declaring weighed heavily upon him: 'I have so little remorse in my
conscience, thinking that if I did continual penance for it all the days
of my life, though I should live twenty years longer than I may do, I
could not yet make sufficient recompense therefor.' And then, even
though he refused to meddle in policy from Winchester, he still
could not concentrate on spiritual matters, for his mind kept dwelling
on the latest twists of diplomacy, as if 'I were daily attending upon

you in the King's Council'. The 'upon you' is a significant phrase.

Thomas Howard, the Lord Treasurer, at this time needed little encouragement to return to East Anglia in vacations instead of holding himself in readiness to follow the King on progress. Restored to the dukedom of Norfolk after his signal victory of Flodden, he did not underrate Wolsey's ability, but feared his ambition. His son, Surrey, who would succeed to the Treasureship in 1522, two years before he came to the dukedom, was more suspicious of the Cardinal and came to be more outspoken. Among the laymen in Council the old guard, represented by Sir Edward Poynings and Sir Thomas Lovell, left the corridors of power. Effectively the older men were reluctant to cling to office in the face of Wolsey's pushing, while the King, inexperienced and conscious of his youth as much as of his dignity, turned to the Cardinal. A few years back Lovell had been reported to have 'exercised extreme authority' but now, with Wolsey's rule, he seemed to the Venetian ambassador 'to have withdrawn himself and interferes but little in the government, so that the whole direction of affairs rests (to the dissatisfaction of everybody) with the Right Reverend Cardinal', aided by Treasurer Norfolk and Bishop Ruthall.

Thomas Ruthall, the new Lord Privy Seal, had been swiftly overtaken by Wolsey. He had been set fair for a most promising career, becoming King's Secretary at the turn of the century and a Privy Councillor in 1504. The month before Wolsey became Dean of Lincoln, Ruthall had been appointed Bishop of Durham, but once the future cardinal had come to court it was clear to Foxe that he had the edge on Ruthall. There is no evidence that the Prince Bishop was jealous of the younger man. Wolsey, invariably a good judge of men, thought him most suitable to act as his principal assistant and Ruthall, for his part, served him loyally. It was the experience of lengthy discussions with the two men at York House in mid-1516 on the threat of French power in north Italy that led the wearied Sebastian Giustinian to make his pithy phrase describing the relationship between Ruthall and Wolsey: 'I was really so tired with this long and laborious negotiation at which the Right Revd the Bishop of Durham assisted likewise, singing treble to the Cardinal's bass, that I had no appetite for dinner.' Ruthall continued in the post of Lord Privy Seal until his death in 1523.

Norfolk had accompanied Mary to France for her wedding with

Louis XII and the Princess had resented his presence. To him she ascribed the ease with which her husband had dismissed her favourite attendants. The Duke had from the start opposed the marriage, not least because it represented a triumph for Wolsey. Mary did not doubt that Wolsey was her real friend at court, the one man besides her brother who realized how painful a duty it was for her to go through the nuptials with the old *roué* Louis. 'Would God my Lord of York had come with me in the room of my Lord Norfolk,' she wrote to Henry, 'for then I am sure I should have been left much more at my heart's ease than I am now.' It was to Wolsey that she turned in desperation to patch up relations with her royal brother when, a widow after about eleven weeks as Queen of France, she made a runaway match with Suffolk. A third marriage had been too much for Louis, still clutching at the idea of a son. In November 1514 Peter Martyr had written: 'If he lives to smell the flowers of Spring, you may promise yourself 500 Autumns', and on new year's day he died, upsetting Wolsey's carefully laid plans. His nephew Francis, Duc d'Angoulême, a prince of twenty who had married Louis's elder daughter Claude, succeeded to the throne, while the Queen Dowager retired to Cluny, though not before the new King had attempted to seduce her. Protocol required the sending of an embassy to congratulate Francis I on his accession and at the same time to forestall French plans for Mary to be affianced to the Duke of Savoy. Through Wolsey's agency this mission was entrusted to Charles Brandon, Duke of Suffolk.

The son of Henry VII's standard bearer, Suffolk had gone far in the world. Proving himself of all the King's boon companions to be the 'most acceptable . . . in all his exercises and pastimes', he had distinguished himself as Marshal of the Army in 1513 and had earned a dukedom. Henry had known of Suffolk's love affair with his younger sister and, indeed, had eventually agreed to Mary's condition of being married off to Louis XII: that on his death she should be free to take a husband of her own choosing. Before Suffolk left on his embassy in January 1515 he had been made to promise on oath that he would not marry Mary. During his private audience with Francis, the latter taxed him with coming to carry off the Queen Dowager and when he denied it the King revealed that Mary had told him as much herself. As he wrote afterwards to Wolsey, the French King had made him blush by retailing details of their affair 'which I knew no man alive could tell them, but she'. Largely to spite Henry, who continued to regard Mary as a valuable piece in the game of international diplomacy, Francis encouraged their suit. The headstrong Mary probably shamed Brandon into marrying her, and then both of them realized they would have to face the consequences of Henry's wrath. They threw themselves on Wolsey to intercede with the King, and he kept his word to prove 'a fast friend'. As Suffolk put it to Wolsey: 'The Queen [Dowager] would never let me be in rest till I had granted her to be married and so, to be plain with you, I have married her heartily. . . . Let me not be undone now, the which I fear we shall be, without the help of you.' When he read this Wolsey advised them both to write in penitence to King Henry, with supporting letters from Francis and Queen Claude, for he knew better than Suffolk how badly the King would take the news and warned Suffolk that he put himself 'in the greatest danger that ever man was in'. He added a homily: 'Cursed be the blind affection and counsel that hath brought you hereunto.' For a subject to marry the sovereign's sister was indeed a heinous crime, and a ceremony performed abroad and in such secrecy compounded the offence. Mary was clearly, Wolsey thought, carrying a child. It is unlikely, as Suffolk feared in his blackest moments, that his life was in danger, though Wolsey, answering the Duke's rebuff in July 1529, chose to consider that it had been. But certainly Wolsey eased the return to England of the couple and skilfully diverted Henry's wrath towards the French King, so that he might accept the *fait accompli* and steer his energies towards recovering Mary's jewels and her dowry.

The lovers were allowed to return to England in May. Henry insisted on a public second marriage at Greenwich, but could not conceal his delight at having them home again. Soon they left court for their East Anglian estates. Henry was now persuaded by Wolsey that he must fine them for their impulsive action to balance the account of the expenses of Mary's wedding to Louis xii, so they were required to surrender Mary's dowry rights and pay the staggering sum of £24,000 by instalments; it was never to be paid off. Brandon's marriage had, however, weakened him politically much more than financially. Once described as 'scarcely inferior to the King himself', he now spent much of his time away from London. 'He has ceased to reside at the court,' it was soon noted, 'secluding himself on account of the accusations prevalent in great courts, where favour does not always remain stable.' Suffolk's absence from the centre was to remove a political check on the Cardinal's power with the King, and the Duke for long harboured a grievance, until fourteen years later he had his revenge.

It was once fashionable to ridicule Wolsey's formidable efforts to keep the peace between the European powers. His edifice of 'a balance of power' was shown to be founded on shifting sands and his coveted role of 'arbiter of Europe' deemed to be nothing more than a diplomatic pose. This view does scant justice to him. The paradox was that Henry viii's chief minister was at heart a good European who, after the French war of 1512–14 that had set the seal on his career, did his best to restrain his master from embarking on continental adventures. This did not imply that England should withdraw into her island shell – rather the opposite. Our present age, which has seen the strengthening of Britain's continental ties, can appreciate something of the Cardinal's vision of a European commonwealth and also grasp the obstacles that lay in the path of achieving it. For Wolsey, as for Thomas More and the other English humanists, England was an integral part of Europe, and Europe itself an entity, the *res publicae Christianae*. Since the Pope was the spiritual leader of the west, Wolsey would so far as possible bring England to support his moral lead, even if the development of the papacy as a territorial power made for awkwardness and inconsistency.

The most notable humanists of the day were pacifists who looked to the establishment of a rule of law, which would leave disputes between nation states to be decided by arbitration. Thus, apart from campaigns against the Turkish infidel, warfare would be banned. In 1511, when Julius ii had formed the Holy League with Spain and Venice to defend the unity of the Church by expelling France from north Italy, Erasmus had written from London deploring the coming bloodshed: 'I was dreaming of an age that was really golden and isles that were truly blessed – and then I woke up . . . when that Julian trumpet sounded all the world to arms.' Seven years later, when Wolsey was persisting with his scheme for collective security, Erasmus greeted him as the saviour of the western world. If only the Cardinal's initiative would be taken up by the other national leaders, sinking their differences, then an age of peace and plenty would be ushered in: 'I see an age truly golden coming, if that mind of yours should persist with some number of our rulers,' he wrote to Wolsey in flattering terms. 'He, under whose auspices they are made, will reward your most holy efforts; and eloquence, alike in Latin and in Greek, will celebrate with eternal monuments your heart, for to help the human race.' This concept of universal peace, however idealistic, Wolsey attempted to translate into political reality with rather more immediate success than the founders of the League of Nations four centuries later.

The origins of the Cardinal's endeavours lay in Pope Leo x's fresh summons for a crusade against the Turk. On 16 March 1517, at the Lateran Council, he issued a bull calling for a five-year truce between the European powers; to finance the armies which would sweep the infidel from north Africa, the middle east and the Balkans, the Pope would send legates to the leading sovereigns to cajole them into levying a tax, like the Saladin tithe of old, on all clerical and lay property. The legate to be sent to England was Cardinal Lorenzo Campeggio, who set out from Rome on 15 April. But when Henry viii heard of his mission he commented: 'It was not the rule of this realm to admit legates *a latere*.' He maintained that it was most unusual for a foreign cardinal to exercise legatine authority in England – and never in an England where the King's chief minister was himself a cardinal archbishop. Wolsey steeled his King into insisting on certain conditions before Campeggio would be allowed to land in England, and so the Cardinal was to be kept kicking his heels in Calais for two months until satisfactory assurances came from Rome. It was demanded that Wolsey should be granted equal authority with the Italian – the status of legate *a latere* – and in addition that the deprivation of Cardinal Hadrian from the bishopric of Bath and Wells should be fully confirmed by Pope Leo. (Hadrian, a persistent opponent of Wolsey, had hoped to avoid being degraded for his intrigues and believed that Wolsey had treated him most unfairly.) Eventually Wolsey obtained all that he wanted, so Campeggio, ill at ease and deflated by his undignified sojourn in Calais, was allowed to cross over to Dover.

Campeggio was outwardly given a magnificent reception as he reached London, being greeted by deputations from the greatest in the land, pealing bells and salvoes from the artillery in the Tower. He listened to a Latin oration from Sir Thomas More at Cheapside before he was received with great honour at St Paul's, though it was noticed that Wolsey, his co-legate, and the King stayed away from these ceremonies – it was said from fear of the plague. He was lodged in Bath Place and kept waiting some days for an audience of the King at Greenwich. Here in the great hall observers saw Wolsey occupying a more prominent gilt chair than Campeggio, and while the King stood for Wolsey's speech, both he and the Cardinal remained seated throughout the Italian's. During the remainder of his stay, too, Campeggio was made to feel that he was inferior to his co-legate: 'less respect for the papal see could scarcely have been shown.' The formal audience was an empty gesture, for Wolsey had no intention of furthering the general idea of a crusade, let alone of England participating in it. Henry himself, devoted Catholic that he was, needed no prompting to see the folly of Leo's grandiose plan, and in any case England was too remote from the Turkish menace to reap any benefits. When the King had heard of Maximilian's offer to fill the role of commander-in-chief, he had laughed and said it was but an adventure to be undertaken 'with other men's money, concluding that this should be only an expedition of money'. He had let the Venetians know that they should be 'more apprehensive of a certain other person than of the great Turk', meaning the King of France. Wolsey made a show of loyalty towards Leo's scheme, which had secured for him the un-covenanted benefit of his legacy. Yet he had already turned to a more practical alternative – a general settlement of international disputes within the concert of Europe for its own sake.

As an essential preliminary to this he had healed the breach between England and France, which had widened since the death of Louis XII. As Campeggio was landing at Dover Wolsey was bringing to a successful conclusion negotiations for what he hoped would be a permanent peace. The loss of Tournai had rankled with the French, but Wolsey, still notionally its Bishop elect, was prepared to surrender the town, in the face of opposition at Henry's court, for an annual payment of £15,000. Wolsey's own pension from Francis I on surrendering his claims to the bishopric was £12,000. To cement the pacification the King's little daughter, Mary, was to be affianced to the Dauphin. This was seen as a deliberate attempt to break the spell cast on Anglo-French relations by Henry's sister's brief, unhappy marriage to Louis XII. Finally the Cardinal was convinced that to avoid misunderstandings in the future the two Kings, who had been fierce rivals since Francis I's accession, should meet one another regularly.

Around this new *entente*, whose spirit was much more conducive to friendly relations than the treaty of July 1514, Wolsey planned to form a much more extensive settlement for guaranteeing the peace of Europe. As early as January 1518 he had drafted the main outline of his imaginative scheme, and now, with the help of the Archbishop of Paris, who had journeyed secretly to London, he had made sufficient progress to write to Pope Leo, to the Emperor Maximilian and to the young King Charles of Spain for their support for a permanent truce. With sufficient moral pressure Habsburg and Valois rivalry would, he believed, cease; Italy would be freed from invading armies and Rome herself enabled to regain her old authority. As the first act of this drama England and France swore to maintain this multilateral peace of London at the high altar of St Paul's Cathedral on 2 October, at the conclusion of a mass celebrated by Wolsey with a splendour that defied exaggeration. After the service the King entertained the principal actors to a modest feast in the Bishop of London's palace, but the Cardinal's state banquet at York House the same evening was reckoned more sumptuous than any feast 'given by Cleopatra or Caligula'.

Before long the remaining powers – the Empire, Spain, the papacy, Venice and the other Italian states, Portugal, Denmark and eleven principalities bringing the total to twenty-five – signed this agreement. Under its terms any state that became the victim of aggression was to appeal to the other signatories, who would make a united demand for the invading army to withdraw. If after a month their summons had gone unheeded, all were to declare war on the aggressor. The war would be conducted by stages of increasing intensity. No state could forbid the passage through its territory of an army coming to the aid of a country in danger; there were strict clauses forbidding the hire of mercenaries from the Swiss cantons, and the treaty explicitly stated that any existing treaty provisions that ran counter to the peace of London were null and void. Wolsey's non-aggression pact redounded to his credit everywhere, except in Rome, where it was regarded with jealousy and seen as a 'takeover bid' for Pope Leo's own plans for the crusade, to which no more than lip-service was paid in the preamble to the London treaty. 'From it we can see what the Holy See and the Pope have to expect from the English chancellor,' commented Cardinal Giulio de' Medici who, in a few years' time, would trump Wolsey's efforts to become Pope.

For the moment other sovereigns respected Wolsey's imaginative lead, even if some of them harboured personal reservations about how his grand design might conflict with their own interests. Since warfare was becoming incredibly expensive, at the very least there was merit in participating in a general moratorium on campaigning, providing potential enemies took the same attitude. Old Bishop Foxe was delighted at his pupil's negotiations: 'Undoubtedly, my Lord, God continuing it, [the treaty] shall be the best that ever was done for the realm of England; and after the King's Highness, the laud and praise shall be to you a perpetual memory.' For once Wolsey could feel justifiably proud of his diplomatic achievement, and the Venetian ambassador shrewdly noted that 'nothing pleases him more than to be called the arbiter of the affairs of Christendom'. The year 1518 was indeed Wolsey's year.

The Cardinal looked forward to arranging an early meeting between Henry and Francis I. Initially he had hoped that the Holy Roman Emperor might also be present, but he soon realized such a summit meeting would have to wait on events; once the principle of periodic meetings of heads of state was accepted, he would endeavour to promote wide attendance. The long-expected death of the Emperor Maximilian in January 1519 produced a mood of uncertainty and suspicion. The fortunes of Wolsey's perpetual peace were to be threatened first by the intense rivalry between Charles of Spain and Francis I and later by the turn of events in Germany, as the challenge to the unity of Christendom at Wittenberg in 1517 unfolded.

Maximilian I had been pondering the fate of the Empire for at least six years before his death and on various occasions had offered Henry VIII what was at face value a reversion of his imperial rights. Henry, so Maximilian claimed, could be elected King of the Romans without difficulty; and that office was deemed to carry with it the right of succession to the Empire. In May 1516 there had been an even more remarkable proposal, for Maximilian then offered to adopt Henry as his son, on condition that he landed on the continent with two thousand horse and four thousand archers, to march to the imperial city of Trêves. Here the Emperor would resign the imperial crown to him and also invest him with the Duchy of Milan; the new Emperor would then have to conquer this from the French before taking the road to Rome for his coronation. No one in England quite knew whether this proposal was a further sign of Maximilian's instability or a piece of bold-faced diplomatic trickery. Richard Pace thought the scheme too bizarre to need any warning to be given to Wolsey for dissuading the King from dallying with it: 'Whilst we looked for the crown imperial, we might lose the crown of England, which is this day esteemed more than the Emperor's crown and all his Empire,' he wrote in xenophobic strain. Henry did not rise to the bait that year, nor in 1517 when the offer was repeated, and Maximilian was to devote his final days following his apoplectic stroke to securing the succession to his grandson, Charles of Spain. Yet undoubtedly the proposals had some effect on the English King and soon after Maximilian's death he began to think about offering himself as a candidate. Once it was known that Francis I was to go all out for the election Henry was determined to stop him. By now, with the passing of the old order, Henry saw himself as the leader, as well as the eldest, of the triumvirate of rulers on the European stage, for he was in his twenty-eighth year, while Francis was three years younger and Charles of Spain a stripling of eighteen. As Francis Bacon put it in his essay 'On Empire', between Henry, Charles and Francis 'there was such a watch kept that none of the three could win a palm of ground, but the other two would straightways balance it, either by confederation, or, if need were, by a war'. Their rivalry was at its keenest in the imperial election and it continued to threaten the Cardinal's plans for European peace until the end of his rule.

Wolsey had done nothing to encourage Henry's ambitions for gaining 'the monarchy of Christendom', which towered above all the monarchies with a mysterious dignity that was half sacred. Next to the papacy itself the Holy Roman Empire was the supreme dignity to which anyone could aspire. Only once in the long annals of the west had there been an English 'King of the Romans', with the appointment of Richard, Earl of Cornwall, brother of Henry III, in 1257, but he had failed to secure his election as Emperor, so the idea was both challenging and romantic. While Campeggio was still in England a letter arrived from Leo x explaining that it would be in the interests of Christendom and of the Holy See if neither Habsburg nor Valois should be elected, but a third candidate should enter the lists. Campeggio was asked to discuss this with Wolsey, who interpreted it as a broad hint that Henry should let his name go forward.

The evidence suggests that Wolsey was very lukewarm about the whole affair – perhaps not much more enthusiastic than Bishop Tunstall, who told the King that if he accepted election this would amount to an admission that England was subject to the Empire, a dangerous notion and likely to be 'a perpetual prejudice' to his successors. Wolsey obviously felt in duty bound to follow through any suggestions coming from Rome and once Henry had decided to contest the election the Cardinal could scarcely do otherwise than support him. Yet at this particular juncture, as architect of the peace of London, he was truly an international figure with very considerable influence, though we see little sign of him using it to gain support for Henry's candidature. Since he knew the continental scene, and its personalities and problems, better than anyone, he would have known that Henry's chances were indeed slight, for right from the start of the campaign everything was in Charles's favour and it was inconceivable that the German princes and archbishops would prefer an outsider to a Habsburg. Wolsey had made his reputation by painstaking attention to detail, yet the campaign undertaken by Pace in Germany was ill-prepared and badly managed. Indeed Wolsey had not issued Pace with his commission before he left England, had failed to write to him for a whole month and had then chosen not to give him adequate funds to influence the electors. A strong case can be made out for Wolsey having, if not sabotaged Henry's campaign, at least failed to back it with any show of confidence. We do know of an urgent late-night discussion between the King and one of Wolsey's servants, John Clerk, at Windsor, about the election, for Clerk reported to the Cardinal: 'Your Grace may be assured that I have answered as deeply as my poor wit would serve me, not varying from your instructions. . . .' At the end of their talk Henry said he would 'sleep and dream upon it'. Whether Wolsey was trying to hold Henry back or even endeavouring to persuade him to withdraw his name entirely we do not know, but it seems clear from this that King and Cardinal had rather different views about the election which Pace was trying to influence at Frankfurt. He had entered the bidding too late and then offered sums to the seven electors that were derisory compared with the funds Charles was able to dispense, thanks to his credit with the Augsburg banking house of Fugger.

Henry swallowed his pride; at least it was Charles, not Francis, who won the day, and he could readily applaud Tunstall's words that 'the Crown of England is an empire in itself', so further dignities were irrelevant. Wolsey, too, was thankful that he had not invested any more time and money in chasing this wild dream.

The imperial election was an interlude in Wolsey's plans for the pacification of Europe. The Cardinal now took up the threads for an Anglo-French meeting, to be arranged on a much more lavish scale than the abandoned state visit of the two sovereigns to Calais in 1519. Notwithstanding their rival candidatures in the imperial contest, Henry and Francis had each vowed that they would not shave their beards until they had met, though Henry had to go back on his word when Catherine disliked his appearance. Personal rivalry had naturally enough bred mutual curiosity and Wolsey firmly believed that relations could never improve until the two sovereigns had actually embraced and their courtiers had mingled. At every level prejudice died hard. French children were brought up on stories about the Hundred Years' War when the English 'Goddams with tails' had ravaged their land, while many Englishmen were convinced that French peasants were so poor that they went barefoot and drank only water. Anglo-French hostility had been for so long an accepted facet of international diplomacy that people on both sides of the Channel found it hard to discard their inherited attitudes, and every sustained attempt at *rapprochement* had been bedevilled by cries of 'perfidy' and fears of double-dealing. Even Wolsey himself had on occasion been guilty of hasty judgements and of believing hearsay. For instance when the Venetian ambassador had tried to assure him that Francis I was a very different fellow from Louis XII the Cardinal had retorted: '*Omnes sunt Galli.*' But now at long last there was a conscious attempt at making a clean sweep of history to tie a 'knot of perdurable amity'. Sir Richard Wingfield, the English ambassador in Paris, had been prompted by Wolsey to declare that the aim of the monarchs' meeting was to 'make such an impression of entire love' that shall 'never be dissolved, to the pleasure of God, their both comforts and the weal of Christendom'. It was throughout 'the weal' of the Christian west to which Wolsey gave priority. So rich were the costumes and pavilions of both courts that the name 'Field of Cloth of Gold' came naturally as an accurate description of the gathering; it was sheer coincidence that the scene of their meeting had once been called the Golden Vale, in the neutral territory between Guisnes and Ardres. As the preparations went forward men prophesied that this would become the eighth wonder of the world.

In March 1520 the Cardinal had been commanded by both Kings to make the arrangements and on the English side there were many parallels with his preparations for the 1513 military campaign, which had brought him such fame. In a fit of enthusiasm Francis had once told Henry that he was determined to meet him, even if he came with no more than a page and a lackey, but as the plans hardened over five thousand English men and women, forming or supporting Henry's court, were to be transported across the Channel with all their requirements for a full month. By comparison the organization of a royal summer progress in southern England was elementary. Provisions costing £8,831 and a further £1,568 for wine and beer were assembled at Calais. The greatest care was taken over transporting the thoroughbred Neapolitan horses for the jousts, while the steel mill at Greenwich was dismantled and set up at Guisnes with other forges for repairing swords and lances. The Field of Cloth of Gold had many facets: it was first and foremost a political conference, yet it was also an athletics meeting, with jousting, tournaments, archery contests and wrestling, a festival of music and drama and a series of state banquets. In his own day and since, Wolsey has been accused of devising the meeting principally as a stage for his own greater glory. Polydore Vergil wrote that he 'longed like a peacock to display his many-adorned tail, that is, to exhibit his special appearance, in the land of France'. Undoubtedly he wished to make the Field a personal triumph and, as always, was eager to be in the limelight, but the two Kings were of necessity the principal actors and had they not dominated the stage, Wolsey would have felt that the meeting had been held in vain. He wanted no cause for jealousy, for his fundamental aim was to improve Anglo-French relations as the first stage in a much wider *entente*, stemming from the peace of London, so that the next meeting could be a tripartite one, with Charles v present. He devoutly hoped that other heads of state might be 'encouraged thereby to repair to such meetings hereafter'.

Since Guisnes Castle was pronounced unsuitable for the royal lodging, ambitious plans were made for a very large temporary palace to be built of brick and timber close by and an army of workmen, recruited by Wolsey, strove to beat the calendar. In the end the idea of a banqueting house was abandoned in favour of a vast, highly ornate tent. Yet the palace proper still included three chambers for the King on the first floor, the largest being more spacious than the White Hall at Westminster Palace, with separate apartments for Queen Catherine, and there was even a secret passage to take Henry to a privy lodging in Guisnes Castle itself to take his ease. Wolsey had a suite next to the King's, while the Duchess of Suffolk, as Dowager Queen of France, was assigned quarters next to Catherine's. These buildings, with a chapel 'painted blue and gold' and a porter's lodge, formed a quadrangle. The whole was made resplendent by heraldic painters like John Rastell, who had married a sister of Sir Thomas More. Following the book of instructions prepared by Garter King of Arms, they illustrated it with 'hearts, fowls, devices, badges and cognisances' meet for the occasion. Here on display were Wolsey's own arms, devised by the heralds, which recalled his East Anglian origins through the sable shield and cross engrailed of the fourteenth-century Ufford Earls of Suffolk and the azure leopards' faces of their successors to the title, the de la Poles. His cardinalate was pictorially shown through Pope Leo x's purple lion and there was room, too, for the choughs that the College of Arms believed to have been the arms borne by Thomas à Becket of Canterbury, whom Wolsey took as his patron. As supporters there were dragons that held aloft pillars, the symbol of his legatine authority.

The canvas roofs were 'gilded and garnished' inside and out and the Black Monk, Alexander Barclay, was given leave of absence to devise mottoes and sayings to be painted on the banqueting house and apartments. Allegory and symbolism were thus in evidence on every side. A notable feature of the palace was the amount of glass in it. The state apartments were hung with the richest tapestries and fitted out with Turkey carpets, chairs of estate, and gold and silver plate brought across by the Lord Chamberlain's men. From two gilt pillars, bearing statues of Cupid and Bacchus, flowed streams of malmsey and claret respectively, free for all. In all this there was intense competition with the French preparations at Ardres. Reports on the progress of the French pavilions spurred on the English workmen to excel themselves and there was welcome relief at Guisnes when it was heard that the roof of the principal French pavilion had been torn off by a high wind. The chief courtiers had been assigned rooms in Guisnes Castle, the others were found accommodation in the encampment of nearly four hundred tents that Richard Gibson, master of the King's hales, tents and pavilions, had erected in neighbouring fields. But Gibson's *tour de force* was the banqueting house, 'the most sumptuous ever', covered outside by cloth painted to resemble brickwork *à l'antique* and decorated inside with cloth of gold and silver, interlaced with the Tudor colours of white and green. One Italian thought this English palace so superb that even Leonardo could not have surpassed it; another compared it to the fairytale palaces of Ariosto's *Orlando Furioso*. If showmanship was all, the Cardinal's men had brilliantly achieved the right setting to show off their King and their master.

On this peaceful expedition to France Henry took with him 114 nobles, ecclesiastical peers and gentlemen, comprising Wolsey, Archbishop Warham, the Dukes of Buckingham and Suffolk, the Marquess of Dorset, 10 earls, 5 bishops, 20 barons, 4 knights of the garter and 70 knights. Also in his retinue were Secretary Pace, the Master of the Rolls, 12 chaplains, 12 sergeants at arms, all the kings of arms, heralds and pursuivants, 200 guards, 70 grooms of the chamber and another 266 additional household officers. All these brought their own servants; Wolsey extravagantly allowed himself 12 chaplains, 50 gentlemen and 237 servants, though he permitted the two dukes to bring only 140 men apiece and the Archbishop of Canterbury a mere 70. The King's entire retinue amounted to 3,997 persons. The Queen's retinue of 267 included the Earl of Derby, Bishop Fisher of Rochester, the Duchess of Buckingham, 6 countesses and 12 baronesses, who with their servants numbered 1,175, bringing the grand total to 5,172 men and women, who required the services of 2,865 horses. Never before had the English court moved abroad in such strength and in such style. In the King's absence the government of the realm was entrusted to Lord Treasurer Norfolk and the Bishop of Winchester, both of them glad to be separated from the Cardinal.

Petty rivalries provoked a series of disputes about the number of attendants each King should bring to the Field, the date of the meeting and the exact place where the monarchs should embrace; there were thorny problems of precedence and etiquette and the rules under which the jousts were to be held had to be agreed. Most of these awkward questions were amicably settled, but there was a much greater cause for friction when Charles v arrived at Dover from Spain on 26 May for discussions with Henry. They agreed to continue these at Calais when the Field of Cloth of Gold was over. The French were intensely suspicious of these developments, which effectively prevented the meeting between Francis and Henry from being more than a spectacular display of national rivalry.

Despite the exceptional preparations being made at Calais and Guisnes for the festivities and the fact that most of the household officials were already out of England, the Emperor was entertained lavishly at Dover and Canterbury during his five-day visit. Wolsey naturally dominated the service held in Warham's cathedral church, and at the state banquet he regarded himself as the King's equal by virtue of his legacy. His insistence on his rightful precedence on this occasion angered the dukes and earls present. At the state banquet at Canterbury 'love-lorn youths' waited at table on the Spanish ladies and, we are told, some of the Spaniards were quite overcome by their amorous pursuits. The Count of Capra, for instance, fainted and had to be carried out. The old Duke of Alva opened the ball by dancing the *Gloves of Spain* to the tune of the fife, and dancing in the Spanish fashion continued until daybreak. They left Canterbury in a torchlight procession, to make their farewells 5 miles outside the city. Charles sailed from Sandwich for Flanders and Henry, accompanied by Wolsey, embarked at Dover for Calais on 31 May. In fact there is no evidence to convict Henry of duplicity in his negotiations, for Charles found that he could not draw him to join the coming struggle against Francis.

On 1 June, the day after Henry arrived at Calais, he sent Wolsey on a solemn embassy to Francis I, who was by now impatient of further delays and full of suspicion about the Dover meeting with the Emperor. The Cardinal rode out on his mule for the French camp at Ardres with great pomp, wearing a robe of crimson figured velvet and his red-tasselled hat. Preceded by his cross bearers, he was accompanied by a large retinue from his own household as well as six bishops and a detachment of royal archers in scarlet and crimson. It was an impressive procession, though not much more remarkable than his routine appearances in England. A delegation of French nobles and ecclesiastics came out to welcome him and escort him through the gates of Ardres, where Francis was waiting on horseback. Here the two embraced, though without dismounting; this was usual with royalty and Wolsey, as his sovereign's personal representative, felt sure he must follow royal practice. There were lengthy conversations at Francis's lodging and these were continued the following day. Italian despatches mention that Wolsey tried hard, first, to obtain Francis's consent to extending the invitation to Charles v and then, when this proved unacceptable, to offer himself as mediator between Valois and Habsburg. The heads of a new treaty, which Henry and Francis would ratify during the month, were agreed. This treaty was designed to safeguard the betrothal of Mary to the Dauphin, a marriage that Francis thought would be vulnerable to imperial advances. French obligations to pay Henry the arrears of the pension due under the 1475 treaty, as well as the compensation for Tournai, were also strengthened. Since French influence in Scotland remained a perennial cause of friction, it was agreed that Anglo-Scottish disputes should be settled jointly by the Queen Mother of France and the Cardinal. The discussions at Ardres cannot have been simple, for there are hints that Wolsey's command of French was imperfect, even though it was vastly superior to the French King's grasp of Latin.

On Corpus Christi day Henry and Francis, supported by the greatest of their courtiers, rode to opposite edges of the Val d'Or at a signal from cannon. For a tense moment they waited, as if in full battle array, and then, as trumpets sounded, the sovereigns galloped forward to the appointed place and, still mounted, embraced. There followed feats of arms in full pageantry, with elaborate symbolism, so that the men could show off their martial prowess before the ladies watching from the galleries. The challenge was in three parts: jousting at the tilt, a tournament in the open field and finally a combat on foot at the barriers, all conducted according to very precise rules, with an elaborate system of scoring. Contestants in the lists had to present their shields and issue challenges at the Tree of Honour, an artificial affair of hawthorn and raspberry (symbols of the Kings) decked out with a miscellaneous array of fruits and leaves. There was a tricky moment when there was doubt among the heralds about which monarch should first hang his shield and in which position, but Henry settled the matter by causing Francis's arms to be placed on the right and his own on the left, at the same height.

The trappings of the horses and the series of costumes worn by the riders from both courts, changed for each course, added to the colour of this midsummer pageantry. The gold-worked 'basil trees' on the clothes of some of the English participants were pulled off at the end of the day and worn in the belts of their French opponents. On one occasion Henry's bay horse had trappings of cloth of gold with waves of 'waterworks', each wave being wrought and friezed with damask gold, symbolizing England's mastery of the narrow seas. It is worth remembering that though the Kings and their parties were the authors of the challenge, at no time did they take part in any joust or combat against each other, so personal rivalry was avoided. When on the spur of the moment Henry asked Francis to wrestle with him, he found himself thrown to the ground in a masterly way by his opponent and was much put out. He did, however, acquit himself well in the archery contest. While the English ladies were watching the jousts they drank rather freely, passing round a large flask of wine, which each put to her lips, and also drank out of large cups that circulated at least twenty times among them and the French nobles who kept them company. It was the English custom of sharing the same cup, rather than the amount of wine consumed, that shocked foreigners. At one banquet King Francis surpassed himself with a display of gallantry by going round the hall cap in hand kissing all the English ladies in turn, 'save four or five that were old and not fair standing together'.

At noon of Saturday 23 June a solemn mass was celebrated by Wolsey in a temporary chapel erected on the site of the lists. The choirs of the English and French chapels royal sang alternately. Cornish had trained his gentlemen and children to perfection; they may well have included in their repertoire a motet by Fayrfax, who was present. Before the benediction Richard Pace faced the illustrious congregation to deliver a Latin speech on the theme that the mass heard by the two courts was to the honour of God and the court of heaven, to confirm good friendship, and that to mark the occasion the

Cardinal would grant plenary indulgence and absolution to all present. During the mass a firework in the shape of a dragon, intended for the evening's St John's eve festivities, was accidentally set alight and caused some confusion. Afterwards Wolsey laid a foundation-stone for a chapel of Our Lady of Friendship, to be jointly built and maintained by the Kings of England and France. Alas, the chapel was never built. At the conclusion of the festivities the new treaty, negotiated by Wolsey with Francis at Ardres, was solemnly ratified by both Kings.

The tide of goodwill was still running strongly when the meeting came to an end, and it is fair to say that only Wolsey could have stage-managed these ceremonies and festivities to avoid friction during the full month. The role of 'arbiter of Europe' required him to deal as impartially with Charles v as he had with the French, making it plain that friendships, even on the scale of the Field of Cloth of Gold, were not exclusive. Henry was now bound to Francis by 'great concordances . . . in personages, appetites and manners', but this was to be balanced by his warm relations of 'fraternal love and consanguity' with Charles. If the Cardinal had his way, England's studied neutrality would prevent the major powers from aggression.

There was no duplicity when Henry again met Charles within a fortnight of bidding adieu to Francis. At first they discussed developments at Gravelines and then the Emperor and the Archduchess Margaret returned to spend two days at Calais as guests of the English in a newly built pavilion of honour, though the entertainments were something of an anticlimax after the French festivities. Their meeting was no less cordial than at Dover, but Wolsey refused to betray England's new accord with France and firmly resisted efforts by the Emperor both to press Henry into an alliance against Francis and to annul Mary's betrothal. King and Cardinal returned to England well satisfied that the peace of Europe embodied in the treaty of London would hold. The Cardinal took a holiday from state papers by going on a pilgrimage to Walsingham.

The splendour of June 1520 saw Wolsey at the zenith of his power and influence in Europe. It was cynical of Erasmus to predict that the meeting would be a waste of time and it was easy for John Fisher, Bishop of Rochester, to preach before the end of the year a telling sermon on the theme of heavenly and earthly joys, in which he lamented the extravagance of the 'midsummer games' between Guisnes and Ardres. Anglo-French friendship was to prove too fragile to survive, but the attempts at understanding and camaraderie were made in earnest. Even if in retrospect the Field of Cloth of Gold settled nothing, the superb vision of what might have been remains.

There was a higher honour still that many of his contemporaries thought was Wolsey's due – the papacy, yet the extent to which he may himself have coveted it has continued to puzzle posterity. It is hard to take his own expressions of unwillingness and unworthiness at their face value. A churchman of Wolsey's stamp, who had so often turned his face to Rome, cannot have been indifferent to the signal distinction of being regarded as a serious candidate, and he was at various times personally assured of the support that both Francis and Charles v could command in the curia, as well as the firm backing of his own sovereign. A man of Wolsey's pride could only have smiled with deep satisfaction when Margaret of Savoy – whom he had flattered by addressing as 'Mother' – wrote to say she looked forward to becoming 'mother' of her 'father', that is the Holy Father. He was so ambitious in his swift ascent through the *cursus honorum* at Henry's court, that it would have been out of keeping if he had not on occasion set his sights on the triple crown, nor considered that he could have worn it with distinction. But the calculating prudence of one well versed in diplomacy made him realize that his chances were slight, for anything could happen in a conclave where there was no obvious candidate.

For a cardinal aspiring to the papacy, however, Wolsey remained surprisingly indifferent to the power struggles within the Roman curia. He had never visited the Holy City and had scant patience with those who thought that he should; the only cardinal with whom he was personally acquainted was Lorenzo Campeggio, whom he had slighted in 1518; and he stayed strangely ignorant of personalities and procedures and made no attempt to build up a personal following by securing the election of Englishmen or people of other nationalities to the cardinalate. Wolsey had even forgotten to collect the revenues of the Church of St Cecilia, to which he was entitled – a strange lapse for a man with a marked trait for levying every penny of his dues. The Cardinal Archbishop of York was, in short, that surprising figure, a 'non-curial cardinal', a type of churchman that the Italians in particular found hard to understand. Pope Leo x was indignant that he should write to him so infrequently, when he had so much to report about diplomatic affairs, while other cardinals wrote regularly about nothing in particular. Consequently, to maintain that Thomas Wolsey had passionate ambitions for the papal crown makes a little sense, unless he deliberately set out to pretend, by his utterly detached attitude, that he was indifferent to the honour of election. It would be as if a modern statesman with ambitions to become Secretary-General of the United Nations had never set foot in a foreign capital or attended a diplomatic reception in his own.

The Emperor Charles v had first suggested to Wolsey that he would back his candidature in 1520, when there was no immediate prospect of an election, and the following year this became a firm offer, both to Wolsey and to his sovereign, with whom Charles discussed it. Henry was immediately captivated by the idea, for he was very conscious of the fact that there had been no English-born pope since Nicholas Breakspear had become Adrian iv in the twelfth century. To secure Wolsey's election would therefore greatly redound to his credit, quite apart from the obvious political advantages. When Leo x died in December 1521, Wolsey's name was vigorously canvassed, though he made clear that he had entered the election only in obedience to his King.

As in the imperial election of 1519, Wolsey sent Pace as a special envoy, and once again Pace arrived on the scene too late. Wolsey had armed him with two recommendations, one for himself and a second in favour of Cardinal Giulio de' Medici; for the Englishman the primary objective was not his own election but the defeat of the French candidate. A letter in which Wolsey had offered to pay for imperial troops to march on Rome to overpower the conclave can be interpreted only as a threat to overturn French intrigues. John Clerk, the English agent in Rome, who worked closely with Pace, wrote to Wolsey when the result was announced: 'I did not greatly labour before their entry into the conclave, because your Grace at my departing showed me precisely that you would never meddle therewith. And on my faith were not the King's persuasions I should stand yet in great doubt whether your Grace would accept it or no.' This speaks volumes for Wolsey's personal attitude. In the event he secured perhaps as many as six votes, possibly more, all in the fifth scrutiny. John Clerk, dependent on what cardinals chose to tell him, was talked into believing that on the fourth count he had won as many as nineteen votes and that had only three other cardinals been prepared to declare for him he would have been home and dry. This in fact seems most unlikely. Giulio de' Medici claimed to have spoken up for him in the conclave, which tallies ill with his remarks three years before about Wolsey's slighting treatment of the Pope and Rome. Significantly Cardinal Petrucci made the point to Pace that the majority of the electors 'would not consent to his election, alleging he would never come to Rome'. Any outside chance he had was ruined in part by his 'non-curial' attitude, in part by Charles v going back on his word, for it was the Emperor's old tutor, Adrian of Utrecht, then residing in Spain, who won the day.

There are indications that this election of a non-Italian in January 1522 encouraged Wolsey to believe that it would be worth fighting another election if the opportunity arose. Certainly the ascetic and aged Adrian vi was in poor health and Clerk made the extraordinary proposal to Wolsey that he might be persuaded to journey to Rome via England, where he would surely find the climate so hard that his end would be hastened – and if he did die in England, 'your Grace might be present at the next election'. When Pace heard of this outlandish scheme he underlined that a papal election could take place only in Rome, regardless of where the reigning pontiff expired. There is not the slightest hint that Wolsey regarded Clerk's suggestion with anything but disdain.

Adrian vi's death on 14 September 1523 after so short a pontificate offered Wolsey a second chance rather too soon, for there had been no time to develop an 'English faction' in Rome. Once more he seems to have been pushed into the election by his sovereign, though he was probably less reluctant than at the close of 1521. He protested privately to Pace that he would rather end his days in the King's service, remaining in England, instead of 'mine old days approaching, to enter into new things', but his master had been adamant: 'The mind and entire desire of His Highness, above all earthly things, is that I shall attain to the said dignity,' he wrote. The way this was put makes one discount as flattery Wolsey's private comment to Henry that he would rather remain his minister than be 'ten popes'.

In the autumn of 1523 he moved rapidly, sending his agents two sets of instructions in the King's name. The first letters recommended the Cardinal of York in forceful terms, praising his diplomatic ability and his character as a statesman who had striven hard for international peace and whose present aim was to bring 'final rest, peace and quiet'. The electors should not think he was another Adrian, all austerity and bleakness – in fact it would have been amazing if Wolsey's reputation for grandeur and high living had not reached Rome – but a churchman who would bring unexampled credit to the highest office. Moreover if some counted it against him that he had so far been an absentee cardinal, they should accept unquestioningly his present pledge to come to Rome within three months of his election, where he would be joined by Henry, ready to lead a crusade against the Turks. The alternative set of instructions, promoting Giulio de' Medici's candidature, was to be produced only if it was clear that there really was sufficient support for him to make Wolsey's bid irrelevant.

In the conclave the key figures were de' Medici himself, Campeggio, Colonna and Pucci. Some energetic canvassing was undertaken for Wolsey but, as previously, his absence counted heavily against him. 'One thing we be right sure of,' reported Clerk, 'if your Grace were here present ye should be as sure of it as ye be of York.' But the Italian cardinals feared that an absentee would move the historic centre of the Church to foreign parts. In one of the scrutinies on 16 October Wolsey appears to have done rather better than in the previous election; some, Clerk wrote hopefully, would rather 'go to Jerusalem upon their thumbs' than pass over Wolsey as a most fitting candidate. Cardinal Colonna, who swayed not a few, was in principle against Wolsey, though he would do all he could to prevent the election of another Medici pope. The election was a long-drawn-out process, lasting from 1 to 23 November, during which time the citizens of Rome became restive. From the interim reports reaching London there seemed a chance that Wolsey might be accepted as a compromise candidate, though this would have been a doubtful victory compared with an unambiguous vote of confidence and would scarcely have been to Henry VIII's liking. In fact almost to a man the cardinals feared the consequences of choosing a non-Italian who was not personally known to them. So once Colonna had been persuaded to withdraw his opposition to the Medici party, Giulio was elected as Clement VII.

When the news reached him Wolsey wrote a warm letter to the

new Pope as 'his singular and especial lover and friend' no less than as 'the Protector of England', telling him how delighted he was to learn of his election, which he had so entirely deserved 'above all spiritual persons living'. His pen could not adequately express his great joy at Giulio's being called to the supreme governance of Christ's religion, 'being far more joyful thereof than if it had happened upon mine own person'. Empty words? Ironical, certainly, in the light of Wolsey's later difficulties with Rome, but not entirely an essay in flattery. Wolsey's disappointment was largely a reflection of the disappointment felt by his master; it was overshadowed by personal relief that he would not after all have to take on an office fraught with so many difficulties at a time when the Church of Rome was being attacked more seriously than ever before. He knew, or thought he knew, where he was with King Henry, but Rome was unknown terrain. Had he won the tiara he would have found his relations with the King of England, no less than those with the Emperor and the King of France, an intolerable strain. He would have found himself in a largely hostile community rent by factions, dealing with institutions, headed by churchmen who were past-masters at obstruction and intrigue. And if by some miracle his elevation had come about it is by no means certain that five years later he would have been prepared to grant Henry his divorce from Catherine of Aragon.

Peace was fragile. From the timber used for the pavilions the French were fortifying Ardres, while the imperialists were urging Henry to violate his promise of amity with France. Wolsey constantly pointed out that his sovereign was bound to Charles v 'by good peace, fraternal love and consanguity', but at the same time held Francis I in special affection. If England could not actually hold 'the balance of power', the Cardinal would mediate between Habsburg and Valois, and advise his King to 'pass between and stay them both'. As he commented in May 1521, mediation was the most honourable and Christian cause to follow: it avoided bloodshed, 'the consuming of treasure, subversion of realms, depopulation and desolation of countries'. Only if mediation and moral sanctions failed would England throw her weight against the aggressor who upset the balance, as the treaty of London required. Once hostilities proper had begun, with France in the role of the guilty party, the Emperor at once called on England to come to his aid under treaty obligations. Henry himself was eager to fight as Charles's ally. But, since money was short, he allowed Wolsey to go to Calais as mediator, though under cover of this attempt to bring the disputants together round the conference table he was required to negotiate an alliance with Charles V, thus postponing England's entry into war – if peace could not be patched up – for as long as possible.

At Calais, where he was supported by Tunstall and Thomas More, the Cardinal worked desperately from early August to late November for an accommodation. His grand edifice of perpetual peace was tottering, but he strained every muscle to preserve it. As always he kept great state while at Calais: £2,400 was spent on clothing his retinue in velvet dress, he was lent the King's best trumpeter, and he had taken with him the great seal of England, 'which had not been seen before'. When it became clear that Charles V would not send representatives to the diet at Calais unless Wolsey journeyed to Bruges to sign a treaty of assistance, the Cardinal accepted the inevitable. The Emperor treated him in his palace at Bruges as Henry's personal representative: they were seen hearing mass under the same canopy and even sharing the same kneeling-desk. There was justice in this, for by going to Bruges the Cardinal had undertaken to carry out Henry's personal policy, which conflicted with his own negotiations at Calais. Inevitably he appeared to be playing a devious role, yet there is not the slightest doubt that in the interests of peace he had been attempting to pursue a policy at variance with his master's. When the King's suspicions were confirmed he showered on his minister one complaint after another, and the fact that they did not see each other for five months accounted for misunderstandings on other matters at the same time.

By the terms of the Anglo-Imperial treaty of August 1521 England was to declare war on France the following May, *provided* peace between the powers had not been signed. Wolsey set much store by that proviso and remained hopeful that before he left Calais hostilities between France and the Empire would have been brought to an end. If he failed to secure peace Henry would be obliged to launch a small naval campaign in 1522 and send an expedition to France the following year. When Wolsey fell ill he left it to his deputies to try to persuade both parties to agree to a truce for two years. When he was well enough to involve himself in negotiations again he determined to break the deadlock, personally appealing both to Charles and to Francis for 'unity, peace and concord' and writing a moving letter to the Queen Mother of France.

At one stage it seemed as though he would succeed. Francis was prepared to accept his demands, but the Emperor, having achieved the treaty with England, proved obstinate. 'The more towardly disposition I find in the French party,' wrote the Cardinal, 'the more sticking and difficulty be showed [by the imperialists].' Such was the lot of the mediator. Time was running out and the series of papal and imperialist successes in the Milanese reinforced Charles's desire to continue the war in which he had already taken Tournai, not so long ago Wolsey's own city. In the end the Cardinal accepted the inevitable, tearing up his draft terms of truce and embarking for home. He arrived on 28 November, worn out and dispirited: 'I have as effectually laboured [for peace] by all the politic ways and means to me possible as ever I did any cause in my life,' he wrote in sorrow, and he meant every word of it. Still he hoped that common sense might prevail and that envoys from each side would accept his invitation to England. Henry was not at all displeased at the prospects of fighting in France again and was happy that Wolsey's treaty of Bruges had included clauses by which Charles would marry his, Henry's, daughter Mary and also compensate him for the loss of his French pension. Like his father, Henry VIII had turned to the Empire and Spain for support, and he argued that the safeguarding of his dynasty was best assured by the marriage of his only legitimate child to the Emperor. The precedent of the Netherlands suggested that England might retain great autonomy while becoming part of the Habsburg dominions through another felicitous marriage. To recompense Wolsey for his heavy expenses at Calais, Henry granted him the Abbey of St Albans, by far the richest monastery in the realm. And at once came news of Pope Leo x's death in Rome.

Preparations were now in train for the state visit that the Emperor was to make to England at the end of May 1522. Wolsey continued to write letter after letter urging Francis to come to England at the same time, but in vain. To his intense dismay no chance of avoiding war remained and during Charles's stay England formally made her declaration of hostilities. The peace which the country had enjoyed for eight years was over and with it Wolsey's scheme for collective security in Europe collapsed, for in spite of the Cardinal's efforts to keep England neutral, Henry had got his own way. Francis I is reported to have remarked: 'I looked for this a great while ago, for since the Cardinal was at Bruges I looked for no other.'

The sustained pageantry in court and city to welcome Charles V was crudely anti-Gallic. In particular a play by William Cornish of the chapel royal 'ridiculed the King of France and his alliances', while Wolsey had perforce to eat all the honeyed words delivered at Ardres and Guisnes in 1520 at the banquets now being given to the imperial embassy, lashing the slippery Francis and his subjects, who must be 'exterminated' if peace were to come again to Europe. The French, he said, were constantly fomenting trouble and people should remember that Henry VIII had a far superior title to the French throne than its present incumbent and 'would assuredly oust him'. On Whitsun day in St Paul's, attended by some twenty mitred prelates, Wolsey celebrated high mass before Charles V and his courtiers, who were 'sore disdained' by observing that he was served with water for his ceremonial ablutions by two dukes, two earls and two barons. De Salino noted that the elaborate service was conducted by 'the Pope who is the Cardinal'.

With Henry firmly committed to the Habsburg cause Wolsey forfeited his cherished role of mediator and at once the weakness of England's changed position became painfully clear. The King placed too much reliance on the Duke of Bourbon's revolt, which he thought would seriously hamper Francis. He overestimated the financial resources he could command for waging a major war and placed far too much trust in Charles V. In 1523 Wolsey found considerable difficulty in extracting from Parliament the unprecedented taxes needed for the war and even greater difficulty in collecting the sums in shire and borough, so he was anxious for an early truce. In 1513 he had shown his great ability by organizing the commissariat for the French campaign, but ten years later he found the task of preparing a great expedition insuperable, since he was starved of funds. He worked as steadfastly towards an accommodation with France 'as may stand with my duty to my sovereign lord and master', so that with Henry's agreement a pact was reached with Francis in the autumn of 1524.

Suddenly, at the end of the following February, came news of the imperialists' overwhelming victory at Pavia, in which the King of

France was captured and the Yorkist claimant to the English throne, Richard de la Pole, was killed. Henry was elated and was determined to exploit the weakness of France to regain England's lost dominions. Wolsey was quite unable to dissuade him from his impracticable plans and was required to organize the collection of the 'Amicable Loan', which earned him far more unpopularity than the heavy taxes wrung from Parliament in 1523. As he had predicted, Charles v discerned Henry's intentions, which did not at all suit his own schemes. He rejected out of hand the request that Princess Mary should take up residence at his court in preparation for an early marriage, and called Henry's bluff by demanding immediate payment of her considerable dowry. He was thus able to break off their betrothal. Everything was going sadly awry and the King more or less admitted that he had misjudged the situation.

Wolsey's treaty of the More, signed at his Hertfordshire manor house in August 1525, ended hostilities with France. Though there was nothing to show for England's intervention in the feud between Valois and Habsburg he was hopeful that he could again steer the country towards firm neutrality. The following January Charles achieved a victor's terms with France and acquired the Duchy of Burgundy. Shortly afterwards he rubbed salt in Henry's wound by marrying Isabella of Portugal.

At last the Cardinal hoped that he might be able to fill once more the role of mediator in international affairs, which he had been unable to do for five years. He was loath to join the League of Cognac formed between France, Venice and the papacy to counter further imperialist designs in Italy. Neutrality was for him the obvious course for England to adopt. To his dismay a series of Spanish successes in the peninsula threatened anew the independence of the Pope, at the very time when Henry required forthright papal assistance in solving the 'Great Matter' of his marriage. Subsidies to the member states of the League of Cognac led, in April 1527, to an Anglo-French alliance and a fresh betrothal of Mary to the Dauphin. But by then French power in Italy was illusory. The sack of Rome in May 1527, which effectively made Pope Clement a prisoner of the Emperor, forced Wolsey to abandon neutrality. He had to do this if there was to be a serious chance of an independent papal ruling about Henry's marriage to Catherine of Aragon. If the Pope were to end his days, as he said, as an imperialist, then Wolsey would, by force of circumstance, end his as a francophile, and in January 1528, to the anguish of city merchants, he declared war on the House of Habsburg – a war that, in the absence of hostilities, quickly passed into the limbo of a truce. The 'arbiter of Europe' had been outwitted abroad at the moment when Henry needed to rely on his international influence. He paid dearly for his failure.

3
The Power and the Glory

Once Wolsey was no longer an *éminence grise*, as in his days as royal almoner, but had become the acknowledged chief minister of the crown everyone commented on his 'great mental activity and diligence'. He was criticized for accumulating offices, yet Henry recognized in him a born administrator with an unquestionable thirst for patient, ministerial paperwork and the stamina for working excessively long hours. 'He, alone, transacts the same business as that which occupies all the magistracies, offices and councils of Venice, both civil and criminal,' wrote Sebastian Giustinian, 'and all state affairs likewise are managed by him, let their nature be what it may.' He seemed 'to have the management of the whole of this Kingdom'. 'All really depends on him.' Above all he took the burden of making decisions, forming policy and other aspects of governance off the King's shoulders and Henry was encouraged to shed even more of the load.

Already in his first year as Lord Chancellor the Cardinal was being styled by one acute observer as 'another King'; a second remarked that he was 'constantly occupied by all the affairs of the Kingdom', and a third noted Henry's devotion to his accomplishments and amusements, day and night, 'leaving business to the Cardinal of York, who rules everything sagely and prudently'. A year later, in 1517, Francisco Chieregeto was reporting: 'The Cardinal does everything. The King occupies himself with nothing but scientific amusements. All negotiations pass through the Cardinal, who manages everything with consummate ability, integrity and prudence. . . .' Foreign envoys were convinced they were negotiating 'not with a cardinal, but with another

53

King'. *Alter rex* was the phrase most regularly used to describe the chief minister. Even Bishop Foxe, who knew far more about power at court from the inside than the Venetian ambassadors, and also knew his Wolsey, came to remark: 'We have to deal with the Cardinal, who is not a cardinal, but King; and no one in the realm dares attempt aught in opposition to his interests.' He kept much not only from the Council but from Henry himself. In the negotiations for the peace of 1518, as Sir Thomas More made clear, 'even the King hardly knows in what state matters are'. At the height of Wolsey's influence Giustinian cast his mind back to his first meeting with him in 1515, when he used to say to the envoy: 'His Majesty will do so and so.' By degrees he came to forget himself and would remark: 'We shall do so and so,' until by 1519 'he has reached such a pitch that he says "I shall do so and so".'

It was to Wolsey or to one of his secretaries that men chose to come, instead of to the sovereign, to seek favours and to make offerings in support of their requests. On occasions his new year's gifts even exceeded Henry's in value. When he was away at the manor of the More in Hertfordshire, people talked about 'the absence of the court' from London. His residences were far superior to the King's. During the years in which Cardinal Bainbridge, his predecessor as Archbishop of York, was living as ambassador in Rome, very little money had been spent on York Place, Westminster, and when its surveyor, James Bettes, suggested that Wolsey might authorize quite modest repairs to the traditional London home of the archbishops of York, he discovered to his delight that the new incumbent had in mind a very extensive programme of rebuilding. Henry Redmayn, whose father was the master mason at Westminster Abbey, was engaged for the Cardinal's service and Richard Russell appointed as master carpenter. Before long Cambridge craftsmen were being impressed to work on Wolsey's building. Bricks made in Battersea kilns were brought by barge to Westminster for the new hall and great chamber, with kitchens and wine cellars appropriate for entertaining on a lavish scale. The existing site was a confined one, already much built upon, so Wolsey did not have the free hand he was to enjoy at Hampton Court. But he did his best to round off the site by purchasing neighbouring properties, including part of Scotland Yard.

It is not easy to determine the extent of Wolsey's alterations, for the whole neighbourhood of York Place was to be transformed even more drastically after the Cardinal's fall, when Henry VIII began to construct Whitehall Palace. Most of Wolsey's new buildings, however, were to the east and north of the older structures and covered an area of 1,000 square feet. In the first year of operations he spent £1,250 on his project and by July 1516 the work was far enough advanced for the King to be entertained there. A new set of 'water-stairs' was built on the Thames and there was a fine chapel, with both an outer and an inner vestry. Yet the chief glory of York Place was the great chamber where Wolsey held his court: 'One traverses eight rooms before reaching his audience chamber, and they are all hung with tapestry, which is changed once a week.' The floors were covered, one suspects, with the damascene carpets that he had wheedled out of the signory of Venice. York Place put Lambeth Palace, renovated by Cardinal Morton, into the shade and it was the finest house owned by a subject since Humphrey, Duke of Gloucester's 'Bella Court' at Greenwich. The entertainments the Cardinal gave here were as lavish as the setting for them. To mark the betrothal of little Princess Mary to the Dauphin in 1518 he gave a state banquet, which was described by one of the guests as 'a most sumptuous supper, the like of which, I fancy, was never given either by Cleopatra or Caligula. The whole banqueting hall being so decorated with huge vases of gold and silver, that I fancied myself in the tower of Chosroes, where that monarch caused divine honours to be paid to him.' Dinner was followed by a masque, led by King Henry and his younger sister, the Dowager Queen of France. While sweetmeats were served Wolsey's serving men placed bowls of ducats and dice on the tables for those who wanted to play at mumchance or other gambling games, and then the tables in the hall were removed to enable the general concourse of guests to dance into the small hours.

The striking improvements at York Place were, however, only one part of Wolsey's grandiose building programme. Within five months of becoming archbishop he had acquired a ninety-nine-year lease from the Knights Hospitallers of the manor of Hampton Court. The extensive operations that now began were to last until 1522. There is a ring of truth in the tale that Wolsey had engaged a physician to visit various possible sites for a suburban residence away from the smoke and the plague of London, and that the man had come down in favour of Hampton. Besides being a salubrious place it was on the riverside, giving easy access to Westminster by barge. The original plans were prepared by Ellis Smith, but without question the chief architect was Henry Redmayn, who was assisted by William Reynolds – the same master mason who had completed Madgalen College tower. Most of the timberwork was prepared under the direction of Humphrey Cook, master carpenter. With his near-obsession about hygiene Wolsey had ordained that there should be brick sewers 3 feet thick, to run from his residence into the Thames, and had required the water supply to be brought by lead pipes from distant springs.

During April 1515 an army of workmen descended on Hampton, to dig the moat, lay out the herb gardens and begin the foundations. Great loads of materials arrived by water – stone from Reigate and Barnet, lime from Ruislip, timber from Weybridge and Reading and many thousands of red bricks baked in nearby kilns. Not yet Lord Chancellor, let alone a cardinal, Wolsey was impatient to see his buildings go rapidly forward and agreed to the expense of having a crane on the site. Progress was so swift that in the middle of the first year's operations a glazier could begin putting in the 65-foot run of windows 'on both sides of my Lord's gallery'. Everything was to be on an elaborate scale. For instance the kitchen was 48 feet long, and we are told that there were, on completion, 280 guest chambers. It is impossible, however, to discern the complex of Wolsey's buildings and the unity of their design, because of the extensive alterations and additions made by Henry VIII after 1529, using the same materials and, indeed, the same craftsmen, headed by Henry Redmayn. In the end it proved impossible to build as rapidly as the Cardinal had wanted. Although he stayed there from 1519 onwards it was probably not until 1522 that the entire residence, as he had envisaged it, was ready for occupation by his enormous household of retainers. In that year the last of the series of tapestries was bought, for hanging in the great gatehouse. Surprisingly the earliest reference to Hampton Court in Cavendish's *Life* is in November 1527, when Wolsey entertained a French embassy there. In preparation for their state visit there was much work for carpenters, joiners, masons and painters.

To embellish this palace Wolsey brought to England a number of distinguished artists and sculptors from Italy. Giovanni da Maiano arrived from Florence to fashion a series of terracotta rondels with the heads of Roman emperors. From the surviving examples that today decorate the gatehouses of Base Court and Clock Court, one can appreciate the intricate workmanship, not least of the borderwork and the emblems, such as the crouching griffon over Otto's bust. Maiano also executed panels to illustrate the 'Historie of Hercules' for the oriel windows of the gateway, which were to be replaced within a decade by the King's Beasts. Yet the finest terracotta work commissioned by Wolsey was perhaps the panel with his arms over the gateway of Clock Tower, showing the cardinal's hat, his archiepiscopal crosses and legatine pillars, with two exquisite nude *putti* as the supporters for the shield. Much decorative work has been superseded – for example the ceiling of Wolsey's closet once bore cardinal's hats and other appropriate motifs, but they were replaced by Henry's monogram and the Tudor rose – and the wall paintings by Antonio Toto have vanished. The work at Hampton Court showed Wolsey to be a patron on the grand scale and the first Englishman to commission Italian artists and sculptors.

The Cardinal had also acquired a small house at Kingston-upon-Thames, which proved useful while Hampton Court was being built, and in 1519 he had persuaded Bishop Foxe to allow him to reside from time to time at his house in Esher. 'Use it all ways, as often and as long as it shall please you, right as your own,' the Bishop generously agreed, 'and make it a cell to Hampton Court.' In due course, when Wolsey had succeeded Foxe as Bishop of Winchester, his informal tenancy was legally recognized. His palaces at Southwell and Cawood in the northern archdiocese he never visited until 1530, and he never set foot in the residences that belonged to the three bishoprics he successively held – Bath and Wells, Durham and finally Winchester (with the exception of the house at Esher). He did, however, take a personal interest in two of the manor houses belonging to the Abbey of St Alban's, once he had become its titular abbot. Of these, Tittenhanger in Bedfordshire proved to be much too far from London to see the Cardinal very often, but the other, the Manor of the More, near Rickmansworth in Hertfordshire, became a favourite retreat from the capital.

Henry VIII marvelled at the splendour of Wolsey's two great residences. They were so much more up to date than any of his palaces, with the partial exception of Richmond, completed by his father at the turn of the century, and his own modest construction of Bridewell. In particular Henry was envious of York Place, since he was desperately short of accommodation in the capital – in April 1512, while Wolsey was still almoner, there had been a disastrous fire at Westminster Palace. Both Westminster Hall and the Painted Chamber had escaped damage, but the rest of the royal apartments, with the extensive domestic offices, were in ruins and were never to be rebuilt as a residence for the royal family. Henry made use of Baynards Castle and the Tower of London and began building Bridewell Palace; but his quarters in the White Tower in the Tower of London were unbelievably cramped and they were badly damaged in another fire later in the year. Compared with what had been lost at Westminster these other London houses were on a most modest scale and could not, even combined, provide the accommodation necessary for his own and his Queen's household staff. For long Henry put up with these makeshift arrangements whenever he had to be in London and he increasingly came to rely on Greenwich Palace, where he had been born, and Richmond. Without those it would have been more than he could have borne to see York House rise in splendour on a marvellously central site. He was to covet that residence no less than Hampton. In the end both came into his grasp.

An Italian, used to the pomp of great ecclesiastics, reckoned Wolsey to be 'the proudest prelate that ever breathed'. At state banquets he would dine at the royal table, from which even dukes were excluded, and whereas in the earliest days of his rule a new ambassador would be entertained by his side, 'now no one is served with the viands of the sort presented to the Cardinal until after their removal before him'. He delighted in elaborate ceremonies and ritual that required peers of the realm to perform 'menial' tasks for him at mass and on other occasions. Both foreign envoys and English nobles were kept waiting for audiences and often would not manage to obtain one until the third or fourth request. Once an audience was obtained, the great man could cut it short without warning: 'I have at this present a great deal of business to despatch; we will confer together more at leisure,' he might say, intending to relegate the visitor to one of his secretaries when he next appeared. The King was much more accessible, yet Wolsey contrived to keep professional diplomats from him. The Cardinal remained exceptionally sensitive about his dignity and the salaams due to one holding his high offices, yet he somehow failed to grasp that others might be no less sensitive.

In attendance on the Cardinal and assisting in the running of his household he employed a staff of no fewer than five hundred. The household was organized on the time-honoured system of the royal court. Down the years this had provided a model for the greatest in the land, certainly for the lay peers, though Wolsey's attachment to Lambeth Palace in the early years of the century had shown him that an archbishop's household could be run on much more modest lines. There were four main departments – the chamber, the hall, the chapel and the kitchen and other 'below stairs' offices from the larder to the woodyard. About a hundred officials served under the high chamberlain, including twelve gentlemen ushers, of whom George Cavendish was one, waiters in the privy chamber, gentlemen ushers and cup bearers. The servants of the chamber were dressed in a livery of crimson velvet 'of the purest colour', with the front and back of their tunics bearing the letters 'TC' in gold – the monogram for 'Thomas, Cardinalis' – with the device of the red hat, all copied from similar monograms decorating the uniforms of the royal Yeomen of the Guard. Wolsey's household had its own professional lawyers, auditors and surveyors. They were primarily concerned with the mass of detailed business that came domestically, preparing litigation, drafting leases and checking accounts, complementing the work of the Cardinal's secretaries, who assisted him in his official business. Thomas Cromwell, as we shall see, rose in the world as Wolsey's solicitor. There was, too, a tutor who instructed the wards in Wolsey's custody, such as Edward Stanley, third Earl of Derby. Cavendish tells us there was always kept in the chamber a mess for 'the young lords'. As we would expect, the household had its own physician and apothecary, and (suprisingly for an ecclesiastic) there were also a personal herald, an armourer and a tent-keeper. The affairs of the hall were overseen by the steward, the treasurer and the controller. Here, at tables where the places were assigned according to rank, the main body of the Cardinal's staff dined. At the lowliest table of all the almoner dispensed food and drink to paupers.

The complement of the chapel was fifty-four. This might seem relatively modest for a cardinal archbishop, but we should remember that it was the staff of a personal chapel and this lay quite outside the establishments attached to his various ecclesiastical preferments, such as York or Winchester. The dean of the chapel was supported by a sub-dean, a precentor, gospeller and epistler and twelve singing priests, while the organist directed a choir of twelve boys and sixteen men, with a servant to help look after the choristers. At special feasts the choir was reinforced by 'divers retainers of cunning singing-men'. The musical standards at Hampton Court were extremely high and the King envied the Cardinal the services of so fine a choir. On one occasion he devised a competition between the chapel royal and Hampton Court choir, requiring each to sight-read in turn the same composition. In Henry's highly professional view the Hampton Court choir 'more surely handled' the piece. Before long Wolsey took the hint and arranged for one of his best choristers to be transferred to the chapel royal, where the boy's new choirmaster was most enthusiastic, 'not only for his sure and cleanly singing, but also for his good and crafty descant'. Under Wolsey's chamberlain there were, too, four 'musicians' – most probably trumpeters. The rest of the chapel staff comprised two cross bearers and two pillar bearers and a yeoman and two grooms of the vestry, who saw to the crosses, candlesticks and other ornaments, the copes, altar frontals and vestments. In addition to the chapel, there was a quite separate establishment of doctors of divinity, chaplains and others, serving the Cardinal in his closet, 'to say daily mass before him'.

The 'below stairs' departments of kitchen and scullery, pastry, larder and pantry, buttery, waifery and bakehouse, which saw to the needs of the inner man, were indeed extensive. Perhaps the most important official here was the master cook of the privy kitchen, 'who went daily in damask, satin or velvet, with a chain of gold about his neck', for he was responsible for the fare that was served at the Cardinal's table. Noteworthy among the rest were the yeomen of the barge, the two tall porters who kept the gate and the four footmen, who were turned out 'in rich running-coats' whenever the Cardinal made a journey. Because Wolsey was Lord Chancellor he would often have attached to him various Chancery officials, including the Clerk of the Crown, who attested all letters and writs issued under the great seal, and the Clerk of the Hanaper, who looked after the fees of the Chancery Court. By virtue of his enormous diplomatic correspondence

Wolsey required two principal secretaries to assist with the paper-work. These were men selected for their outstanding ability, such as Brian Tuke, William Knight and Stephen Gardiner, and all rose high in the King's service.

The daily procession of the Cardinal in term time from York Place to Westminster Hall was a remarkable sight. Two great crosses of silver went before him, the first a double cross, like that of Lorraine, symbolizing his power as legate, the second his office of archbishop; and the two crucifers were the tallest priests that could be found in the realm. Next were borne the two heavy pillars of silver, two gilt pole-axes, followed by Wolsey's serjeant-at-arms with his mace. A hand-some page walked bare-headed, carrying the great seal of England in its silk purse, and then (if a peer was not available for the task) a gentleman usher bore the red hat with its great tassels. At length came Wolsey himself, riding the mule that symbolized humility – yet the beast was decked out with crimson velvet trappings and gilt stirrups. The procession made its stately way to the shouts of the gentlemen ushers, 'On, my lords and masters! Make way for my Lord's Grace! Make way for his Grace the Cardinal Legate of York, Lord High Chancellor of this realm!'

Like his sovereign, Wolsey had a massive frame and was physically strong. William Tyndale, a severe critic, described him as 'a man of lust and courage and bodily strength to do and suffer great things.' He was able to control his temper better than his sovereign, but was given to fits of impatience. This was most noticeable when he was waiting for news of his election as a cardinal and was seen to be gnawing at his cane. Like Henry, too, he had a gargantuan appetite for food and drink, freeing himself from the stern requirements of abstinence and fasting that the Church expected lesser mortals to obey, on pain of penalties in the spiritual courts. As he was a butcher's son there would have been no shortage of meat in his childhood and he came to take an intense personal interest in the building of his kitchens at Hampton Court. The menus for the banquets he gave at York House provoked foreigners present to consider that gluttony was a national vice. But whereas the King took regular, vigorous exercise, which until middle age kept his figure trim, Wolsey did not, and his work was essentially sedentary. His single-minded devotion to government affairs worried

Henry, who thought there was something odd in a man – even a churchman – who did not enjoy hunting or the tennis court. Once, as he sat comfortably after a good day's sport and thought of his minister, tied to his desk, he wrote in his own hand – a rare honour, since he found all letter-writing 'somewhat tedious and painful':

> Mine own good cardinal, I recommend unto you with all my heart, and thank you for the great pain and labour that you do daily take in my business and matters, desiring you (that when you have well established them) to take some pastime and comfort, to the intent that you may the longer endure to serve us, for always pain cannot be endured.

Henry always made the most of colds, headaches and minor ailments as sound excuses for taking a holiday from the paperwork of the palace. Wolsey, by contrast, driving himself so hard, failed to grasp that relaxation paid dividends for both work and health. When he was feeling very unwell as a result of over-work at Calais in 1521 he made a virtue of putting his illness down to the 'unwholesome air of Calais'. He would never admit that ceaseless labours caused strain.

Both King and Cardinal were compulsive worriers about their health, though as Henry was so much the younger of the two this trait was less marked in the years of Wolsey's primacy. The Cardinal, who had been so anxious about the drainage system at Hampton Court, was for ever taking medicine of one kind or another as a preventive against illnesses. Henry did not approve of his reliance on pills and was glad (in 1519) to be assured that his persuasiveness had been effective, and that Wolsey was restraining this bad habit. He asked Thomas More to write to Wolsey that if he continued to forgo the frequent taking of medicine, 'ye shall not fail of health'. A few weeks before the Field of Cloth of Gold Wolsey went down with colic and jaundice, and Francis I offered to send him his best physicians.

In June 1517, a month after the 'evil May day rising' (see page 83), Wolsey had been seriously ill: '. . . his life was despaired of and for many days neither the grandees,' wrote the Venetian ambassador, 'nor other members of the privy council, who are wont to be so assiduous, went near him.' This was his first enforced break in the royal service since 1512 and for two to three weeks, while he was convalescing, diplomacy came to a halt. Notwithstanding recurrent bouts of 'the sweating sickness' that summer, which only a man of exceptionally good physique and strong will-power could have thrown off so easily, Wolsey felt compelled in September to make a pilgrimage to the shrine of Our Lady at Walsingham in Norfolk, perhaps in fulfilment of a vow made during his illness in June, when he feared he was *in extremis.* (His journey, if he took the traditional pilgrim's road, which was one of the best roads in the kingdom, would have taken him near his native Ipswich. Nor was this his last pilgrimage to the Walsingham shrine.) In later years, certainly from 1523, he had a Venetian physician in his household – Agostino degli Agostini, known more generally as 'Master Augustine'.

One fear King and Cardinal shared with the majority of urban Englishmen was dread of the sweating sickness. The plague had, since Henry VII's accession, visited parts of England in most summers and in particular struck terror into the hearts of Londoners – because it was so densely populated, the capital usually suffered most casualties. Though the epidemic rarely arrived before June it could persist until November, throwing the government machine out of gear. The symptoms were frightening and the danger-point could be reached with little warning. 'One has a little pain in the head and heart; suddenly a sweat breaks out and a physician is useless, for whether you wrap yourself up much or little in four hours, sometimes in two or three, you are despatched without languishing.' One could, as the chronicler Edward Hall disarmingly put it, be 'merry at dinner and dead at supper'. At the first hint of the plague Henry would speedily leave London to shut himself up in Windsor Castle, or to settle down in Hunsdon Manor in Hertfordshire, which he bought as a country retreat from the noxious air of the capital. Yet the Cardinal remained at the helm in Westminster until public business allowed him to depart. Despite his very real fear he would remain on duty, displaying singular courage while wondering each day how long he might survive, for numbers of his household died, as in the 1517 epidemic, 'and not merely his under-attendants, but some of the principal ones'. In the space of nine weeks he was himself laid low with the frightening symptoms on four separate occasions, yet he always pulled through. During another serious outbreak of the infection in 1528, when members of the King's and the Cardinal's households were dying like flies, Henry asked Sir Brian Tuke to write to Wolsey, advising him to follow closely his own procedure: he should keep clear of all places

where there might be the slightest risk, and if anyone in his company
should fall a victim he must at once move on to another of his country
residences. 'His Highness desireth your Grace to use small suppers and
to drink little wine.' He now also advocated his own specific remedy:
Wolsey should once a week 'use the pills of Rasis'; if he did become ill
he must order his physician to prepare a posset made with clarified
herbs, for this would induce moderate and continual sweating.

Wolsey had found it impossible to fulfil the canonical obligation to
chastity that a priest's orders demanded. In this he was no better, and
no worse, than several high ecclesiastics of the Renaissance, whose
personal conduct followed the pattern set by various fifteenth-century
cardinals. On some occasions in Rome, it seemed almost as if any
cardinal without a natural son lacked stature. The mealy-mouthed
talked of uncanonical unions that begat nephews; the forthright spoke
of mistresses and bastards. The demand for reform of the Church
included a return to celibacy and chastity at every level, yet very few
regarded sexual misconduct as the worst feature of the age. The
visitation reports of English and Welsh dioceses and religious houses
showed how widespread were breaches of the seventh commandment.
There was less to deplore in a churchman who broke the rules of
celibacy to keep a mistress and remained faithful to her, than in a
layman who formed liaisons outside marriage, as did Henry VIII,
Ferdinand of Aragon and successive kings of France.

The Cardinal did not flaunt his mistress publicly, but behaved with
considerable discretion, for the liaison that he formed, in about 1511,
with Mistress Lark, most probably the daughter of a Thetford innkeeper, might easily have counted against him when he was still on the
fringe of the Council. The 'lusty Lark' – well known to a fellow East
Anglian, Skelton (who could no more live the life of a bachelor than
Wolsey) – bore Wolsey two children. A brother, Thomas Lark, was
taken up by the Cardinal, who – incongruous as it may seem to us –
appointed him to be his own confessor and later secured for him a royal
chaplaincy; he played a minor part in Buckingham's downfall. Though
his chance came when his sister began to cohabit with Wolsey, it is
clear that Thomas Lark had considerable ability and he proved himself
to be a most capable member of Wolsey's secretariat. In the early
1520s he was Master of Trinity Hall, Cambridge, but he returned to

the Cardinal's service and died at Southwell in 1530. Another brother, Peter Lark, also took orders and came into the service of Stephen Gardiner.

Wolsey's daughter was born in 1512, christened Dorothy and adopted by John Clansey. In due course she was placed in Shaftesbury Nunnery, which had the reputation of being the finest 'finishing school' in England. Yet she stayed in the house, conscious of her vows, and at its dissolution under Cromwell received a pension. The Cardinal's son, given the name of Thomas Wynter, was placed with a family in Willesden and remains unknown until 1521, when a lively correspondence began between his father and his tutor, Maurice Birchinshaw. Wolsey, perhaps thinking back to his own prowess as a 'boy bachelor', was frankly disappointed with his offspring's attainments. Birchinshaw apologized for the boy's 'speaking less Latin' than Wolsey desired and defended both himself and his pupil: the fault was in the shape of the curriculum they were required to follow. Subsequently young Wynter became rather ill from a fever near Trent in north Italy. At this point Erasmus offered to help with his schooling, though, fortunately for all concerned, Wolsey did not pursue the idea.

When Henry VIII brought his own natural son by Bessie Blount, Henry Fitzroy, out of the shadows in 1525, to create him Duke of Richmond, with the intention of grooming him for the succession, Wolsey decided that the time was ripe to bring Wynter, who was six years older than the king's son, to public notice. He therefore had his feet firmly placed on the ladder of ecclesiastical preferment. Garter King of Arms granted him a coat of arms with a defiant bar sinister, and Master Wynter, still in his early teens, soon became Dean of Wells, a prebendery of Beverley, Chancellor of Salisbury, Archdeacon of York and of Richmond and much else besides, including rector of a church in his father's native Ipswich. Meanwhile he was taught by the humanist Thomas Lupset. When old Foxe of Winchester died, Wolsey tried in vain to secure the bishopric for the boy, who had still not taken priest's orders. After Wolsey's death Henry appointed him a chaplain, though he lived mostly on the continent, toying with scholarly pursuits. Wynter told Thomas Cromwell in dilettante vein in 1534: 'I am devoted to letters, but desire to keep my preferments' – sentiments of which the Cardinal would indeed have approved. He is last heard of in 1543, in connection with the revenues of the archdeaconry of Cornwall, which he was still enjoying, but he apparently survived for a further decade.

Wolsey's exceptional authority was to be resented on all sides for his manner of wielding it. His love of pomp was at first seen as the besetting sin of an upstart, at last able to draw attention to his remarkable success. Yet far from coming to terms with this trait in his character he instead increasingly revelled in the ritual displays of power for their own sake. Puffed up with pride, he showed what Polydore Vergil termed 'a brazen insolence'. He was as incapable of tact as of humility. Peers, such as Buckingham and Norfolk, who smarted under the Cardinal's rule and feared the next show of hubris, would have found in Caxton's *Reynard the Fox* an apt passage: 'When a covetous man of low birth is made a lord, and above his neighbours hath power and might, then he knoweth not himself, ne whence he is common. . . . All his intent and desire is to gather good and to be greater.'

This unprecedented power provoked personal polemics against him to a hitherto unknown degree. His most persistent critic until 1522 was John Skelton, once Henry VIII's tutor, who had written a treatise for his young charge on how royalty should behave and later claimed to have introduced him to the muses. For some years he had been away from the centre of events, but in 1512 he left his Norfolk rectory to return to court. Long before, the Lady Margaret had praised his verse, while Erasmus had predicted that he would make a singular contribution to English letters. Now he was appointed poet laureate in succession to the blind French priest, Bernard André. Skelton's unorthodox ways had an electric effect. He may, indeed, have dazzled people by appearing at court in a robe of white and green, embroidered in silken letters of gold with the one word 'Calliope' (the ancient muse of epic poetry). He may have shocked people with bawdy tales of his tribe of illegitimate offspring. Yet it was his verses that jolted readers out of their complacency. Skelton was determined to voice his unfettered opinions, mocking pretentiousness and laughing at pomp. In a year or so Wolsey became the obvious target for his shafts and he did not shrink from tackling so *risqué* a theme, and indeed relishing it.

Skelton may not have been an entirely independent critic, for he was taken up by the Howard faction, led by the victor of Flodden, the second Duke of Norfolk, who like his son after him quickly realized that his position as Lord Treasurer was being undermined by the Cardinal. The Countess of Surrey, old Norfolk's daughter-in-law, took special interest in his writings, notably after the execution of her father, the Duke of Buckingham. We know that Skelton stayed at her household periodically and that his conservative attitude to the New Learning made him a not disagreeable companion for her husband.

Before launching his diatribes against Wolsey, the poet took the precaution of securing a residence within the sanctuary of Westminster Abbey, where he would be safe from arrest. Here for long periods Abbot Islip befriended him. His lodging was on the south side of the great belfry, for which he paid the very steep rent of £50 a year. His earliest shafts at Wolsey's expense had been tucked away in his poem *Against Venomous Tongues*, where there are lines poking fun at the monograms embroidered on the liveries of Wolsey's uniformed attendants:

> For before in your breast and behind on your back
> In Roman letters I never found lack.

Magnificence, probably written in 1516, contained only vague allusions to the Cardinal, but it was inevitable that the minister whose love of pomp was even then a byword should feel he was being lampooned in this 'goodly interlude'. It circulated in manuscript, though it would have been surprising if it had not been performed. The main theme of *Magnificence* was the squandering of the King's wealth by a mistaken foreign policy. *Colyn Cloute*, a cruelly barbed attack on the corruption of the Church, contained more pointed allusions, with scarcely veiled references to Wolsey's riding on his mule, to his amassing ecclesiastical preferment and to what is often interpreted as a prophecy of his fall from grace.

Once Wolsey had obtained his wide legatine authority he decided to launch an assault on the sanctuary-men in general and Skelton in particular. Nothing would induce Abbot Islip to give way, for he maintained that the perpetual sanctuary enjoyed by inmates within the Abbey's hallowed precincts was above the law of the land. Islip was summoned to the Star Chamber in November 1519, but would not be moved, so the Cardinal legate had to admit defeat. Skelton's next composition, *Speke Parrot*, written in the autumn of 1521, begins most obscurely and then suddenly the mysterious bird cries out with unmistakable clarity, once it has been persuaded to forsake sophistry. We read of 'so bold a bragging butcher' who 'carrieth a King in his sleeve'. It is to Wolsey that the parrot ascribes the decay of monastic life, the decline of fasting, sanctuary breaking and other evils:

> So hot hatred against the church, and charity so cold,
> So much of my lord's grace and in him no grace is;
> So many hollow hearts, and so double faces.

Skelton, who, as we have seen, had once written a poem *Against Venomous Tongues*, now dipped his own pen in the blackest gall. Wolsey was

> So bold and so bragging and was so basely born,
> So lordly of his looks and so disdainsly,
> So fat a maggot, bred of a flesh fly,
> Was never such a filthy gorgon, nor such an epicure.

Papal bulls, legatine crosses and archiepiscopal blessings were of no avail, for everything the man meddled with 'came to small effect'.

The most virulent and detailed tract of all was *Why Come Ye Not to Courte?*, written in 1522, which demands extensive quotation:

> Once yet again
> Of you I would frain,
> Why come ye not to court?
> To which court?
> To the King's court,
> Or to Hampton Court?
> Nay, the King's court
> Should have the excellence;
> But Hampton Court
> Hath the pre-eminence.
> And Yorkes Place,
> With my lord's grace,
> To whose magnificence
> Is all the confluence,
> Suits and supplications,
> Embassies of all nations.
> Straw for the law canon,
> Or for the law common,
> Or for law civil!
> It shall be as he will.

There was not a nail that Skelton did not drive home. The man who had ousted the ancient families from their traditional place in the government of the realm was himself of ridiculously humble birth:

> His base progeny
> And his greasy genealogy;
> He came out of the sink royal
> That was cast out of a butcher's stall.

His education was suspect. The achievements of 'the boy bachelor' are forgotten; instead, he was

> But a poor master of art;
> God wot, had little part
> Of the quadrivials,
> Nor yet of trivials
> Nor of philosophy . . .
> His Latin tongue doth hobble
> He doth but clout and cobble
> In Tully's faculty,
> Called humanity.

He had always been ambitious, crafty and vicious; and now

> He ruleth at will
> Without reason or skill!

No man could have gained such an ascendancy over the King through normal means. It was remarkable that His Majesty was

> . . . so far blinded
> That he can not perceive
> How he doth him deceive,
> I doubt lest by sorcery
> Or such other loselry
> As witchcraft or charming;
> For he is the King's darling.

The nobility whose authority he had usurped had a special fear of him. There was no need to allude to Buckingham's recent fate:

> The great peers of the realm
> Dare not look out at doors
> For dread of the mastiff cur;

> For dread of the butcher's dog
> Would worry them like a hog . . .
> For all their noble blood,
> He plucks them by the hood.

Wolsey is portrayed as forging papal briefs, tearing up royal letters that favoured men of whom he disapproved and waxing fat on bribes. The prince of the Church is presented as a loose-liver and a glutton, who constantly breaks the rules of Lenten fasting. As Lord Chancellor he turned the law to his own advantage:

> He is set so high
> In his hierarchy
> Of frantic phrenesy
> And foolish phantasy
> That in the Chamber of Stars
> All matters there he mars,
> Clapping his rod on the board
> No man dare speak a word;
> For he hath all the saying
> Without any renaying,
> He rolleth in his records,
> And saith, 'How say ye, my Lords?
> Is not my reason good?
> Good even, good Robin Hood. . . .'

He had become even more insufferable on being appointed a papal legate, which was for the poet a mere 'title of pride'. These powers gave him an unprecedented control over the Church, so that

> All places of religion
> He hath them in derision.

Never before had an English statesman been so extensively libelled and lampooned. John Wilkes's scurrilous articles in the *North Briton* two and a half centuries later are mild outbursts on men and manners compared with Skelton's insistent blasts directed at the Cardinal. Skelton threatened him with a fall no less dramatic than Lucifer's and urged him to repent before it was too late:

> And lay down thy pillars, poleaxes and crosses
> By the which this land hath had great losses
> And pill the people no more.

Even so the attack in one way lacked real teeth, for it is worth emphasizing that these verses circulated in manuscript and were not to be printed for some years to come, so their potential readership in Skelton's lifetime was extremely limited. The bitter scorn poured out in *Why Come Ye Not to Courte?* could itself be scorned, since the Cardinal could afford to ignore with dignity a tract of this nature, providing manuscript copies reached neither the King nor the Pope. He considered, however, that as it would be impossible to silence Skelton there would be merit in attempting to win over to his side so forceful a writer, who might be persuaded to direct his shafts at his own political enemies. The poet had by now had enough of the near-imprisonment that a sanctuary-man faced – and his was a high rent to have to pay indefinitely. Having spoken his mind so fully about the Cardinal, there was effectively nothing more to be said. There would therefore be a point in coming to a truce with the great man, assuming the terms were satisfactory. In his *The Merrie Tales* he shows himself kneeling to beg forgiveness; and if the words 'I pray your Grace to let me lie down and wallow, for I can kneel no longer' are a bit far-fetched, at least there was some show of penitence for the past and an assurance of turning over a new leaf. The two strong-willed men reached a concordat and within as little as two months after the completion of *Why Come Ye Not to Courte?* Skelton abruptly changed his tune from being Wolsey's 'dearest foe' to his 'humble client', most probably with a firm promise of preferment. In 1523 he dedicated to the Cardinal his poem on the Duke of Albany and was to write his final verses, *Replication Against Certain Young Scholars*, at his new patron's request.

Alexander Barclay, the Black Monk, who was himself a victim of Skelton's taunts, had in 1509 achieved fame with his version of Sebastian Brant's *The Ship of Fools* – it was more than a translation for it carried so obviously an English crew. Like Skelton, Barclay enjoyed Howard patronage, which involved praising the Duke of Norfolk, 'the flower of chivalry', and making pointed comments about Wolsey. His first eclogue on the miseries and manners of the court and courtiers, written before Wolsey became Cardinal, has a slighting reference to him as well as to Bishop Foxe. Yet the former was subsequently glad to employ him in writing mottoes and epigrams for decorating the pavilions at the Field of Cloth of Gold. Later on, when

Barclay had deserted the Benedictine order to become a Franciscan friar, he was quick to brand the Cardinal as a tyrant, making his criticisms in 'opprobrious and blasphemous words'. In 1528 Wolsey's spies reported on his hob-nobbing in Lutheran Germany with Tyndale, Jerome Barlow and William Roye, whom we shall meet in a minute.

It was not surprising that George Cavendish, the Cardinal's servant and earliest biographer, should open his work by castigating those who 'with their blasphemous trump ... spread innumerable lies', before bracing himself to set the record straight.

In addition to the biting wit of Skelton and the sarcastic asides of Barclay Wolsey also suffered the vituperation of the red-headed Greenwich Franciscan friar Jerome Barlow. At the suggestion of another apostate friar in exile, William Roye, Barlow wrote *The Burial of the Mass*. For long it was thought that Roye was himself the author of this rhyming dialogue, which was generally known by the title *Rede me and be not Wroth*, from a couplet on the title-page. Roye was more interested in denigrating his order of Friars Observant, which was the theme of the second half of the dialogue, but Barlow devoted the first half to a vehement attack on Wolsey, beginning as it were where Skelton had left off, with stinging comments on his private life no less than on his mismanagement of public affairs. The work was printed in Strasbourg in 1528, though the preface made a brave attempt at pretending that the printer's copy had been sent from England. The title-page warns the reader of what is to follow, with an unusually bold piece of mock heraldry that linked a cardinal's hat with a mastiff cur, and told how the upstart from Ispwich had broken the ancient nobility. In its way this colourful illustration ranks as the earliest political cartoon in England. An apposite verse explains the details of the drawing:

> Of the prowde Cardinall this is the shelde,
> Borne up betweene two angels off Sathan,
> The sixe blouddy axes in a bare felde
> Sheweth the cruelte of the red man
> Which hathe devoured the beautifull swan*
> Mortal enmy unto the whyte lyon†
> Carter of Yorcke the vyle bochers sonne.

---

* Edward Stafford, Duke of Buckingham.
† Thomas Howard, third Duke of Norfolk.

The Sixe bulles heddes in a felde blacke
Betokeneth his stordy furiousnes.

The bandog in the middes both expresse
The mastif Curre bred in Ypswitch towne
Gnawing with his teeth a kings crowne.

The dialogue is memorable for the detailed description of Cardinal Wolsey riding in procession. Despite the malicious undercurrent, the versifier cannot help conveying the true magnificence of the scene and the greatness of the figure commanding the centre of the stage:

More like a god celestial
Than any creature mortal
    With worldly pomp incredible
Before him rideth two priests strong
And they bear two crosses right long,
    Gaping in every man's face:
After them follow two laymen secular,
And each of them holdeth a pillar
    In their hands, stead of a mace.
Then followeth my lord on his mule
Trapped with gold under her cule,
    In every point most curiously;
On each side a poleaxe is born
Which in none other use are worn,
    Pretending some hid mystery.
Then hath he servants five or six score,
Some behind and some before,
    A marvellous great company.
Of which are lords and gentlemen
With many grooms and yeomen
    And also knaves among
Thus daily he proceedeth forth . . .

When a copy of the book came to his notice, Wolsey was furious and sent two friars to the continent to track down the author. By the time they discovered Barlow it was too late, for the Cardinal had already fallen and was in no position to trouble him. Barlow may even have prided himself that his tract had played a part in his dismissal from power. If all England from the King downwards was rejoicing it would be foolish not to make capital of his authorship. Accordingly Jerome Barlow wrote to the King, confessing that he was the author and acknowledging his faults in attacking the friars. He was now allowed to return to England and, apparently, to his order, for Thomas More noted that the apostate had 'graciously turned to God again'. He was to be employed by the government to write a polemical *Dialogue Against the Lutheran Faction*. William Roye, who had commissioned *The Burial of the Mass*, unwisely stayed abroad and was soon reported to have been burned as a heretic in Portugal.

Wolsey had reacted far less strongly to personal criticisms that came from a Cambridge pulpit. The preacher in question was Robert Barnes, an Augustinian friar, who spent his life speaking and writing in so forthright a manner that he was always in trouble. In 1524, after returning to Cambridge from Louvain, Barnes, with Hugh Latimer, the university chaplain, had experienced the truth of the Gospel. He was the leading spirit in advocating a thorough reform of the church's doctrine and organization and tradition has it that he was the first Englishman to say divine service entirely in the vernacular. The Cardinal and all that he stood for were anathema to the friar, whose other-worldliness led Martin Luther to nickname him 'Saint Robert'. The occasion of his outburst against Wolsey at the end of 1525 was a testamentary dispute. The executor of a man of very modest means had found himself unable to carry out the terms of a bequest to St Edward's Church, Cambridge, of a kettle valued at 28d, whereupon one of the churchwardens had him imprisoned. Barnes intervened with the church officials, making plain the sinfulness of prosecuting such a suit, but to no avail. When on Christmas Eve he saw the churchwarden in the congregation he referred to the matter by way of a parable in his sermon. Yet he went on to contrast the simplicity of Christ's nativity with the pomp of contemporary proud prelates – a favourite theme of Luther's – and ended the address with some injudicious gibes at the Cardinal. 'He wears a pair of red gloves – I should have said bloody gloves.' The friar's enemies, bent on denouncing him for heresy, found no fewer than twenty-five points in the sermon requiring answers. The clerks of Cambridge were divided on this *cause célèbre*, but as Barnes would not submit to the Vice Chancellor it seemed best to the authorities to have him cited to appear before Wolsey.

At this stage Barnes was befriended by Stephen Gardiner, who had known him years before in Cambridge as 'a trim, minor friar Augustine and as a good fellow in company was beloved by many'.

Gardiner arranged for him to have a private interview with the Cardinal, who commented on the offending sermon in most charitable terms and went out of his way to explain to the hot-head that if he continued to maintain his innocence of heresy then the machinery of a dread law would inevitably have to be put in motion. By all accounts Wolsey treated him with great fairness. After his trial Barnes made public penance and was then placed under house arrest, first in the Austin Friars, London, and then at Northampton. He escaped from the latter house and made it appear that he had drowned himself by leaving a pile of clothes and a 'farewell' letter to the Cardinal. In London again, he succeeded in finding a passage to the Netherlands. As an abjured heretic who had broken penance he was in an unenviable situation. Wolsey was understandably annoyed at being deceived and swore that he would take him captive, even if it 'cost him a great deal of money'. Robert Barnes stayed securely in Wittenberg, living by his pen, until 1534 when, as we shall see, he found himself by a strange twist of policy employed by Cromwell on diplomatic missions in northern Europe.

Secular drama, though in its infancy, could make apt comments on political themes. A play produced at Gray's Inn for the Christmas festivities in 1526 had as its plot that 'Lord Governance was ruled by Dissipation and Negligence, by whose misdemeanour and evil order Lady Public Weal was put from Governance'. This topical drama was written by John Rouse, a serjeant-at-law; the dialogue was enlivened with masques and morris dancing. The production was 'highly praised' by everyone who saw it, except the Cardinal, who was convinced that the play had been written about him. He sent both Rouse and one of the actors, Thomas Moyle, to prison and would have dearly liked to lay his hands on another, Simon Fish of Gray's Inn, who played the leading role. But Fish escaped abroad, where he took refuge with Tyndale and began work on his tract against the clergy, *A Supplication for Beggars*. Archbishop Warham was 'sorry such a matter should be taken in earnest' by Wolsey and before long Rouse and his friend were released. Even if there was no intention to attack Wolsey directly, it seems obvious that Rouse expected his audience to make its own comparisons with the Cardinal's rule – were this not the case the production would have been rather pointless.

The great man's swiftness to pounce on those he suspected of mocking him in public shows how on edge he was at this time. Once his position was seriously threatened the ballad makers felt safe to publish their popular prophecies and 1529 produced a spate of verses, such as *An Impeachment of Wolsey*:

> Thou knowest that Lucifer had a fall
> And all that follow him shall,
>   Into the pit of hell.

Though his history of these years was not revised for publication until after Wolsey's death, Polydore Vergil's comments on the Cardinal show the strength of feeling against him. A native of Urbino, Polydore had come to England in 1502 to serve as sub-collector of Peter's Pence and soon obtained preferment, including the archdeaconry of Wells. His contributions to humanist studies encouraged Henry VII to invite him to write a detailed history of England from the earliest times. Wolsey, as we have seen, made use of his services in 1514 on a visit to Rome, when he was angling for a cardinal's hat. While Polydore was away, however, Wolsey had been persuaded to support a rival Italian, Andrea Ammonio, one of the King's secretaries, in his bid for the papal collectorship. When Polydore discovered these moves on his return he wrote complaints in an indiscreet vein to his master, Cardinal Adrian, of the curia; the letters were intercepted and Vergil was sent to the Tower in April 1515. As Wolsey had hoped, the sub-collector's friends in Rome worked hard to influence his promotion to the cardinalate and once he had been elected he set Polydore free. Thereafter Polydore contrived to steer clear of politics, though he remained on friendly terms with Archbishop Warham and the busy diplomat Pace; yet he never forgot Wolsey's treatment of him. When in the later years of Henry VIII's reign he came to write up his contemporary notes for Book XXVII of his history, covering the years from 1513 to the birth of Prince Edward, he unleashed his unmitigated hatred of the Cardinal. This final book was to be first published in the third edition of the *Anglica Historia* in 1555.

Polydore portrays him in one purple patch after another as a man feeding on vanity. Having described his appointments as Archbishop of York and Lord Chancellor, the chronicler adds a pointed homily:

The enjoyment of such an abundance of good fortune is to be reckoned most praiseworthy if it is showered upon sober, moderate and self-controlled men, who are not proud in their power, nor are made arrogant with their money, nor vaunt themselves in other fortunate circumstances. None of these characteristics could be described in Wolsey, who acquiring so many offices at almost the same time, became so proud that he considered himself the peer of Kings. He soon began to use a golden chair, a golden cushion, a golden cloth on his table, and, when he was walking, to have the hat, symbol of the rank of cardinal, carried before him by a servant, raised up like some holy idol or other, and to have it put upon the very altar in the King's chapel ... Thus Wolsey, with his arrogance and ambition, raised against himself the hatred of the whole people and, in his hostility towards nobles and common folk, procured their great irritation at his vainglory. His own odiousness was truly complete, because he claimed he could undertake himself almost all public duties.

In another passage Polydore relates that 'nothing so much pleased him as worldly vanity, in comparison with which he held true glory of small worth. Hence when he saw himself elevated to the loftiest rung of the ladder his first consideration was by some vivid symbol to demonstrate his superiority over other people.' His foundations at Oxford and Ipswich, for whose sake he had despoiled religious houses, were 'intended to enhance his own empty glory, rather than serve the interests of religion or scholarship'.

This is far too harsh a verdict. Vergil can produce no word of praise for the Cardinal's extraordinary abilities or for his devotion to work; in his prejudiced view it was an utter disaster for England that he was at the helm for fifteen years. He piles on the vituperation and slips in pithy phrases as asides in his narrative. Wolsey was 'headlong and erratic in all his judgements', 'a man unique in his irresponsibility', a devious intriguer who would sell his country for a crock of gold; the churchman was 'to be taken by preferment as a fish by a worm'. No one could trust a man who so readily accepted bribes, and to his mind Wolsey's habit of untruthfulness went far beyond the bounds of diplomatic necessity; 'Nothing was more old-established in Wolsey (indeed from his youth onwards) than lying, which is the mark of a shameless man.' For Polydore Vergil the Cardinal is the villain of the piece as soon as he makes his début; only he was black enough to devise the scheme for Henry's divorce from Catherine of Aragon, so events are twisted to make him the architect of the 'King's Great Matter'. The chronicler's obituary notice is terse, when he describes

Wolsey's death at Leicester: 'How uncertain is the lot of man at birth! How equally inconstant in living! Wolsey flourished in importance and wealth. When he set in motion the marriage project, which he considered would be a fine thing for him, it brought him ruin.'

Polydore's dislike of the Cardinal coloured his whole approach. While all the earlier books of his *Anglica Historia* display a refreshingly critical attitude to the interpretation of events, so that Vergil may fairly be termed the first 'modern' historian of England, he could not hold in check his anti-Wolsey bias when tackling contemporary affairs. That this prejudice reached such intensity indicates the extent of the opposition that Wolsey's personality and policies had provoked.

4
The Sinews of Power

Authoritarian in his rule, Wolsey's goal was to preserve the status quo in church and state by maintaining, as he saw it, the internal harmony of the kingdom. Disaffection and injustice were the main evils that could disrupt internal peace, weaken the country he wanted to make a force in European affairs and undermine his own supremacy; as a benevolent despot he sought to cure those ills by firmness and by fair judgements. He had no scheme for introducing a body of reforming legislation, no vision of a new social code (such as Thomas Cromwell was to possess). Parliament played no part in Wolsey's system of government, for to him it was no more than a body for voting taxes in times of crisis and he never appreciated the aspirations of elected members to discuss the affairs of the commonwealth, to share in the forming of policy and to promote bills that might remedy the state of the law. Seemingly secure in his own power as the King's Lord Chancellor and the Pope's Cardinal legate, he was destined to be at the mercy of Parliament once he had lost Henry's confidence.

Contemporaries, English and foreign, saw the Lord Chancellorship as the greatest administrative and political office under the crown: the Chancellor was head of the oldest department of state, the dominant figure on the King's Council and the principal spokesman in Parliament, though his majestic office in its origins considerably ante-dated Council and Parliament. Effectively he was the King's principal minister, and it was this that appealed to Wolsey, this that gave him the status on the continent to negotiate with the Emperor, the Pope and Kings. Though he was also a judge, the head of the English judiciary, sitting in his own court in Westminster Hall in term to dispense justice, it was for him a secondary consideration, for he was not a lawyer and, unlike many ecclesiastics, he had not even taken a degree in canon or civil law. As a man unversed in pleadings at moots, who had never studied year books or forms of action and had never practised in any court, it is remarkable that Wolsey left such a mark upon the Court of Chancery. He took immense personal interest in the development of equity and appreciated more clearly than any of his predecessors the significance of Chancery as a 'court of the King's conscience'.

As a judge Wolsey quickly found his feet. His zeal for swift and impartial justice earned him early on the praise of Thomas More and impressed Sebastian Giustinian, who wrote that he had 'the reputation of being extremely just; he favours the people exceedingly, and especially the poor, hearing their suits and seeking to despatch them instantly. He also makes the lawyers plead gratis for all paupers.' (There was, however, nothing new about legal aid, which had been the predominant feature of the Court of Requests, the 'court of poor men's causes'.)

Cavendish in retrospect regarded Wolsey's Chancellorship as a golden age and at no time in his later years did he see 'justice better administered with indifference'. He was a layman's hero, not a lawyer's judge, for he had no time for legal artifice or the niceties of a well-argued case. Certainly his exercise of his judicial powers aroused antagonism from the legal profession, who resented being put in their place by an amateur, and his vigorous extension of the Chancery's equitable jurisdiction disturbed the harmony that had existed during the previous half-century with the common law courts of King's Bench, Common Pleas and Exchequer. The volume of Chancery litigation increased very noticeably during his rule, partly because he removed suits into Chancery from other courts by writs and injunctions, partly because his own court attracted fresh business since many litigants came to prefer pleadings in Chancery to proceeding by writ at common law. On his fall Wolsey was to be accused of abusing the system of injunctions to remove cases into his jurisdiction as well as of making insulting remarks about common law judges. Naturally, too, his ingrained arrogance and love of dignity counted against him with lawyers schooled in the Inns of Court, who were dismayed that the Cardinal, for a personal grudge, should order the confinement of one of their most distinguished brethren, Sir Amyas Paulet, to the Middle Temple. Under his long Chancellorship the conflict of jurisdiction became critical and it was perhaps the need to appease the common lawyers elected to the House of Commons in 1529 that led Henry VIII to appoint an outstanding lawyer as the Cardinal's successor. It was Wolsey's dual role as keeper of the King's conscience and as papal legate controlling the church courts that gave him his extraordinary power.

To maintain public order the Chancellor developed the Council's special jurisdiction, created in 1487, to enforce legislation summarily against riots, livery, maintenance and other breaches of the peace – the ancestor of the later Tudor Court of Star Chamber. Wolsey dominated this specialist committee of the Council, which sat regularly term by term; indeed, the room called the Star Chamber in Westminster Palace was enlarged at this time through fines levied by the Cardinal for breaches of the statute of *praemunire* – a strange irony. He thus reintroduced Henry VII's policy of clipping the wings of overmighty subjects, which had been in abeyance since 1509, and extended it.

The chronicler Edward Hall noted the immediate change that came with Wolsey in 1516: besides correcting perjurors, 'he punished also lords, knights, and men of all sorts for riots, bearing and maintenance in their countries, that the poor men lived quietly, so that no man durst bear for fear of imprisonment ...'. That year the Earl of Northumberland was sent to the Fleet Prison and other peers were heavily fined for keeping retainers. Forgery, perjury, slander and other offences that tended to threaten the King's peace were grist to his mill under 'the new law of the Star Chamber', as he put it. In the high summer of 1517, three months after the 'evil May day' riots in London, the Cardinal wrote proudly to his sovereign: 'And for your realm Our Lord be thanked, it was never in such peace nor tranquillity; for all this Summer I have had neither riot, felony, nor forcible entry, but that your laws be in every place indifferently maintained without leaning of any manner.' It was true, he continued, that there had been an affray between one Pygot, King's serjeant, and the servants of Sir Andrew Windsor about a wardship, in which a man had been slain, yet 'I trust the next term to learn them the law of the Star Chamber, that they shall ware how from henceforth they shall redress their matter with their hands.' He underlined the point: 'They be both learned in the temporal law, and I doubt not good example shall ensue to see them learn the new law of the Star Chamber, which (God willing) they shall have indifferently administered to them, according to their deserts.' A few months later he wrote to Rome in even prouder terms: 'Never was the kingdom in greater harmony and repose than now; such is the effort of my administration of justice and equity.' 'Justice' and 'equity', through the work of the Council in the Star Chamber and the Chancery respectively, preserved the common-wealth. Such iron-handed methods alienated many of the great land-owners, who came to regard Wolsey as the enemy of the nobility. There was soon 'a great snarling at court'.

Despite these legal developments Wolsey made no innovations in the staid routine of Chancery as an administrative department. Certainly the creaking machinery of the old departments of state needed more than minor adjustments to fit them for administering a modern kingdom, yet Wolsey was in such matters a traditionalist and it was left to his ultimate successor, Thomas Cromwell, to overhaul the entire system of government. The only practice of the Cardinal to attract attention was his taking of the great seal of England with him on his visits to France in the autumn of 1521 and again in 1527. It has been suggested that this was less for symbolic reasons, to enhance his stature, than to ensure that the fees due to him for issuing instru-ments under the seal were not diverted; and of course custody of the seal ensured the rigid control of new patents of appointments and royal grants, in which he was keenly concerned.

The Council, which Wolsey had entered in 1510, became largely transformed into the small body of councillors who in term time administered 'the new law of the Star Chamber'. There was a group of councillors attendant on the King, an ad hoc body of men who rode with him on progress from residence to residence in the summer season, but the Council proper had become eclipsed by Wolsey. The King sometimes complained that he was poorly attended by councillors when away from London and would feel deserted 'without some noble and wise sage personages about him'. Yet these never included the Cardinal, who abstained from royal progresses and kept his own rival court in term and vacations. In 1524 Henry issued a standing order to ensure that there was always a quorum of councillors in attendance on him. The first to be nominated were John Clerk, Bishop of Bath and

Wells, Secretary Knight, Sir Thomas More and the Dean of the chapel royal. 'Two of them at the least to be always present every day in the forenoon by 10 a.m. at the furtherest, and at afternoon by 2 p.m., in the King's dining chamber, or in such other place as shall fortune to be appointed for the Council Chamber.' There was no power sharing. This division suited Wolsey, for had there not been this informal group of councillors in the royal entourage, he could not have enlarged his own authority so effectively. He fed the King and those with him such information as he considered good for them, and they thus remained in ignorance of various details of policy. Only with the collapse of Wolsey's position in the autumn of 1529 did the shadowy 'council about the King' come into its own. From it was to develop the Privy Council proper.

Since King and Cardinal were rarely together a massive correspondence grew up between them, or rather between their secretaries. The key intermediary was the King's secretary, who read out most of the letters forwarded by Wolsey and wrote out the replies, though Henry would generally read the Cardinal's own letters himself. The secretary, whose office was to be elevated by Cromwell into a post of the first importance, remained under Wolsey's rule very much a personal servant of the King. Though he was rather more than a clerk and was privy to state secrets, he was certainly not an individual of ministerial rank. But because of the King's abhorrence of paperwork Wolsey feared the secretary might come between him and the sovereign. (This was in fact to occur with a vengeance with Stephen Gardiner's appointment in 1529.) Richard Pace, who became secretary in 1516, was a man of much less weight than his predecessor Ruthall, who had been Bishop of Durham; and so was his successor in 1526, William Knight. Because secretaries Pace and Knight were in turn employed on diplomatic missions overseas, in their absence Wolsey would be required to second a substitute to serve the King from his own secretariat – men such as Richard Sampson, Sir William Fitzwilliam and Brian Tuke. Henry thought Wolsey's household the finest training ground for secretaries and both Knight and Gardiner had graduated in that hard school.

The incident of the 'evil May day rising' in London served to strengthen Wolsey's authority. The city apprentices and the craft guilds had long envied the prosperity of the foreign communities, and agitators worked on their fears of unemployment and loss of trade through foreign competition. Dr Beale, a canon of St Mary Spittal, exploited this xenophobic mood in a notable sermon after Easter, inciting the apprentices to violence: 'As birds would defend their nest, so ought Englishmen to cherish and defend themselves and to hurt and grieve aliens for the common weal.' Trouble flared up in the streets at the end of April and there were rumours that on May day all foreigners within the city's bounds would be massacred. The Cardinal summoned the lord mayor to discuss the crisis. They decided that it would be folly to call out the watch, who would be easily overpowered by the mob, and instead ordered a curfew until seven o'clock on May morning. As expected, the apprentices and watermen thronged the streets to the cry 'Prentices and Clubs!'. There were ugly scenes in which the property of aliens was looted. Prominent men such as the Spanish and Portuguese ambassadors and the King's French secretary were lucky to escape with their lives, while the mayor and sheriffs were forced to release the prisoners in Newgate. Wolsey had prudently had some pieces of artillery installed for defending York Place if need be, and he had alerted Norfolk, Surrey and Shrewsbury to be in readiness with troops. The Howards, leading 1,300 soldiers, succeeded in restoring order, capturing many rioters. Thirteen of them were summarily dealt with and gibbeted. The rest were kept close prisoners to await the King's decision.

'This has been a great commotion,' wrote one eyewitness, 'but the terror was greater than the harm done.' He paid tribute to Wolsey's precautions for dealing with the touble, without which 'much greater mischief and bloodshed would have taken place'. Shortly afterwards a remarkable scene was staged in Westminster Hall, when some four hundred prisoners, with halters round their necks, were brought before the King. The Cardinal made a lengthy plea to Henry for clemency, but the latter at first disregarded it. Then the cry, 'Mercy, gracious Lord', was taken up by everyone in the hall and the King agreed to pardon the men. Wolsey conveyed this news to the prisoners, urging them to obey the laws in future and to ensure that all strangers were well treated. Overjoyed, they threw away their halters. 'It was a very fine spectacle and well-arranged,' we are told. Undoubtedly the Cardinal had stage-managed the scene and for the moment he earned no less popularity for the pardons than Henry.

Wolsey seemed to be deliberately edging the established families from their traditional places in government, though the evidence for this is slender. Buckingham, who had held the chief honorific offices at the coronation, never held a ministerial post, largely, it was felt, because there was such antipathy between him and the Cardinal. Norfolk largely shared Buckingham's view that Wolsey was a *parvenu*. (While Wolsey was still almoner and he was Earl of Surrey, Thomas Howard was 'discountenanced by the King', and when he left court in a pique Wolsey remarked it would be good 'if he were ousted from his lodging there altogether'.) Yet the Lord Chancellor and the Lord Treasurer could hardly avoid each other in term time. They eventually came to achieve a working relationship, which led one ambassador to consider that they were 'very intimate'. When the Cardinal became Princess Mary's godfather, Norfolk's Duchess became godmother. The Duke was not sorry to be left behind as guardian of the realm when there was a general exodus of the great in the land to support Henry at the Field of Cloth of Gold, for he disliked the courtier's life as much as Wolsey. The second Duke was, by Tudor standards, an old man and he wanted to live out his days in peace without too much friction with Wolsey; but his son was impatient and outspoken.

Surrey had become Lord Admiral when his younger brother, Sir Edward Howard, was killed at Brest in April 1513. By May 1516 he was on the Council – an unusual combination of father and son serving together. With the benefit of hindsight it is easy to suspect disagreements concerning men and measures between Surrey and the Cardinal in those years. There are indications that the Earl spoke out against Wolsey when he first became a legate and Shakespeare has him saying that the Cardinal 'wrought to be a legate without the King's assent or knowledge'. There is no firm evidence for Polydore Vergil's accusation that in 1520 Wolsey 'decided to isolate him, or rather to banish him, to some place or other', because he had married Buckingham's daughter and was 'a violent man'. Surrey was appointed Lord Lieutenant of Ireland for no other reason than that he was the fittest man for the job; he would have stayed longer in the post but for dysentery and the need to employ himself, when he was fit again, against the French. It was only with Buckingham's fall that Surrey became noticeably critical of Wolsey and encouraged Skelton to lampoon him (see page 66). Yet the Cardinal took no steps to prevent

him succeeding his father as Treasurer – as was certainly in his power –
when the old man, who had wept as he presided at Buckingham's trial,
decided to retire to Framlingham.

Another peer in disgrace for his friendship with Buckingham was
Henry Percy, fifth Earl of Northumberland, who had fought for
Henry VII at Blackheath and for his son at the Spurs. In 1516 Wolsey
sent him to the Fleet. This sentence probably increased his unpopularity with the nobility, but there was nothing savage about his
verdict. Much is sometimes made of Wolsey's imprisonment, in 1518,
of Sir Robert Sheffield, an old servant of the Tudors who had been
Speaker of the House of Commons in 1510 and 1512. By 1517,
however, he was remote from politics and the charge of harbouring
murderers that cost him his freedom was not invented. Even Polydore
Vergil omits a charge against the Cardinal on this count.

In 1519 the palace was purged of a group of 'young minions', who
were thought by staid courtiers to be over-familiar with the King and
to show scant respect for councillors and senior officials. Men such as
Sir Edward Neville and Sir Francis Bryan had become too informal
with their sovereign 'and played such light touches with him that they
forgot themselves'. Wolsey was not himself the instigator of this
palace revolution, though once the problem of taming the wild bucks
was raised officially he added his voice to the complaints of Norfolk,
Worcester and Sir Thomas Boleyn. The Cardinal was, indeed, too
little at court to be much plagued by the mimicry and tomfoolery of
Bryan and his friends of the Privy Chamber, who ran down English
tradition as prim and pompous whenever their elders lifted reproving
fingers. Secretary Pace had warned him that Sir Nicholas Carew was
up to no good and had returned to court 'too soon'. As far as Wolsey
was concerned there was no harm in their revelry, providing the young
sparks did not attempt to interfere with policy or to influence the King
over appointments, and so long as such behaviour did not debase the
monarchy. Once they overstepped the mark and clipped the divinity
that hedged the King, something had to be done and Wolsey led the
councillors' request for their banishment for a season. Henry did not
disagree. While he regretted the need to discipline his boisterous
companions, he accepted the Cardinal's complaint and agreed to a
purge of the Privy Chamber. Herbert, as Lord Chamberlain, was to
summon the offenders and dismiss them from their posts about the

King, warning them to concern themselves with their other appointments in the administration, which must no longer be reckoned as sinecures. In part this purge was an attempt to reform the household administration by preventing offices from being discharged by deputies. The places of the 'young minions' were filled by 'four staid and ancient Knights', headed by Sir William Kingston. All were nominees of Wolsey.

Following this incident the King decided to make a personal effort to devote much more of his time to public affairs. Some talked of him 'leading a new life' and were convinced that he had put away childish things. The Cardinal was expected to be less in command. As an earnest of his good intent Henry caused three memoranda to be compiled about this time. The first and most important of these was 'A Remembrance of such things as the King's Grace will have to be done and hath given in command to his Cardinal to put the same in effectual execution as hereafter ensueth'. The financial changes included payments to the Privy Purse of £10,000 a year by quarterly instalments at the hands of the Treasurer of the Chamber, and they envisaged close control by the King himself of all royal revenues. The Lord Treasurer, the Chancellor of the Duchy of Lancaster and other officers were to make their reports to the sovereign 'in his own person'. In the judicial sphere the Lord Chancellor and the judges were to make reports to him on the 'whole state of the realm and order of every shire'. The organization and financing of the royal household was to be reformed 'without any further delay'.

The second memorandum was an agenda listing topics that Henry intended to debate with his Council. The items included the impartial administration of justice, improvements in the government of Ireland, the problem of the unemployed and, most significantly, the state of the financial machinery, for the King 'intendeth to reform his Exchequer to establish substantial order in the same'. The third document concerned measures for the King's safety, the succession, potential rebellions and various miscellaneous topics of much less weight. It is hard to believe that Wolsey was not behind these three papers, which purported to be Henry's personal views, or at any rate that he did not encourage his sovereign's sudden urge to take a more active part in administration and be better informed about the state of the realm. (Certainly in the previous year he had been writing

various papers and collecting facts and figures about the royal household.)

By now Wolsey was firmly established in power and he knew
Henry's character too well to imagine his interest would persist: there
would be no threat to his own supremacy from a master who had no
application and became easily bored, a man who always procrastinated
when it came to setting pen to paper or settling down to despatches,
who when the sun shone laughed at the pile of papers and said, 'I will
read the remnant at night', who used every little ache and pain as an
excuse for taking a holiday from public affairs. Even as late as 1526
Henry was reported to have spent the entire five months from the
middle of May in hunting, and much of his admiration for the Cardinal
derived from his amazement that anyone could concentrate to such
effect through a long day at his desk. Sir Thomas More once conveyed
to Wolsey the King's marvel at his stamina when a reading of the
letters he had written occupied more than two hours.

The main reforms adumbrated in these three memoranda all
depended on the King's active participation, as if the clock were being
put back to the days of the first Tudor, who so regularly checked
accounts and signed warrants. Had these reforms come to pass Wolsey
would indeed have become very much of a junior partner of the King
in the government of the realm, but as it was his position remained
unchanged. In his relations with officials and courtiers it would have
suited him to have the need for change presented as a royal command
'to his Cardinal to put the same into effectual execution'. For the Lord
Treasurer and his under-treasurer and barons of the Exchequer to have
to report regularly to the sovereign was a requirement that Norfolk
could not escape. Yet there was every likelihood that Henry would
depute the receiving of these financial reports to Wolsey, who would
thus be in a position to interfere in the affairs of the Exchequer. In the
event these plans for widespread 'economical reform' were stillborn.
Perhaps formal discussion with councillors satisfied Henry that all was
well or that a radical overhaul of the system would create more
problems than it solved. The only area where reforms were introduced
by Wolsey was in the organization of the royal household, and then
not for another six years.

In 1519 it had been announced that 'the King's pleasure is that his
household from henceforth shall be put in honourable, substantial and

profitable order, without any further delay'. Henry himself lost interest in the proposal and Wolsey, too preoccupied with foreign affairs, had no time to work out the details. The problem was accordingly shelved. In 1525, however, when the financial crisis demanded retrenchment and the Cardinal's position was for the first time seriously challenged, he revived the proposals, embodying detailed reforms in the Eltham Ordinance, which was endorsed by King and Council in January 1526. The Eltham Ordinance recognized two basic weaknesses in the time-honoured system: there were too many officials at court, many of them without any definite job to do, and the frequent absence of royal servants (notably accountants on special duties such as purveyance for the army) robbed the Lord Steward of professional men essential for the good administration of his department. In short there were too many of the wrong people in the Chamberlain's list at court and too few of the right people in the Steward's list.

Henry had been lavish in granting posts in his Chamber, with the result that there were far too many carvers, cup bearers, ushers and sewers, all of whom brought their own servants to court, to be housed and fed at the King's expense. Even when some of the masters were absentee sinecurists, their servants clung to the privilege of free board and lodging at court. Those with duties to perform too often collected their fees but had their functions discharged by deputies, and the ranks of hangers-on were swollen by servants of servants of royal servants. Brawling was commonplace among this army of pensioners, and the King's Guard was in no better state than his Chamber. The chronicler Hall remarked that the 'great number of the yeoman of the guard were very chargeable and ... there were many officers stricken in age which had servants in the court, and so the King was served with their servants and not with his own'. The supernumeraries were now dismissed with suitable pensions, as recommended by Sir Henry Guildford, the controller. The gentlemen of the Chamber, for instance, were reduced from 112 to 12, the sewers from 45 to 6 and the grooms of the Chamber from 69 to 15. 'Alas, what sorrow and what lamentation was made when all these persons should depart the court.' But if the dismissed men could no longer cheat their sovereign, it was said that they would pillage the countryside! Henceforth ability was to be the sole criterion for filling posts at court and a ladder of promotion was devised, with weight given to seniority. Regular attendance was now obligatory, unless leave of absence had been granted, and no duties could be performed by a deputy. In particular no serjeant of arms, herald, messenger, minstrel, falconer, huntsman or footman was to bring to court 'any boys or rascals'.

These reforms intimately affected Henry. He was to have his Privy Chamber 'and inward lodgings reserved secret, at the pleasure of his Grace, without repair of any great multitude' – except for the favoured few, no courtier was to presume to cross the threshold. The staff of the Chamber were to be circumspect, careful of their language and 'expert in outward parts'. At any one time there were now fifteen of them on duty, headed by the Marquess of Exeter, Henry's first cousin, 'who has been brought up since childhood with the King'. Henry Courtenay, born in 1498, who had succeeded to his father's earldom of Devon in 1511 and taken Buckingham's place as a knight of the garter, was appointed 'privy councillor immediately attendant on the King' in the autumn of 1525, a few months after his promotion to the marquisate of Exeter. Under him were six gentlemen-in-waiting, two gentlemen ushers, four grooms, a barber and a page. The servants of the Chamber were to be 'loving together and of good unity and accord, keeping secret all such things as shall be done or said in the same'. They were not to be curious about the King's movements, not to gossip about his pastimes and habits, the company he kept, his 'late or early going to bed, or anything done by his Grace'. If they were, they would incur the King's displeasure. The gentlemen-in-waiting spent the night on the pallet inside the Chamber, to be ready in the morning to dress the King, but of the six only Norris attended Henry in his bedchamber. The ushers reported by seven o'clock, to guard the door during the day, and the grooms by that hour had swept the Chamber, put down fresh straw and laid and lit the fire. Each morning the King's doublet, hose and shoes (though not his gown) were brought to the Chamber door by the yeoman of the wardrobe and handed to one of the grooms, who would warm the garments by the fire and then deliver them to the gentlemen-in-waiting. (No groom or usher was to presume to lay hands upon the royal person or interfere with the preparations for his dressing.)

Whenever the King was away from the Privy Chamber the staff were not to gamble immoderately at dice or cards – as happened in the groom porter's house; they could play cards or chess, provided voices were not raised, but immediately the sovereign returned they were to abandon their game. Penny, the barber, was to be ready each morning with water, cloths, knives, combs and scissors to trim the King's beard and hair, and, because of his daily contact with his sovereign, was required not only to be scrupulous about his cleanliness but to avoid bad company.

In the Lord Steward's 'below stairs' departments officials were required to attend to their specific duties and no other. In the future, for instance, it would not be possible for a clerk of the royal larder to be away from court arranging for military provisions. The laziness (Barclay had taunted) that seemed to go with the Tudor household livery ('They have no labour, yet are they well beseen/Barded and guerded in pleasant white and green') was now outlawed. The establishment of each department was set down, with the wages and allowances for each individual and a precise statement of his or her duties. The scullions who washed up the crockery had been found to be working in most unhygienic conditions, and as most of them worked naked, the rest clad in garments of 'vileness', the master cooks were now allowed 20 marks a year to provide them with proper clothes. Leavings from the dinner plates and the dregs from tankards and glasses were no longer to be left in the courtyard for flies and vermin to feast on, but were to be collected after every meal under the supervision of the almoner's staff and given to the beggars at the gate. No dogs were to be kept within the palace buildings, 'other than some few spaniels for the ladies', but they had to be left in the kennels, in order that the palace might remain 'sweet, clean and well-furnished', and the keeping of hawks, ferrets and other animals required a royal permit. There were rudimentary arrangements to prevent embezzlement and to ensure economy in fuel and lighting. Every morning by nine o'clock the remains of all candles and torches were to be collected for re-use, instead of being pilfered or thrown away. Specimen menus were set down for each rank in the ladder of court society and there were detailed instructions about the allocation of horses. (Significantly, 'a cardinal' was allowed stabling for twenty-four horses when lodged at court, a duke for no more than eighteen.)

Changes of such magnitude involved changes in command. The old Lord Chamberlain, the Earl of Worcester, had been getting decrepit and had been too feeble either to play a part in bringing in the reforms or to try to obstruct their introduction. Lord Sandys, the treasurer of Calais, was appointed to succeed him; and in fact Worcester died in April 1526. In place of Sir Thomas Boleyn, Sir William Fitzwilliam became treasurer of the Household, and Edmund Peckham replaced John Shurley as cofferer. Master Shurley had gone about his duties in his own quaint way and when Wolsey was working out details of the reforms had gone off to his Sussex home for the summer, setting a lamentable example to his staff.

By ancient custom all men and women who had lodgings at court took their main meals together in the King's hall, grouped with their servants into messes. But, just as Henry dined in state in the hall only on red-letter days and ate most of the year in his Privy Chamber with his personal attendants, so other officials took to dining in their own lodgings, inviting their own guests to their table at the King's expense. By 1526 this practice of 'sundry noblemen, gentlemen and others' delighting 'to dine in corners and secret places' had got completely out of hand and as a result much of the food sent up to the hall was wasted or misused. From now on the number of tables in lodgings was limited to those of the Lord Chamberlain, the Vice-Chamberlain, the Captain of the Guard and the Lord Steward. It was to the last table that councillors, henchmen and the Steward's senior staff repaired. At one stroke the number of hangers-on who had found ways of eating free was drastically reduced and it was possible to enforce stricter control over the amount of food supplied. At the same time the list of those receiving the traditional allowance of 'bouche of court', consisting of a daily ration of firewood, candles, bread, wine and beer sent to their rooms, was pruned and the amounts were firmly fixed according to rank.

Wolsey's ordinance achieved notable economies and introduced a new principle of service to the crown that should have strengthened the *esprit de corps* of officials, high and low. Yet unfortunately his reforms did not go far enough, for there was no provision to guarantee that they would be fully implemented, and the hope that the chief officers of the household (steward, treasurer and controller) would achieve these ends by meeting round the Board of Green Cloth only once in the whole year shows a surprisingly poor grasp of administrative matters. It was not until thirteen years later, under Thomas Cromwell, that the root of this problem was tackled with the formation of an adequate organization, with stricter control by the Board of day-to-day affairs.

Wolsey's principal attempt to use controls to remedy social injustice was in the sphere of agrarian reform. He sought to restrain the enclosure movement, mainly because large-scale sheep farming by both lay and monastic landowners was causing depopulation of hamlets that had once prospered under the plough. Unless administrative action was taken an act of Parliament of 1515, requiring land enclosed for conversion to pasture to be restored to cultivation within a year, seemed likely to remain as ineffective a law as the earlier statute of 1489 'for keeping up of towns for husbandry'.

As a first step the Cardinal needed to obtain full information about the state of enclosures up and down the land, so in May 1517 he appointed commissioners of enquiry to establish all enclosures that had been made since 1485, requiring them to send their returns into Chancery. These returns furnished a great mass of detail about the state of the countryside and are a tribute to Wolsey's driving force. There was a further commission in 1518. Then in July of that year he issued a decree ordering all enclosures, hedges and ditches made in the past thirty-two years to be demolished, on pain of fines of £100, unless cause could be shown that they both benefited the commonwealth and were within the law. The crown entered proceedings against many landowners in the Court of Chancery, among those pleading guilty through ignorance of the law being Bishop Foxe of Winchester. Many offenders were compelled to enter into recognizances to pull down their quickset hedges. Yet this policy was bitterly resented by landowners as a whole – the very people on whose shoulders lay the burden or local administration, including the execution of the laws 'for the improvement of tillage'.

For all his reforming intentions, Wolsey could not hope to do more than slow down the pace of the enclosure movement. The reissue of proclamations in the mid-1520s increased the suspicion that he was seeking to court the populace, though a truer interpretation is that he did not shrink from arousing the hostility of landowners when he was convinced that his policy was for the 'good of the common weal'. It would have required the utmost persistence for a statesman to swim against the strong tide of the enclosing movement. In fact Wolsey became distracted by other problems and had not created adequate machinery for dealing with the situation, though even in his final months of power writs were issued from Chancery to sheriffs in Kent and Northamptonshire to destroy enclosures. John Longland, Bishop of Lincoln, wrote in 1528, 'There was never thing done in England more for the commonwealth than to redress these enormous decays of towns and making of enclosures.' Yet he implored the Cardinal to redouble his efforts. If only he would visit the countryside, he went on, he would weep at the sight of ruined hamlets, the ploughs forsaken and great poverty. His enemies, however, did not underrate the campaign Wolsey had mounted and one of the charges brought against him when he was at the King's mercy was that he had sought 'to execute the statute of enclosing', for it was judged that he had acted *ultra vires* in carrying out the provisions of the limited statute of 1515.

In the spring of 1521 the court was dumbfounded at the reports of the Duke of Buckingham's alleged treasons. The fall of the Duke, who headed England's most illustrious house, was later to be laid at Wolsey's door, partly because the two men were poles apart in origin and outlook, partly because of Polydore Vergil's prejudiced account. The chronicler wrote that Buckingham met his heavy personal expenses of attending the Field of Cloth of Gold grudgingly and knew not 'what could be the cause of so great an expenditure of cash unless it was for the future spectacle of foolish speeches, or for a conference of trivialities. Hence he decided it truly unbearable to be subservient to so base and uncivil a fellow. Wolsey's ears readily drank in these and similar opinions which the Duke imprudently put about . . .'. Yet there is no shred of evidence that Buckingham found the costs involved in any way difficult, or indeed unacceptable. Polydore has the Cardinal 'flaming with hatred and lusting to sate it' with Stafford blood. He therefore 'induced the King to consider the Duke as someone to fear and, at length, as someone to get rid of'. Even after such strong words, however, the chronicler has to admit that Buckingham fell 'because he had coveted the crown'. Wolsey felt no subsequent remorse at 'devouring the beautiful swan'. In his view the Duke was guilty of constructive treason and his schemings for the succession had quite shaken the King.

Henry Stafford, Duke of Buckingham, was head and shoulders above the rest of the nobility. His father had led a rebellion against

Richard III with the aim of putting Henry Tudor on the throne, and had paid the supreme penalty. The son revelled in his Plantagenet blood, for he was descendant of Thomas of Woodstock, youngest son of Edward III, and nephew of Edward IV's queen, Elizabeth Woodville. He was bound by family ties to many other noble families (his wife was a Percy, their son had married a Pole and their daughters had married a Howard and a Neville respectively). These were formidable connections. Stafford himself seemed to be a survival from an older feudal age, with his great castle at Thornbury in Gloucestershire and his fine residence at Penshurst in Kent, with his liveried retainers and a rent roll that was easily the most valuable in England. He was popular, except with his own tenants, to whom he appeared as a tyrannical magnate. The King had known him for as long as he could remember. They had often been together in the tiltyard, on the tennis court and on the hunting-field, and his appointments as Lord High Steward of England and Lord High Constable at the coronation were taken as an indication of his exceptional position. Buckingham was, too, a close friend of Queen Catherine and his sisters were both ladies-in-waiting. The Duke was in short a man of regal lineage, a prince in all but name. Yet until the close of 1520 no one had suspected his ambitions.

When in 1518 Catherine of Aragon gave birth to yet another stillborn child Henry despaired of having a legitimate son. If Princess Mary married a Valois or a Habsburg, as seemed most probable, there was the terrible risk of England becoming an appendage to a continental power. Yet an unmarried Mary was an even greater hazard for the peace of England. Inevitably people commented on the claims that Buckingham might put forward to the succession if something should happen to the King. In consequence he became a marked man. King and Cardinal had overheard these whisperings and Henry became sure that the Duke was at the centre of a fearful web of conspiracy. The King wrote to Wolsey asking him to 'make good watch on the Duke of Suffolk, on the Duke of Buckingham, on my lord of Northumberland' and other peers: 'No more to you at this time, but *sapienti pauca*.' Wolsey did not 'frame' Buckingham, for the King was already convinced of the threat offered by his Plantagenet blood. The Cardinal's eyes and ears found out much about the Duke's vainglorious boasting and his indiscreet prophecies. Men in his service reported him to be lamenting the execution of Warwick in the last days of the fifteenth century, for God was now punishing Henry VIII for his father's ruthlessness over the White Rose of England 'by not suffering the King's issue to prosper'. The Duke had allegedly listened too eagerly to those who foretold his own accession.

Naturally in this atmosphere of scare and suspicion there was a degree of hearsay and invention, but none of it was prompted by Wolsey. Certainly the Duke was looked on as the spokesman of the great nobles who resented the Cardinal's extraordinary power – courtiers remembered that when Buckingham was holding the basin for the King to wash his hands at a banquet he had deliberately spilt water over Wolsey's shoes. But even systematic opposition to the Cardinal was insignificant compared with angering the King by idle speculation about the succession, and an unwise remark about his desperate lack of a prince touched him on a raw spot. In such a mood the years of royal friendship, far from excusing the offence, served only to aggravate it. Buckingham was rash, proud and ambitious and at his trial proved to be unable to convince his peers of his innocence. It is true that Wolsey told the French ambassador after his execution that the Duke had fallen because he had intrigued against his policy, but this was a typical piece of boasting. It was the Cardinal who in vain recommended that Henry should send letters of condolence to the Duke's widow and her son. Moreover the spoils of the Stafford inheritance went chiefly to men Wolsey trusted little more than he had trusted Buckingham – Norfolk and Suffolk.

Parliament met only once throughout Wolsey's rule, from April to August 1523, and no Lord Chancellor has ever spent so little time on the Woolsack. In the stormy session of 1515, when the Commons were giving vent to the latent anticlericalism provoked by the case of Richard Hunne, Wolsey, newly created Cardinal, had advised the King on a speedy dissolution to prevent a sustained attack on the Church. On the day Parliament was dissolved Archbishop Warham resigned the Chancellorship. It was not until he had served seven and a half years as Warham's successor that Wolsey presided in the Upper House for the first time. At the time of Buckingham's conspiracy Henry had urged the issue of writs for summoning another Parliament to strengthen the position of the crown and also to deal with the state of Ireland, but Wolsey had been able to persuade him not to do so. He had no wish to give the knights from the shires and the burgesses a forum for attacks on his own administration. Even less did he want to give them an opportunity to bring forward legislation that would cut at the heart of clerical privilege, the concept of benefit of clergy and the whole apparatus of the church courts.

With Parliament in abeyance, Convocation could not meet for its parallel purposes, though with the King's leave there was nothing to prevent the holding of provincial convocations. As Archbishop of York Wolsey chose not to summon a single convocation of the northern province until November 1530, while by his legatine authority he did his utmost to prevent Warham from holding effective gatherings of clergy from the southern province. Just as the administration of the Church was for the Cardinal a matter entirely for himself as legate, so in secular affairs he regarded the administration of the State as his prerogative as Lord Chancellor. He saw no place for the regular meeting of representative assemblies, which were inefficient vehicles for conducting business, unreliable and always tending to question the higher powers, to open the flood gates of controversy and to talk endlessly – largely about matters that were no proper concern of theirs and on which they had little to contribute. In taking this attitude towards Parliament Wolsey was very much a child of his time, for throughout Europe the fortunes of representative assemblies were at a low ebb. The years from December 1515 to April 1523, and again the interval from August 1523 to November 1529, which was nearly as long, formed a period of personal rule that can be compared with Charles I's eleven years of ruling without Parliament.

It was only the need for finance on a massive scale for the war that convinced Wolsey that he could not avoid summoning Parliament in 1523. In the previous year he had raised £352,231 by forced loans and a further sum by borrowing from the City of London. The legality of the loans was questioned no less than the principles of the assessments, yet at court there was no little admiration for Wolsey's ingenuity and dexterity. It is worth noting that he himself had been assessed at £4,000, while Archbishop Warham's figure was no more than £1,000. Essentially the loan was a tax (in the tradition of 'Morton's fork') on those who could afford to pay, even if a London alderman moaned: 'For God's sake remember this, that rich merchants in ware be bare of money.' Wolsey had agreed to citizens being allowed to make their own returns, which would not be made public. He also laid down that the laity should not be permitted to know the details of clerical wealth. But as the considerable sum provided by the forced loan proved to be nowhere near sufficient for the war, there was no alternative to summoning Parliament, which was now asked to find the unprecedented sum of £800,000.

On 15 April the Commons assembled in the great hall of Blackfriars and elected as Speaker Sir Thomas More, who had been a Councillor for five years and had then held the office of Undertreasurer at the Exchequer. Members knew that he would be a choice acceptable to the King, though there is no evidence that Wolsey was responsible for arranging his election. More began by making an historic request for the Commons to be allowed to speak freely, without fear of the sovereign's 'dreadful displeasure, every man to discharge his conscience, and boldly, in everything incident among us, to declare his advice'. This petition was granted and Wolsey feared that members would range critically over every aspect of policy before getting down to the task for which they had been summoned. They were indeed opposed to the attempted conquest of French territory on the grounds of expense, and one member, Thomas Cromwell, prepared a long speech claiming that Thérouanne, captured in 1513, had cost 'more than twenty such ungracious dogholes could be worth' (see page 146). There was, surprisingly, no immediate move to limit benefit of clergy, perhaps because Speaker More was able to steer men away from this dangerous topic.

After a fortnight of debating, the Cardinal came down to the Commons to make a statement about the King's desperate need for £800,000 for the continental war, which could be raised by taxing every man's lands and goods at a rate of 4 shillings in the pound. His words were coolly received. Next morning the Speaker repeated the demand, but members groaned at what was expected of them: loyal subjects would be reduced to 'barter clothes for victuals and bread and cheese'. Because of the recent forced loans money everywhere was tight and further attempts to collect taxes at the high rates proposed led some to predict that 'the realm itself for want of money would grow in a sort barbarous and ignoble'. After a long and acrimonious debate a deputation was sent to the Cardinal, beseeching him to move the

King 'to be content with a more easier sum'. Wolsey remained unmoved and told the deputation he would 'rather have his tongue
plucked out of his head with a pair of pinsons than to move the King'
to accept a lesser total. As a rich man he could not see how others
could find the tax an impossible burden. He was quite aware, he told
them, of the luxury in which people lived, as if 'he grudged that any
man should fare well and be well clothed but himself'.

What amazed him even more than the Commons' initial refusal to
grant supplies on the scale demanded was the way in which the subject
of the Blackfriars debate and the deputation to him was being noised
abroad 'in every alehouse', making people panic. Impatient to settle
the matter and to put the Commons in their place, he determined on
30 April to go to their Chamber a second time. The Speaker, sensing
the feeling of the House, skilfully put the question of whether Wolsey
should be admitted with his customary retinue.

Masters [began More] forasmuch as my Lord Cardinal lately, ye wot well,
laid to our charge the lightness of our tongues for things uttered in this house,
it shall not in my mind be amiss to receive him in all his pomp, with his maces,
his pillars, his poleaxes, his crosses, his hat, and his great seal, too, to the intent
that if he find the like fault in us hereafter, we may be the bolder for ourselves
to lay blame on those that his Grace bringeth hither with him.

When Wolsey arrived he was heard in silence and then irritated the
House by asking individual members their opinions. Since he came
from the King himself he demanded a reasonable answer, yet not a
man replied. He addressed them again: 'Masters, unless it be the
manner of your House, as of likelihood it is, by the mouth of your
Speaker, whom you have chosen for trusty and wise – as indeed he is –
in such cases to alter your mind, here is without doubt a marvellous
obstinate silence.' More at once fell on his knees to excuse the silence
of the House. Of course, he said, the members, however wise, were
'abashed at the presence of so noble a personage', yet their custom was
that while the Commons might listen to communications from
outside, they did not debate with strangers present. The Cardinal
could only retreat, thoroughly put out.

After another sixteen days the House agreed to vote supplies but
on a far from generous scale: 2 shillings in the pound from people with
incomes of £20 and over; 1 shilling from those with between £1 and

£20; and 4 pence a head from the poorest subjects. In each case the payments were to be spread over two years. Such parsimony irked Wolsey, who now put up Sir John Hursey, Member for Sleaford and Master of the King's Wards, to agitate for voting the original amount, by offering a further 1 shilling in the pound for a third year from men owning land worth more than £50 a year. When the House re-assembled after the Whitsun recess a split developed between land-owners and the men from the boroughs on a proposal that an extra grant of 1 shilling in the pound on goods (moveables) should be levied in a fourth year. At length More healed the breach and the tax was voted. Far from being grateful to More for achieving this outcome, Wolsey (according to Roper) said to him in the gallery of York House: 'Would to God you had been at Rome, Master More, when I made you Speaker.' 'Your Grace not offended, as would I, too, my Lord,' replied the other, and tactfully changed the subject by saying how much he preferred the gallery at York House to the one at Hampton Court. Yet Wolsey did not harbour any grievance and almost at once wrote to the King asking for More to be given £100 from the Chamber in addition to the usual Speaker's 'reward' of £150. No man, wrote the Cardinal, 'would better deserve the same than he hath done', and he is 'not the most ready to speak and solicit his own cause'.

The experience of the summer of 1523, added to that of the winter of 1515, made Wolsey determined as far as possible never to call another Parliament. He had no intention of abiding by the terms of the subsidy bill that had received the royal assent and, overriding the Commons' stipulation that the money voted should be collected over four years, he issued commissions in October 1523 for the collection of the full amount 'by anticipation'. But not even he could achieve this and in the counties there were plots to seize the tax officials. He was no less high-handed over clerical taxation for the war emergency. Although sums could be voted only by the two separate convocations, by virtue of his legatine powers Wolsey ordered the Convocation of Canterbury, which Warham had summoned to meet at St Paul's, to join representatives from the province of York at Westminster to levy a tax of fifty per cent of one year's revenue on all benefices in England, payable over five years. England had never previously experienced a legatine synod usurping the role of the ancient convocations. 'Gentle

Paul, lay down thy sword, for Peter of Westminster hath shaven thy beard,' wrote Skelton.

The final straw came two years later with the 'amicable loan', as it was euphemistically termed, imposed by the King's prerogative. Henry needed a great deal of money if he was to take advantage of the French defeat at Pavia by leading an army to Normandy, and after the troubles of 1523 neither he nor Wolsey dared face another Parliament. So Wolsey devised the 'amicable loan', a compulsory tax, assessed by the King's commissioners on lay and ecclesiastical property. The Cardinal refused to listen to those who warned him that the country could afford no more, that the cupboard was bare and that the commissioners would be resisted in city, village and monastery. To the lord mayor and aldermen of London he said, 'Sirs, resist not and ruffle not in this case, for it may fortune to cost more than their heads.' The citizens of London became so vociferous that instead of being assessed they were allowed to vote the King a benevolence. But when the Cardinal asked the lord mayor how much they were prepared to grant he and the aldermen procrastinated. 'If I enter into any grant,' said the mayor, 'it might fortune to cost me my life.' Wolsey could not believe his ears. 'Your life! That is a marvellous word. For your will towards the King will the citizens put you in jeopardy of your life?'

He had entirely misjudged current opinion, and once he had given way in the capital it was impossible to expect the commissioners to carry out their assessments in the rest of the kingdom. Sir Thomas Boleyn was roughly handled in Maidstone, while East Anglia was on the verge of civil war. Norfolk (the third Duke, who had succeeded his father the previous year) came to the Suffolk cloth-weaving area, where labourers had assembled, and demanded who was their leader. One of the men answered that their captain's name was 'Poverty', 'for he and his cousin Necessity have brought us to this doing'. The Duke advised them to submit and disperse peaceably; they submitted, but there was little chance of the revenue being collected. It was the same all over the country. The 'amicable loan' devised by Wolsey had utterly failed and Henry had perforce to abandon his grandiose plans. As we have seen (page 51) Wolsey, greatly relieved, now arranged for a truce with France to be signed on 14 August. Far from keeping England settled, internally at peace and strong enough to enable him to make it a power in Europe, the affair of the loan had provoked difficulties on a scale he had never experienced. The undercurrent of opposition to his rule swelled and ballads lampooning him circulated more freely.

For the first time in a dozen years the King was displeased with the Cardinal. Wolsey had just embarked on ambitious plans to found Cardinal College, Oxford, and his wealth emphasized the King's own straitened circumstances. Henry had long envied Hampton Court and to regain royal favour Wolsey now considered it politic to present the splendid palace with its rich contents to him. The King did not hesitate to accept the gift – the most lavish that any English subject had given any sovereign. Wolsey continued to use the residence himself, much as a life tenant, but Henry now came there more frequently, delighting in the fact that it was his own.

At home the Cardinal's policy became increasingly based upon his extraordinary powers which derived from Rome. 'All his grandeur', remarked Wolsey's co-legate, Cardinal Campeggio, 'is connected with the authority of the Holy See.' On 17 May 1518, less than three years after receiving the cardinalate, Leo x appointed him a legate *a latere* as a temporary measure to watch over Campeggio (as Henry VIII had requested) during his visit to England to raise funds for a crusade. These wide powers were gradually extended by successive papal bulls, until in January 1524 Wolsey was created legate for life by Clement VII, 'with the faculties he had and those he wished for . . . which was never heard before'. Such authority was indeed unique. The individual who suffered most was Archbishop Warham. Already in 1519 Warham's chaplain was referring to Wolsey as 'this great tyrant' and soon many other ecclesiastics were complaining bitterly of the Roman tyranny over the English Church that Wolsey embodied. There was a personal edge to the Cardinal's relations with Warham, for Wolsey resented the old man's unexpected longevity and had early on regarded himself as the rightful successor to the throne of St Augustine. Indeed most of Wolsey's cajoling of successive popes to secure an increase of his legatine authority can be interpreted as a determination to out-manoeuvre Archbishop Warham, a weak character who never recovered from the shock of being eclipsed in the Church when his fellow archbishop became a cardinal.

As the special envoy of the Holy See Wolsey erected a corpus of emergency powers into a permanent system of church government controlled entirely by himself. Effectively the separate jurisdiction of the province of Canterbury ceased to exist, and the Cardinal amalgamated the two convocations of Canterbury and York into a legatine council under his own presidency. He saw himself grandly as pope in England; others saw this, too, and were aghast. As legate *a latere* he was empowered to reform the entire clergy, from the lowliest cleric to the highest dignitary; to issue dispensations of all kinds; to absolve individuals from the excommunications and other sentences pronounced on wrongdoers by other ecclesiastics; to make appointments to benefices; to grant degrees; and to make bastards legitimate. The exercise of each of these powers produced a steady flow of fees. Wolsey enjoyed the revenues of vacant bishoprics and, to the dismay of wealthy laymen, derived a considerable income from the probate of wills.

The English clergy had never known so ruthless a master, one who overrode their ancient privileges and sapped their powers of resistance. Warham himself was threatened with the penalties of *praemunire*, the Bishop of Coventry and Lichfield was charged with treason, and Stokesley, like the young Wolsey a royal almoner, so high in favour that he was destined for a bishopric, was sent to prison. No ecclesiastic was safe from the legate's attack. When, in 1515, the case of the Lollard Richard Hunne had produced in London a violent outburst of anticlericalism, Bishop Fitzjames had implored Wolsey, only recently a cardinal, to support the clergy in their vulnerability, for then, he said, all would be bound to him for ever more.

Yet though Wolsey had well appreciated the danger from without and had been as insistent as any cleric at that time on the force of the sacred text, 'Touch not mine annointed', all his actions as legate served to alienate the laity from a seriously weakened Church. Instead of closing the ranks to withstand the charge, 'Down with the Church', he had undermined the confidence and loyalty of the defenders of the citadel. Through his attitude the Church as a whole, and more particularly the Roman supremacy that Wolsey represented, had acquired a bad name. One cannot explain the subsequent success of Cromwell's measures in breaking with Rome to erect a national church without taking into account the pronounced xenophobia that the Cardinal's rule provoked. Some years before the break with the papacy, while Wolsey's power was still undisputed, the city of Rome was sacked by imperialist troops. The chronicler Edward Hall records that 'the King was sorry and so were many prelates, but the commonalty little mourned for it, and said the Pope was a ruffian and was not meet for the room . . .'. Indeed enough was known of the standing of Renaissance popes, their behaviour and moral standards, to shatter the Church universal even before Luther's stand. It was a curious attack of myopia that made Wolsey fail to appreciate the consequences, for papal claims to supremacy, of the basic fact that in Renaissance Italy, the papacy had become a temporal power. The logical consequence was that if the Pope had become an Italian ruler there was full justification for the creation of separate national churches owing no allegiance to Rome.

The real indictment of Wolsey's legacy was his utter failure to use his exceptional powers to reform the Church in his care. For half a century thoughtful men had been insisting on the need for such reforms and the Lateran Council had at last made a constructive stand. Wolsey, clinging to the status quo, did nothing. It became painfully obvious to those who desperately wanted to see a renewal of the Christian life, with the correction of all the blatant malpractices and injustices apparent in the Church, that the Cardinal was behaving with unpardonable dishonesty. He had sought wide powers to enable him to achieve a thorough reform of the English Church, but once these had been accorded him, he had gloried in this unprecedented authority for its own sake and failed to undertake what had been expected of him. It came to be seen as the worst case of a political confidence trick, yet the damage was incalculable; after he had gone reform could be achieved only through revolution. Moreover, his own manner of life flatly contradicted the spirit of reform. Never before had an archbishop held *in commendam* an English bishopric; never before had a secular priest of his status been titular head of an abbey of the importance of St Alban's. The Cardinal was judged to have broken all the rules at a time when those rules were expected to be tightened. In consequence the moral force of the Church wilted. 'Blessed are the meek' was a text he never attempted to understand. When in the autumn of 1529 his legacy was abolished he knew he was finished, for – as he lamented to Norfolk – it was the fount of 'all my high honour'. The Duke retorted: 'A straw for your legacy. I never esteemed your honour the higher for that.' Wolsey could never believe that any man could hold this attitude, and it was as if the Lord Treasurer and the Cardinal described circles that never intersected.

In his own day, and since, Wolsey was accused of being the architect of the King's Great Matter. It was natural that Catherine of Aragon should regard him as the instigator of her troubles, for she had gradually seen her own political influence with Henry wither away with the Cardinal's rise and she had resented his intrusions. As an unbending imperialist she had come to fear him for his pro-French policy, first exemplified in Mary Tudor's marriage to Louis XII and then made a thousand times worse by the betrothal of her own Mary to the Dauphin. She blamed Wolsey for Henry Fitzroy's elevation to the dukedom of Richmond, interpreting this as a sure sign that this natural son that the King had fathered on Bessie Blount was being groomed for the succession – which, she felt, belonged as of right to Mary, in view of her own inability to present him with a son. Indeed Richmond's peerage convinced her that Wolsey had prejudged the matter of her fecundity. She hated him when Mary, aged nine, was taken from her side to fulfil her duties as Princess of Wales at Ludlow, which had such bitter memories for her. She felt humiliated when Wolsey contrived, on the pretext of an economic reform of the royal household, to dismiss her favourite ladies-in-waiting, replacing them with women of his own choosing who, she feared, spied on her. She knew he intercepted her correspondence and prevented her from seeing the Spanish ambassador alone. Accordingly, when she finally discovered that Henry had so turned against her that he was bent on ridding himself of her, she could only believe that the Cardinal must be at the back of it all. By 1527 her conviction that he was her implacable enemy, and had probably always been so, coloured the despatches sent by Charles V's envoys. After Wolsey had fallen and she in turn had been cast aside, with her Church and her daughter, her sympathizers fixed the blame for these disasters firmly on him.

A Spanish chronicle, composed in London perhaps in the early 1540s, opens with a chapter headed, 'How the Cardinal was the Cause of all the Evil and Damage that Exist in England'. This is followed by a second chapter entitled 'How the Cardinal Made the King Believe he was Badly Married and Living in Mortal Sin':

After the devil had put it into the head of the Cardinal to do all the ill he could to the sainted Queen Katharine, and the Cardinal, knowing that the King was very much enamoured of one of the Queen's ladies, called Anne Boleyn, he went to the King one day, and finding him very merry, he said, 'Sir, your Majesty must know that for many days I have wished to say something to you, but I do not dare, for fear you should be angry with me'. The King wishing to know what it was said, 'Cardinal, say what is in your heart; you have my leave'. The mischief-maker was nothing loth, and kneeling on the ground he said, 'Your Majesty must know that for many years you have been in mortal sin and living in adultery, for you are married to the wife of your brother, the Prince of Wales'. The King was struck with astonishment, and said 'Cardinal, you deserve heavy punishment if this be so, and you have not told me before. If I really am in mortal sin, God forbid that it should go on; but if it be not so, take care what you say.'

The Cardinal repeated his assurance; and to turn his wickedness to account, he said, 'Your Majesty will see to it and undo the error'. The King, as I have said, being in love with Anne Boleyn, answered him, 'Well, but Cardinal, in what manner can I free myself from it?' Then said the Cardinal, 'Sir, your Majesty must speak to the Queen to this effect: "My lady, you well know that you were married to my brother and lived half a year with him, so by the divine law I could not marry the widow of my brother"; and when your Majesty has spoken thus, you will see what she will say, and we will proceed accordingly'. The King liked the Cardinal's advice, and presently, on the same day, he went to the sainted Queen and said, 'Well you know, my Lady, that on the command of the King my father I married you, and now it seems to me that for many years we have lived in mortal sin. I know you are holy and good; let us then undo the error of our consciences, and you shall be Princess of Wales and we will part.' From that hour forward the King was only happy in the thought of getting rid of her. . . .

This is of little worth as a piece of historical evidence, yet it sets down the gossip of fifteen years back, handed down with suitable embroidery.

For a much more serious writer, Polydore Vergil, who claimed to set down a faithful record of events, the Cardinal remains the villain of the affair, for example throughout Book XXVII of his history. 'It came into his head to change his Queen and to find a new one, whom he wished to be like him in conduct and character.' Bringing John Longland, Bishop of Lincoln and the King's confessor, into his conspiracy, they confronted the King, relates Vergil, with the suggestion that his marriage was uncanonical and endeavoured to persuade him 'to arrange a divorce at the earliest moment', so that he might marry a French princess. This was, indeed, the popular view of the origins of the 'King's Great Matter', which began to spread abroad at the time of the proceedings before Wolsey and Campeggio in their court at Blackfriars, for, when Catherine appeared before them, she complained they were not impartial judges. It was in fact after the Queen had left the court that day that Wolsey asked the King to state publicly his own position: 'Sir, I beseech your Highness to declare before this audience whether I have been the chief inventor or first mover of this matter.' The royal denial absolved him: 'Nay, my lord Cardinal, I can well excuse you herein. Marry, ye have been rather against me in attempting or setting forth thereof.' There is no reason to doubt the truth of Henry's words. It is worth noting also that Bishop Longland, who features in Vergil's account, made plain that it was the King, not the Cardinal, who first discussed the matter with him 'and never left urging him until he had won him to give his consent'. What the King of France whispered to Cardinal Valviati in January 1529 – that Wolsey 'repents having been the inventor of this affair' – is irrelevant.

Henry's awkward conscience about the lawfulness of his union with Catherine had been pricked long before he set eyes on Anne Boleyn. He had been desperate for a son from the earliest days of his marriage and his joy when, on new year's day 1511, Catherine was delivered of a boy, who was christened after him, gave place to bitter grief when the infant died. Catherine's unenviable record of stillbirths and miscarriages continued: there was a stillborn son in September 1513 and at the end of November 1514 came another 'prince, who lived not very long after'. Mary's arrival in February 1516 seemed to be a turning-point in the royal parenthood, for she appeared to be a healthy child. 'The Queen and I are both young,' Henry told the Venetian ambassador, 'and if it is a girl this time by God's grace boys will follow.'

Yet Catherine's unsuccessful confinement in 1518 proved to be her last, and soon her husband was swearing that he would lead a crusade against the infidel if he could have the gift of a son. The gift was denied him. But even if he remained young and virile, the proud father of a bastard, Catherine was six years his senior and, worn out by the disappointments and strains of her miscarriages, looked much older.

Henry had a nagging feeling that she was beyond the age of child-bearing. If God withheld his blessing from their marriage there must be some fault in it. Now at last he saw the significance of the 'protest' he had been made to enter as long ago as 1505 about marrying Catherine, Arthur's widow, when some of the ablest canon lawyers had questioned the validity of Pope Julius II's bull. In 1525, with his natural son Richmond's elevation to the very title Henry Tudor had held before Bosworth, the King had given up all hope of a son by Catherine; by the spring of 1527 his study of the scriptures had convinced him that in the eyes of God he was still a bachelor. The only interpretation he could give of *Leviticus* 20:21, was that he had been living in sin for eighteen years with his deceased brother's wife and the Almighty had given judgement by denying him a son. Nothing would shake him from his new-found conviction that Catherine had never been his lawful wife. The burden on his conscience was by then becoming insupportable. He prayed for relief so that his unhappy alliance could be annulled by the Church, to enable him to remarry and beget a male heir. It was fortunate for him that he had already found a young woman with whom he was deeply in love, though he was absolutely sure that his overriding need for a legitimate son came before any desire for Anne Boleyn.

Always attracted to theological problems, Henry soon became extremely knowledgeable about the canon law on divorce. Cardinal Campeggio was not intending to flatter him when he said the King knew more than any divine on the topic. Yet biblical teaching about a man's relations with his widowed sister-in-law was by no means clear-cut. For years learned men would argue whether the one verse of *Leviticus* had not been abrogated by the teaching of *Deuteronomy*; whether the Jewish law of Moses was binding on Christians; and whether or not holy scripture was giving anything more than general, theoretical guidance on matrimonial affairs. The chances of Henry receiving a straightforward answer to his own practical problem were extremely limited, largely because of the political overtones. Yet he could never appreciate this fact. It was well known that Louis XII had easily secured papal agreement to cast aside his first queen, Joan the Lame, to marry his predecessor's widow, Anne of Brittany. Henry's own elder sister, Margaret of Scotland, had in 1527 been granted a divorce from the Earl of Angus to enable her to wed Henry Stewart –

'a shameless sentence from Rome', as the King of England remarked. Suffolk, the husband of his younger sister, had also received confirmation from Clement VII of the dissolution of an earlier union that had been set aside on very dubious grounds. As so stalwart a supporter of the papacy, the Defender of the Faith felt that a considerate ruling by Clement on his own case was due to him. If royal families could not ease their matrimonial affairs by papal dispensations, he reasoned, the whole system of dynastic marriages and matrimonial diplomacy would collapse. Having convinced himself of his need for a divorce, Henry turned to Wolsey to have it accomplished speedily. Here at last was a matter in which the Cardinal's comprehensive legatine powers would be put to good use, for if Catherine should prove obstinate and insist on appealing to Rome, Henry was in no doubt that Wolsey's great influence in the curia would procure a satisfactory solution.

Though Cavendish's account is confused, there is no reason to doubt his story about Wolsey's reaction when Henry first broke the news: 'The long hid and secret love between the King and Mistress Anne Boleyn began to break out in to every man's ears, the matter was then by the King disclosed to my Lord Cardinal, whose persuasion contrary, made to the King upon his knees, could not effect; the King was so amorously affectionate that will bear place and high discretion banished for the time.' Wolsey did not underrate the difficulties; he was afraid that Catherine would be stubborn and appeal against any judgement he made to the Pope and he knew how little chance he had of influencing a verdict in Rome. He was enough of a realist to fear that if he failed to secure Henry's wishes he would lose the Lord Chancellorship and all it implied.

In May 1527 the Cardinal established a secret legatine court at York House, sitting with Archbishop Warham, who had long ago harboured doubts about the sufficiency of Pope Julius's bull of 1503, as assessor. The Queen's attendance was not required. It was not even necessary for her to be represented. (It was vital from the King's point of view that she should have no suspicion that proceedings questioning the validity of her marriage were being instituted.) Henry was before the court not as a petitioner seeking redress, but as a defendant. The Cardinal had cited him to answer the charge that he was living openly in sin with Arthur's widow. He explained to Henry that, as legate, he was bound to correct offences against the marriage law and, in view of his holy office and his concern for the King's spiritual welfare, he, with Warham, had visited His Majesty at Greenwich to request him to appear before them. Since it was not fitting for a subject to cite his sovereign, Wolsey went on, he begged the King to state formally whether or not he consented to the proceedings and was agreeable to Warham acting as his assessor. Henry gave his assent and then asked leave to be represented by Dr John Bell as his proctor. The citation was an ingenious legal device that stood a good chance of success. Even at this stage Wolsey had no inkling that the King had set his heart on marrying Anne Boleyn when he became free. In answer to the citation Henry claimed that he was legally married to his Queen and to substantiate this produced Pope Julius's dispensation. Had all gone as he hoped, the court would have ruled that the document was insufficient and he would have been over the most difficult hurdle. In further sessions of the court, formal arguments were developed by Dr Bell and answered by the prosecutor, Dr Richard Wolman.

The legatine court held its last session on 31 May and then adjourned. Wolsey now shrank from taking on himself the responsibility of giving an authoritative ruling on so intricate a point of canon law. He could go no further than to find that the King's marriage was open to doubt. In these circumstances the court decided to seek the expertise of such learned canonists and theologians as the Bishops of Rochester and London. Two factors account for this change of heart: first his conviction that Catherine would insist on appealing to Pope and Emperor to support her case, which would transform a domestic event into a key issue in international diplomacy; secondly, the disturbing news of the sack of Rome.

On 6 May Charles v's Spanish and German troops had mutinied because of lack of pay and sacked the Holy City. Several cardinals and bishops were taken as hostages, perhaps a quarter of the entire population of Rome was killed, while the Pope saved himself only by fleeing to San Angelo. Wolsey's letter to Henry of 2 June not only breathes the urgency of the situation but indicates that the curia would have to be influenced in the great matter: 'Sir, if the Pope's Holiness fortune either to be slain or taken (as God forbid) it shall not a little hinder your Grace's affairs, which I have now in hand; wherein such good and substantial order and process hath hitherto been made and used.'

For Wolsey, Clement's plight was much more serious than Henry's. To resolve the crisis he would himself travel to France to convoke an assembly of cardinals at Avignon, in order to oversee the administration of papal affairs while the Pope was in captivity. The anchor man of the Church, he saw this as his finest hour. As the leading ecclesiastic of the west not under imperial sway he would induce Clement to assign to him full authority to act on his behalf throughout his captivity; then by deft diplomacy he would secure his freedom, and arrange a favourable settlement of Henry's suit. But for Wolsey this last was no more than an incidental advantage of a far grander design, since his concordat, bringing liberty to the Holy See and peace to Europe, would make his own sovereign the most effective and respected power in the west. He did not see his mission to Avignon as a desperate gamble, but as the supreme moment for which all his earlier life had fitted him, as saviour of the spiritual and temporal power of the papacy. He was convinced that he would become papal vicegerent without opposition and before he left England had drawn up a communication for Clement VII to sign, bestowing on him absolute power, as if he were indeed pope – power 'even to relax, limit or moderate divine law' – which meant that Clement would be undertaking to ratify all Wolsey's actions once he regained his freedom. He crossed over to France on 22 July with tremendous pomp, for he was not only a King's plenipotentiary but a Cardinal legate about to become, as he thought, papal vicegerent. This, in his own eyes, was the high-water mark of his career.

Wolsey knew that the King was far less interested in the general European situation than in being freed from Catherine, yet – still unaware of the strength of Henry's feeling for Anne Boleyn – he hoped while abroad to arrange a marriage for him with a French princess, such as Renée, Francis I's sister-in-law, which would cement the political alliance. He had arranged to meet Francis at Amiens early in August and had despatched letters to all cardinals inviting them to proceed to Avignon, where they would be reimbursed for their travelling expenses. An agent had also set out for San Angelo to obtain Clement's signature to the draft communication.

Initially two things went wrong for the Cardinal. First, when Henry had confronted Catherine, just a month before Wolsey left England, to tell her of his grievous doubts, which would make their separation inevitable, she had succeeded in obtaining a passport for Felipez, a trusted servant, who was to journey to Spain to warn Charles V of what was afoot. Despite careful arrangements to have him detained in France, Felipez managed to elude his captors and reach the Emperor. Secondly, Wolsey's own absence from England played into the hands of his potential enemies, who were able to influence the King. The Cardinal learnt with dismay that His Majesty had had supper in the Privy Chamber with the Dukes of Norfolk and Suffolk, the Marquess of Exeter and Lord Rochford. This was an ominous sign and, to counter the efforts of Norfolk and the others, he sent back to England John Clerk, Bishop of Bath and Wells, who was to explain to Henry the state of the negotiations and Wolsey's plans for the immediate future. Clerk brought with him a personal letter from Wolsey to the King, written in most obsequious terms 'with the rude and shaking hand of your most humble subject, servant and chaplain', assuring him that it was his daily study to bring to pass 'your secret matter' with the Pope.

All this was of no avail, for Wolsey now had news that Henry was bypassing him to make a direct appeal to Pope Clement by sending William Knight, ostensibly to convey his condolences for the indignities he had suffered in Rome. Knight was to meet Wolsey at Compiègne, pretending that his visit to Italy had nothing to do with the divorce but was solely concerned with the Cardinal's scheme for overseeing papal affairs during Clement's captivity. (Knight's instructions had underlined the importance of defending his secrets from 'any craft the Cardinal ... can find'.) A member of the King's household now revealed Henry's intentions to Wolsey and the knowledge stunned him. He had left England full of confidence, and now he had fallen flat on his face. Not only was his sovereign going about this business in a way that courted disaster; much worse, he was acting behind Wolsey's back, as if he had lost all confidence in his ability and trustworthiness. Nor was this all, for when Knight came to him at Compiègne, Wolsey discovered without difficulty that the King wanted to be free of the Queen in order to marry Anne, a young nobody who came from a family hostile to the Cardinal. For the first time in his long service to the crown the Cardinal felt truly vulnerable. His worries were very different from those that had beset him in 1525 with the failure of the 'amicable loan', and his distance from Henry made him feel much more insecure. That the King should have sunk to such duplicity was the worst blow he had suffered. He was now expected to go to extraordinary lengths with the curia to enable Henry to marry a woman who was Wolsey's avowed enemy. (Beside the political hostility of her relations Anne Boleyn felt personal hatred towards the Cardinal because he had prevented her marrying his ward Harry Percy a year or so before, when she was deeply in love with him.) Wolsey read the writing on the wall and tried in vain to dissuade Knight from riding on to Rome.

Much more was at stake than his own position, for the whole Church was in danger. Men such as Anne's father, the recently elevated Rochford, envied the wealth and influence of churchmen. In effect Anne was buttressed by people who were anticlerical in principle and to these were attracted others with their own reasons for disliking the Church that was embodied in Wolsey – men such as Thomas Cranmer, the Boleyn family's chaplain, who saw in a union between Anne and Henry a glorious opportunity for reform and the triumph of the true gospel. It was irrelevant now that only a handful of cardinals were prepared to accept his invitation to Avignon, for he must return to England to be with the King. In desperation he sent a letter on 13 September assuring Henry of his devotion to his cause, 'enduring the travails and pains which I daily and hourly sustain, without any regard to the continuance of my life or health'. He was travelling home as speedily 'as mine old and cracked body may endure' and – a typical touch – he added that 'there was never love more desirous of the sight of his lady than I am of your noble and royal person'. Once he was at the palace he found it impossible to talk with Henry unless Anne, too, was present. Yet when Knight signally failed to obtain from Rome the assurances that Henry sought, the field was clear for Wolsey to take control of the negotiation once more.

Clement VII had remained a layman until the age of thirty-five when his Medici cousin, Leo X, appointed him Archbishop of Florence. Ten years later he had himself become head of the Church, as Pope Adrian's successor. From the first he showed himself to be a muddle-headed, indecisive procrastinator. It was said that he was 'the most secretive man in the world', and that this trait had been developed to conceal his weakness of character. A victim of the struggle in Italy between Habsburg and Valois, he was anxious to upset nobody and

he continued to make promises he could never honour. The imperialists had allowed him to escape from San Angelo, late in 1527, to the
ruined castle of Orvieto. While Knight was still in Rome Wolsey
instructed his agent, Sir Gregory Casale, to go in disguise to Orvieto
and persuade Clement to send a document, 'without disclosing the
affair to anyone', empowering Wolsey and one other cardinal to
determine in England whether the 1503 bull of dispensation was
sufficient in canon law. 'Since I am a cardinal and legate *a latere* of the
Holy See, the honour of the Pope and the integrity of his conscience
can come to no harm in my hands,' he wrote in grand style. Casale was
given letters of credit for 10,000 ducats to use if necessary as bribes to
any third party who caught wind of the affair. The document Wolsey
had prepared for Clement limited the judges to a consideration of the
points in Henry's suit that were favourable to him, made reasonably
obvious the nature of the sentence to be delivered, empowered Wolsey
alone, if need be, to deliver judgement and promised to ratify whatever
he decided. This chicanery was too much for the curia. Cardinal
Lorenzo Pucci said that if Wolsey's draft had been translated into a
bull it would have disgraced Pope, King and Cardinal.

In the spring of 1528 Wolsey entrusted further negotiations to two
lawyers from his own secretariat, Edward Foxe and Stephen Gardiner,
who were to browbeat Clement into granting all the powers for which
he had earlier asked. They argued succinctly that since Henry's case
was so patently just, the Pope could not but agree to a decision in his
favour. But while Clement was fully sympathetic, he could not
endorse the validity of such special pleading. Foxe and Gardiner
asked that the co-legate might be the canonist Lorenzo Campeggio.
This was granted, but Clement hesitated over agreeing to the heart of
Wolsey's request – that there should be automatic confirmation of the
legates' judgement. But soon Wolsey felt he was home and dry. While
the papal commission omitted the clauses about confirmation of the
legatine court's decisions and forbidding the revocation of the suit to
Rome, since (as Clement explained to Gardiner) 'in a matter that
involved the rights of a third party he could do nothing without their
counsel', Wolsey soon received a secret letter, dated 23 July 1528, in
which the Pope fully gave these assurances. He had no reason to think
that when Campeggio arrived in London he would not sing treble to
his own bass.

5
Fall from Grace

News that his co-legate to hear and determine the King's Great Matter was to be none other than Lorenzo Campeggio must have cheered Wolsey, for Cardinal Campeggio knew England, its King and his court at first hand as a result of his visit at the time of the proposed crusade. Since 1524 he had been Bishop of Salisbury. He was an expert canon lawyer and had enhanced his reputation by his legacy in the German states, which he had discharged in a statesmanlike way. As we have seen, in 1519, when Wolsey was angling for his own legatine authority, he had kept Campeggio waiting interminably in Calais before he would allow him to cross to England, but now the boot was on the other foot. Because of painful gout his journey from Rome was very slow and it was not until October 1528 that he at last arrived in England, where he was initially assigned quarters in Suffolk's London house, before moving to John Clerk's residence. When Wolsey met him on 9 October for preliminary discussions on the case he impressed on him the acute danger to all concerned if Henry did not secure the judgement he desired. As the Italian put it in his despatch: 'There would speedily follow the complete ruin of the Kingdom, of his Right Reverend Lordship and of the prestige of the Church throughout the Kingdom.' Wolsey had, as he thought, his own trump card, for Pope Clement had written to him on 23 July promising that he would never revoke the suit to Rome, but confirm the judgement the legates might give in London.

All that Wolsey had said about the importance of Henry having his way was borne out by the King himself when Campeggio had his first audience. Henry's grasp of the theological aspects of his case seemed to the legate remarkable. He was also impressed when the King said that he would not be persuaded that his marriage with Catherine was valid even if an angel were to descend from heaven. On the following Sunday Campeggio was persuaded to produce the decretal bull – in which Clement had in fact granted *all* that Henry had asked for. Wolsey must have felt, as he and Henry read through the stately pleonasms to the heart of the matter, that their difficulties were at an end. What Campeggio did not tell them was that the Pope had firmly instructed him that this document could not be produced in court, was not to be shown to anybody except Henry and Wolsey and was on no account to be executed.

While the King was anxious for the legatine court to begin its sessions without delay Campeggio procrastinated. Neither of them could accuse him of feigning illness, for it was painfully clear that the Italian was tormented by his gout, which kept him bed-ridden for days on end. This enabled him to fulfil Clement's last-minute instructions to delay sitting in court and to search for a compromise settlement. Many hours were spent exploring the possibility of a reconciliation between King and Queen, assuming that Clement would confirm the Julian dispensation, even though Campeggio knew that Henry would never agree to continuing his life with Catherine. Alternatively the Queen was to be prevailed upon to enter a nunnery, on the precedent of Jeanne de Valois, Queen of France. But she remained unmoved by the careful arguments of Campeggio, by the violent cajolings of her husband, by the sight of Wolsey on his knees begging her to listen to the voice of the Church, and by the entreaties of a score of holy and learned men. God had called her to the vocation of holy matrimony, she sighed, and she would live and die in that estate. There was now no option for the legates but to begin their proceedings. Yet Campeggio still delayed. Realizing that neither side would yield, he wrote to the Pope to make clear that in his view it was unfitting for the case to be heard in England. Wolsey, too, had written to Rome in alarm, throwing himself 'at the holy Father's feet', to bring home to him even at this late hour the grave danger to the Church if Henry, Defender of the Faith, should not receive his due in his 'most just, most holy, most upright desire'. He foretold the destruction of papal authority in England in telling phrases, but closed his eyes before such a horror. Clement's response was merely to order Campeggio not to proceed to sentence without further explicit instructions from him. As the legate spun out the preliminaries, one Spanish success after another over England's continental allies was reported.

Meanwhile Henry had summoned a gathering of magnates from court and city to Bridewell Palace to give the equivalent of a press conference, in which he sought to recover some of the popularity he had lost to Catherine. He assured the assembly that Campeggio had come to England to pass judgement with Wolsey on the state of his marriage, which had for so long troubled his conscience. If the cardinals pronounced that he was in fact lawfully wedded to Catherine, there would be nothing 'more pleasant nor acceptable to me in my life'. But if their union were found to be against God's law so that he had been living all these years in mortal sin he would have no alternative but to leave her. 'These be the pangs that trouble my conscience and for these griefs I seek a remedy.' In mid-November, just as it seemed as if the proceedings might formally begin, Catherine showed Campeggio a copy of a papal brief which she had been sent from Spain earlier in the year and which, if it were not a forgery, turned the tables on Henry's argument. This was a *second* dispensation of 1505, hitherto unknown in England, permitting Henry to marry his sister-in-law. It avoided the flaws in the earlier document, on which both the King's case and the terms of the decretal commission were based. In desperation King and Cardinal decided they must send a further embassy to the Pope, led by Sir Francis Bryan, who was to urge his Holiness to have the document declared spurious. If he refused, Bryan was to press him to remit the case at once to Rome for his personal judgement – once he had extracted a solemn promise to decide it in Henry's favour. The terms of this unrealistic ultimatum indicate how desperate the situation appeared to Wolsey as 1528 drew to a close.

Before Bryan and the others could arrive in Rome, which they did on 19 January 1529, Henry had sent Stephen Gardiner, Wolsey's secretary and high in the royal favour, as bearer of a further threat (though the details of his mission were to be kept from Wolsey): unless Clement immediately instructed Campeggio to hasten his hearing of the suit, the King would throw overboard his allegiance. At this point most disturbing rumours reached England about Pope Clement's state of health and for the next six months reports continued to suggest that his life was in the balance: he had 'escaped death by a miracle', 'another relapse will finish him', 'he is worse than ever'. His condition obviously meant that he was unable to transact business, yet *if* he were to die Sir Gregory Casale and the other English agents in Rome were ordered to be ready to seize what would be a golden opportunity. Wolsey sent instructions that in the event of the Pope's death the cardinals were to be bribed most lavishly to support his own candidature; if there were serious opposition his party was to withdraw from the sacred college and bring about a separate election. He wrote to Gardiner to say that although in his old age he would find the office of pope burdensome, yet 'when all things be well pondered and the qualities of all the cardinals well considered (*absit verbum iactantiae*) there shall be none found that can and will set remedy in the foresaid things, but only the Cardinal Ebor, whose goodwill and zeal is not to you, of all men, unknown.' In readiness for Clement's likely death, a commission was sent to Gardiner, Bryan and the resident Casale, duly signed by the King, empowering them to treat with the college of cardinals about the election of a successor.

But Clement lived on and his secretary wrote to tell Campeggio that if Henry continued to expect the impossible he would most certainly be disappointed. By Easter Sir Francis Bryan had concluded that Henry's cause was hopeless in Rome and, unlike Gardiner, had the nerve to tell him as much without dissimulation: 'Were I to write otherwise, I should put you in hope where none is, and whoever has told you that he [Clement] will, has not done you, I think, the best service.' He dared not, he added, write so freely to his cousin Anne Boleyn. Though Bryan and Gardiner made further attempts to wring further concessions out of the Pope, their separate missions were effectively ended, so they were ordered home to be at hand for the royal proceedings. Henry had decided that the legates should sit as soon as possible under the terms of Clement's original commission, since there was no other way out of the *impasse*, and on 29 May he issued his licence to Campeggio and Wolsey to proceed. Two days later they met to make formal arrangements for Henry and Catherine to appear before them at Blackfriars on 18 June. In their final private discussions before the case opened Wolsey wondered whether Clement would even now remove the case to Rome, quite unaware that this was what his fellow-legate had intended as long ago as the previous

Right Wolsey's arms in terracotta over the gateway at Hampton Court. The motto reads: 'The Lord is my succour.'

Below A panoramic painting of the famous meeting between Henry VIII and Francis I on the Field of Cloth of Gold, by an unknown artist. It hangs at Hampton Court Palace.

Bottom A view of Whitehall from the river, sketched by Anthony van Wyngaerde in about 1555.

Sir Thomas More: portrait after Holbein, 1527. He wears the collar of 'Esses' with the Tudor rose hanging from it.

Portrait of Henry VIII by an unknown artist, painted in about 1518.

Catherine of Aragon, who regarded Wolsey as the author of her misfortunes. The portrait is by an unknown artist.

Anne Boleyn, painted by an unknown artist. She was an ardent opponent of the Cardinal.

Thomas Cromwell:
Holbein's portrait
shows the King's
secretary at the
height of his power
(see p. 150–1).

Archbishop
Cranmer, who
pioneered the
innovations of
the new Church
of England:
portrait by
Gerlach Flicke,
1546.

Jane Seymour, Henry's third queen and mother of Edward VI: portrait by Holbein.

Anne of Cleves: portrait by Holbein, who misled Henry about her charms to Cromwell's cost.

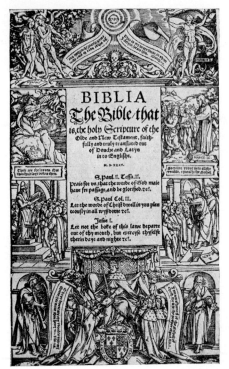

The title-page of the first printed English Bible, in Coverdale's translation, 1535.

Title-page of the King's Book, or *Valor Ecclesasticus*, in which Cromwell's commissioners recorded the valuations of church property in England and Wales in 1535. The initial 'V' contains a characteristic drawing of Henry.

November. But Campeggio merely underlined the Pope's dilemma, which touched them all, and ingenuously left Wolsey 'betwixt hope and fear'.

When the proceedings proper began in the great hall of the Dominican monastery at Blackfriars on 18 June, Henry appeared by proxy. To everyone's surprise Catherine came in person before the court to read a carefully worded protest about the fitness of the legates to determine the case, which, she said, was already pending before the papal curia; furthermore she feared that the two judges, being subjects of her husband (for Campeggio was also an English bishop), would not be impartial. When the hearing was resumed on 21 June Henry spoke at length on the justness of his cause and about his devotion to the Pope before allowing the legates to make their ruling on Catherine's objections. They in fact overruled them – they formed, they said, a court that was in every way competent to determine the issue. Queen Catherine now rose to make an appeal to have the case tried by Pope Clement and then movingly appealed to her husband, the plaintiff, protesting at the likely fate of her being cast aside. She had been, she maintained, 'a true, humble and obedient wife, ever comfortable to your will and pleasure. . . . And when ye had me of the first, I take God to be my judge, I was a true maid, without taint of men. And whether this be true or no, I put it to your conscience.' There was more, and she was heard in silence; but when she had finished she curtseyed and withdrew. The court crier called her back three times, of custom, but she did not return, and never would, for she placed her faith in John Fisher and the others forming her counsel.

Wolsey remained outwardly confident, for under the existing papal commission he had power, if necessary, to act alone. With luck he could still pull it off, providing there were no delays, and – as Henry intended – present Clement with a *fait accompli*. The withdrawal of Catherine from the suit alarmed Campeggio, who was now afraid there would be no formal opposition. He wrote to Rome on St Peter's Day that the King's party had 'full scope to go on as they choose and to bring the suit to an end with all the means which they can, carrying it in their favour'. In fact the previous day Fisher of Rochester had fought tooth and nail for Catherine, claiming he was ready to stake his own life, like John the Baptist, on the sanctity of marriage. He was ably supported by Standish, Bishop of St Asaph, Nicholas Ridley and the Dean of the Court of Arches. John Clerk in Rome was no less worried than Campeggio in London, for the latter's reports flatly contradicted the assurances of Henry's new ambassador, William Bennet, that no proceedings were in progress. And then, on 5 July, there arrived in Rome Catherine's personal appeal. The imperialists now increased their pressure on Clement for action. The Pope was said to be 'in great anxiety and, weeping, prayed for death'. If popes were to do more than play at politics and act as rulers of Italian states, they needed to be men of greater strength of purpose than the timid Clement. On 13 July, ill in bed, he at last realized that he had no alternative but to revoke the case. He therefore formally quashed the proceedings.

The decisive event was the Spanish victory over the French army at Landriano on 21 June, for it confirmed Habsburg rule in Italy. Clement VII could no longer hope for effective French aid and he told the Archbishop of Capua, 'I have quite made up my mind to become an imperialist and to live and die as such.' Truly the old waverer's mind had been made up for him. In the settlement made by the Treaty of Barcelona the Pope's nephew was pledged to marry Margaret of Parma, Charles v's illegitimate daughter. As the puppet of the Emperor, Clement could never permit Henry to divorce his queen, the Emperor's aunt, so he speedily revoked the commission to Campeggio and Wolsey – the papacy had joined a Habsburg family compact and Wolsey was acutely aware that in leaning on France he had backed the wrong horse. Francis I had no alternative but to come to terms with the Emperor, so in August he bade his mother Louise sign the treaty of Cambrai with Margaret of Savoy – 'the Ladies' Peace', as it was called. Wolsey had earlier denied most vehemently to Henry that Habsburg and Valois were negotiating, yet he now accepted that England would have to accede to the general peace. It was an inglorious end to his career as a diplomatist.

The court at Blackfriars was crowded on 31 July, for it was expected that the legates would give judgement. The King sat in a gallery near the door, from which he had a commanding view of the judges. Courtiers and ecclesiastics packed the hall, hanging on the words of Campeggio, when the King's proctor demanded sentence. In polished Latin the Italian cardinal briefly explained that in accordance with the practice of the papal courts the legatine court would stand adjourned for the summer vacation, that is, until the beginning of October. Most present, however, saw his postponement of judgement as rather more than legalistic procrastination and interpreted it as the end of Henry's chances of securing a divorce through a papal court, certainly through a legatine court sitting in England. Only a month before Wolsey had written that if the case was removed to Rome it would 'utterly destroy him for ever'. Now, as Campeggio sat down, he knew that he would be hounded from office by his enemies at court and deserted by the King whom he had assured so often that he would obtain the decision he so desperately wanted.

As Henry left his gallery dazed by what he had heard, Suffolk gave vent to his rage at the intransigence of papal dignitaries by banging his fist on the table and shouting, 'By the mass, now I see that the old said saw is true, that never cardinal or legate did good in England.' For Wolsey it was the equivalent of being brutally told, 'In the name of God, go!' Suffolk's remark expressed the pent-up anticlericalism and nationalist feeling, the all-round dissatisfaction with Wolsey's rule and with the Church for daring to refuse the King his due. Possibly (as Cavendish later wrote) Wolsey calmly made a rejoinder to this outburst: 'Sir, of all men in this realm, ye have least cause to dispraise or be offended with cardinals; for if I, simple cardinal, had not been, you should have had at this present no head upon your shoulders.' (In fact, 'simple cardinal' was a phrase that would certainly have riled the Duke.)

The King now retired to Greenwich before going on progress to Woodstock and Grafton. Though he appointed Stephen Gardiner as secretary, it was by no means clear that Wolsey's service to the crown was over, for Henry needed time to plan his future moves. For the present, however, his extreme displeasure was obvious to all: he refused to write to the Cardinal, except through Gardiner, abruptly declined his invitation to stay at the Manor of the More, on the pretext of the plague, and would not allow the Lord Chancellor to come to court. Wolsey's enemies, headed by the two Dukes, were doing their best to prevent King and Cardinal from meeting one another, and, if it was one thing to escape the wrath of the sovereign until his anger had cooled, it was far more serious to be exiled from his presence. As early as May 1529, when there was still reasonable hope concerning the outcome of the legatine court, the French ambassador could report, 'Wolsey is in the greatest pain he ever was in', simply because Henry had been persuaded by Norfolk, Suffolk and Rochford that the Cardinal had not been doing all he might to advance Anne Boleyn's marriage. When the imperialist Chapuys arrived in England at the end of August for an embassy that was destined to last until 1545, he noted: 'It is generally and almost publicly stated that the affairs of the Cardinal are getting worse and worse every day.' The three new favourites 'transact all state business'; not long past 'no one dared to say a word against the Cardinal, but now the tables are turned and his name is in everybody's mouth'. Yet Henry still shrank from removing him from office. Their partnership, one-sided though it had so often been, had persisted for so long that he could not believe it was nearly breaking up. He could remember the administration of Warham and Foxe before Wolsey had come to dominance only with difficulty. Half of him mistrusted the motives, as well as the abilities, of Norfolk and Suffolk and there were still moments when, despite the adjournment at Blackfriars, he was convinced that if anyone had the talent and the connections to achieve a diplomatic *coup* with Pope Clement, it was Thomas Wolsey.

Cardinal Campeggio, surprisingly, was the one person who attempted a *rapprochement*. When he was due to take his leave of the King on Sunday 19 September he asked Henry if Wolsey might travel with him to Grafton; this was granted, providing that both of them came without their wonted show of arrogant display. Cardinals, as Suffolk had made clear, were unpopular. Before leaving for North-amptonshire Wolsey had a meeting with du Bellay in which he complained of 'the practices of this court, but [was] still hoping to reassert himself, now he had the chance of talking to the King face to face', yet the Frenchman was despondent – 'I have less hope than before of his influence, from the conversation I have had with him.' No lodging had been prepared for Wolsey at Grafton, but Sir Henry Norris, groom of the stable, befriended him and allowed him the use of his room to change from his riding clothes. In the great chamber he saluted the lords of the Council with unusual deference. Then the King entered. Wolsey knelt humbly and Henry, 'with as amiable cheer as ever he did', raised him to his feet and led him away to the great window for private discussion. The two had not met for two months and courtiers watching them laid bets on how the audience would go. It seemed to some likely that Wolsey would dazzle his sovereign with all the old magic, that he would not merely make his peace with the King to save his position but actually dominate the conversation.

A serious disadvantage for Wolsey was that his return to court was being made in company with Campeggio, who had earned even more general hostility than himself. During their discussions Henry produced a letter and, raising his voice, asked Wolsey, 'How can that be? Is not this your own hand?' In Shakespeare's play much is made of the incident; though the document cannot be identified, it most probably related to diplomatic negotiations over the divorce and the contents had convinced the King that Wolsey had not been straightforward with him. But the Cardinal appeared to have satisfied his sovereign almost without effort, at least for the present. If we bear in mind the voluminous correspondence Wolsey had undertaken over the past two years of very complicated negotiations, we can see that it would have been easy for him to make out a case for the apparently incriminating letter being no more than an astute diplomatic move to confound opponents in France, the empire or the papacy.

Henry left to dine with Anne Boleyn, now 'more like a queen than a simple maid', in the privacy of his chamber. During the meal she worked very hard, as her father had instructed her, to persuade the King not to be forgiving towards his minister. The waiters at table reported their conversation to Cavendish, who was himself present at Grafton:

'Is it not a marvellous thing to consider what debt and danger the Cardinal hath brought you in, with all your subjects?' Anne asked him.

'How, sweetheart?'

'Forsooth, Sir, there is not a man within all your realm with five pounds, but he hath indebted you unto him by his means' [referring to the amicable loan].

Henry was not so easily taken in.

'Well, well, as for that there is no blame in him, for I know that matter better than you or any other.'

'Nay, Sir, besides all that, what things hath he wrought within this realm to your great slander and dishonour. There is never a nobleman within this realm if he had done but half so much as he hath done, but he were well worthy to lose his head. If my lord of Norfolk, my lord of Suffolk, my lord my father or any other noble person within your realm had done much less than he, they should have lost their heads ere this.'

'Why, then, I perceive you are not the Cardinal's friend.'

'Forsooth, Sir, I have no cause, nor any other man that loveth your Grace; no more have your Grace, if ye consider his doings.'

If the waiters heard this conversation correctly, Wolsey's fate was still far from settled and Anne's antagonism may have provoked Henry into flying to his defence.

At the councillors' table, meanwhile, there were awkward exchanges. When proposals for summoning Parliament were discussed Wolsey suggested that the King would do very well to send his bishops and chaplains to their cures of souls. He played straight into Norfolk's hand, for the Duke retorted, 'Yea, marry; ye say very well, and so it were for you too.'

'I could be contented therewith very well if it were the King's pleasure to grant me licence with his favour to go to my benefice of Winchester [answered Wolsey].'

'Nay,' Norfolk countered him, 'to your benefice of York, where consisteth your greatest honour and charge.'

To the Duke and his friends Winchester was far too close to the court for comfort and they had already decided that the Cardinal must be banished to the north.

After dinner Henry resumed his conversation with Wolsey by the great window and then, to the dismay of Norfolk's party, led him off to his Privy Chamber, where they were alone together for several hours, until after dark. The apparent reconciliation, perhaps even a rekindling of the King's confidence in his minister, was a bitter blow for his enemies 'and made them to stir the coals'. When the Cardinal left for Easton House, three miles away, to find the rooms Cavendish had prepared for him, his rivals brought home to Anne Boleyn how critical the situation was. She therefore devised a scheme for taking the King on horseback to inspect Hartwell Park nearby the next morning. Henry, who felt he had earned a little holiday in Anne's company after the weighty business of the Sunday, readily agreed and was about to leave when Wolsey returned to Grafton for their adjourned discussions. As luck would have it, Campeggio was taking his leave of the King and Wolsey was required to return with the Italian to London. He still refused to give up hope, for Henry gave him an 'amiable' farewell. He rode off via St Alban's, the More and finally reached York Place, to prepare for the opening of Michaelmas term in Westminster Hall, while Campeggio crossed over to Calais on the first leg of his journey to Rome. In a day or so the King would move on to Windsor to complete preparations for the assembling of a new Parliament on 3 November.

An ominous letter from Stephen Gardiner, written on Michaelmas day, required Wolsey to send to the King various Parliamentary writs, which were to be despatched to the shires 'by the hand and advice of the Duke of Norfolk'. This was no part of a Lord Treasurer's business, yet the Cardinal could not but comply. There were comforting signs when, for instance, he was asked to receive the imperial ambassador, Chapuys, with other councillors on 6 October. Then arrived his own summons for Parliament, which he took as a token that he was not to be cast down. In the council room at Westminster, wrote the chronicler Edward Hall, 'the Cardinal showed himself much more humblier than he was wont to be, and the Lords showed themselves more higher and stronger'. Two days later Henry made a flying visit to London from Windsor, but Wolsey was ignorant of it. 'At present,' wrote du Bellay in that first week of October, 'the King takes the management of everything himself.' For the first time since his accession he considered that he was his own master.

The storm broke on 9 October, the first day of the new legal term. Wolsey came to Westminster Hall with rather less pomp than usual, for 'none of the King's servants would go before him'. And even as he was sitting in Chancery, the Attorney-general, Christopher Hales, was preferring a bill of indictment for *praemunire* against him in the neighbouring Court of King's Bench, on the grounds of receiving bulls from Rome in contravention of the Statutes of Provisions and *Praemunire*. Henry was not leaving the removal of his minister to Parliament, but was bent on achieving this as soon as possible through the courts. In the event the Cardinal was to be given the choice of answering the charges against him either in King's Bench or before Parliament. He chose without hesitation to surrender to the common law, since an Act of Attainder for treason could well involve his life. That evening he sent an abject letter hoping to move the King to pity:

'Most gracious and merciful Sovereign Lord, Thou that I, your poor, heavy and wretched priest do daily pursue, cry and call upon Your Royal Majesty for grace, mercy, remission and pardon, yet in most humble wise I beseech Your Highness not to think that it proceedeth of any mistrust that I have in your merciful goodness. . . .' He prays for the 'forgiveness of his trespass', for 'the sharp sword of the King's displeasure had so penetrated his heart'. Jesus Christ himself said, 'Blessed are the merciful, for they shall obtain mercy', and the Cardinal hopes that Henry will extend his mercy to him – 'Your Grace's most prostrate poor chaplain, creature and bedesman. *T. Cardinalis Ebor*, *Miserimus*'. How were the mighty fallen!

Shortly afterwards Wolsey was visited by his friend du Bellay, who was amazed to find him so shaken:

He has represented his case to me in the worst rhetoric I ever witnessed, for heart and words entirely failed him. He wept much and prayed that the King [of France] and Madame [the Queen Mother] would have pity upon him. . . . I assure you that his misfortunes are such that his enemies, even though they were many, could not fail to pity him. Yet, notwithstanding, they will not forbear from persecuting him to the last extremity and he sees no means of safety, nor do I, except it should please the King and Madame to help him. He desires not legateship, seal of authority, nor influence. He is ready to abandon everything, even to his shirt, and to live in a hermitage, provided his King will not hold him in disfavour.

Though du Bellay overstated what the Cardinal was prepared to sacrifice it was obvious that there was no fight left in him.

On St Valentine's day 1527 Sebastian Giustinian, by then the Venetian ambassador in France, had delivered an oration before Francis I in which he described Wolsey as that great Lucifer, following the course of the Sun King, Henry VIII. That 'most invincible Lucifer' was the brightest star in the firmament, 'a divinity on whom the greatest reliance will be placed on earth'. Yet within two years Lucifer had fallen.

When he heard of the indictment Wolsey had cried out, 'My legacy is gone.' His other offices and the trappings of power were a minor consideration compared with this supreme blow. On Sunday, 17 October Norfolk and Suffolk came to York House to demand the surrender of the great seal of England, but the Cardinal, insisting that they should show written authority, claimed that he held the office by the King's own patent. After 'many great and heinous words' the Dukes rode back to Windsor, returning the next day with a royal mandate for him to deliver the seal into the custody of Dr John Taylor, Master of the Rolls. His successor as Lord Chancellor was still undecided. Henry 'much consulted with his Council' on this appointment. Since another ecclesiastic was ruled out and Norfolk was adamant that the post should not go to Suffolk, the obvious candidate was the one English lawyer with an international reputation, Sir Thomas More. On 26 October More agreed to serve, on the understanding that he would not be required to play a part in the King's Great Matter.

The two Dukes, meanwhile, had announced in the Star Chamber that they had been appointed to sit there to deliver judgement if subjects should complain of lack of justice. The same day Wolsey signed a document in which he acknowledged that through his legatine authority he had 'vexed the prelates and others of the realm unlawfully', incurring the full vigour of the penalties of the Act of *Praemunire*. He admitted that he deserved to suffer perpetual imprisonment at His Majesty's pleasure and to forfeit his lands and offices. To atone for these offences he begged the King to take into his hands all his temporal possessions. Yet he was still a cardinal of the Church. Henry now ordered him to move to Esher, so he prepared to leave York House for good. He had a full inventory drawn up of all its furnishings, which included the copes and altar frontals for service in the chapels of his colleges at Oxford and Ipswich. For many years the King had envied Wolsey his palace at York House because of its central position and its grandeur, particularly because he had no residence of his own in Westminster. With the Cardinal's fall York House began to be transformed into Whitehall.

As Wolsey boarded his barge for the last time at the privy stairs of York House he found that great numbers of Londoners had turned out on the river in small boats or were crowding the banks to see him depart. Some had certainly expected the barge to be going downstream, to the Tower, not upstream to Putney. Recalling this incident, the faithful Cavendish commented, 'I cannot but see that it is the inclination and natural disposition of Englishmen to desire change of men in authority – most of all where such men have administered justice impartially.'

At Putney Wolsey mounted his mule and on the ride to Esher was overtaken by Norris, who had behaved so generously towards him at Grafton, bringing a jewelled ring as a token of the King's favour and bidding him be of good cheer. The Cardinal was so overwhelmed at hearing this that he knelt down on the filthy road, to thank God as well as his sovereign. A little later on the ride he remembered that his much-reduced train of attendants included his fool, Master Williams, nicknamed Patch from his parti-coloured livery. He therefore asked Norris to take 'this poor fool' as a present to the King, for he was worth, he said, £1,000. But Master Williams was reluctant to leave the Cardinal's service and it took six tall yeoman to take him back to London. In gratitude to Henry Norris, Wolsey gave him a little gold cross that he regularly wore round his neck, which was reputed to contain a relic of the true cross. There was further assurance of the King's goodwill when Sir John Russell brought him another ring on the evening of All Saints' day, just before Parliament opened. Wolsey snatched at this token of comfort and asked that as soon as possible 'it may openly be known to my poor friends and servants that Your Highness hath forgiven me mine offence and trespass and delivered me from the danger of your laws; for the attaining whereof I shall incessantly pray, cry and call. Written this morning with the rude and trembling hand of Your Grace's most humble and prostrate subject and priest.'

Henry read that cringing letter an hour or so before the opening of Parliament, on 3 November. Sir Thomas More, the new Chancellor, compared the office of his sovereign to that of a shepherd, charged with the task of preserving his flock from danger and infection. It was a travesty of the parable of the Good Shepherd: 'As you see that amongst a great flock of sheep, some be rotten or faulty, which the good shepherd sendeth from the good sheep, so the great wether which is of late fallen, as you all know, so craftily, so scabbedly, yea, and so untruly juggled with the King' that men must surely think he was either unable to see his wrongdoing or had counted on the King being unable to detect him. 'But he was deceived, for his Grace's sight was so quick and penetrable that he saw him, yea and saw through him . . . and accordingly to his desert he hath had a gentle correction.' Such a 'gentle correction' as the sentence in King's Bench was not thought to be a sufficient punishment by More's hearers, who wanted Wolsey's head on a charger. Above all most of them wanted to take steps to prevent the Cardinal from being restored to his former dignities and to make it impossible for the King to reappoint him to high office in the state. Accordingly a disabling Bill (which we should think of in terms of a Bill of Attainder) was introduced in the Lords, where it passed on 1 December. The charges were originally drafted by Lord Darcy, who had a grudge against Wolsey for removing him from the captaincy of Berwick and was intimate with Norfolk. The committee in the Lords appointed to draw up the detailed articles comprised twelve temporal peers, including More, Norfolk, Suffolk, Rochford, Northumberland and Darcy, two judges and two officials of the royal household who were also members of the Commons. The bishops and mitred abbots stood aside, because they knew, as the French ambassador put it, that the 'heart of these things . . . will cost him his head'.

Whereas the proceedings in King's Bench had been confined to the breaches of the law committed by Wolsey in his capacity as papal legate, the peers ranged widely. There were forty-six articles, 'but a few in comparison of all his enormities, excuses and trespasses against Your Grace's Laws'. The Cardinal was accused of infringing the liberties of the Church by wrongfully making appointments to benefices, pillaging monastic foundations, depriving them of free elections and holding vexatious visitations; he had deprived bishops and archdeacons of their time-honoured jurisdictions in testamentary affairs and had annulled their efforts to stamp out heresies. He was guilty of embezzling the goods of his predecessors in the archbishopric of York and in the sees of Lincoln, Durham and Winchester. His offences against the crown proper included the making of treaties with foreign powers without proper authority, pretending equality with his sovereign by using such phrases as 'the King and I', putting the cardinal's hat on the coinage of the realm and (a rather ludicrous charge) risking the King's health through infection from contagious diseases. He was also accused of insisting that foreign envoys came to see him before they called on Henry, of withholding information on foreign affairs from the Privy Council and of inhibiting councillors from discussing policies. In the Court of Chancery he had reopened cases that had already been determined in the common-law courts, removed other actions into Chancery of his own volition, made injunctions by writs, suspended pardons and deliberately delayed justice, while in the Star Chamber he refused persons committed their right to sue the King for pardons. Wrongful imprisonment, illegal demands for purveyance and the dispossession of tenants featured in the catalogue, while Englishmen great and small had suffered intolerably as a direct result of his greed, extravagance, briberies, extortions and partiality, through which he had 'subverted the due cause of Your Grace's laws'.

Many of the charges were preposterous, some were but generalities, others were grounded on hearsay. There remained a number that were clearly true and could be substantiated, though it is hard to deny the force of Wolsey's plea in a letter to Thomas Cromwell that 'those which be true be of such sort that, by the doing of them, no malice or untruth can be justly directed to me, neither to the Prince's person, nor to the incommodity of his realm and subjects'. Yet proof by the accusers was not required, for the main intention of drawing up the articles was to blacken further the Cardinal's character and so to bring into effect a loyal request that 'he be so provided for that he never have any power . . . hereafter to trouble, vex and impoverish the Commonwealth'.

The articles were signed and presented to the King on 1 December and then sent to the Commons. The suggestion has been made that this was not part of a legislative process, but was being tabled in the Lower House to reinforce the chorus of criticism against the Cardinal. The articles had certainly been framed with a Bill of Attainder in mind and Wolsey's biographer Cavendish mentions the discussions on them in the Commons as if they still formed the basis of such a Bill. At any rate in the debate on Wolsey's crimes and misdemeanours Thomas Cromwell, his solicitor, ably defended his master as we shall see (pages 153–5) and the whole affair was dropped.

When Parliament was prorogued just before Christmas the King announced that he would merely make due provision for Wolsey as the articles had requested. He had no intention for the present of having his hands tied by giving an undertaking never to re-employ him. (He had already taken him into his protection as a precaution against the likelihood of an irate Parliament demanding his execution.) Indeed Henry remained enigmatic for some time to come. Even in his present anger he could not forget that Wolsey had for many years served him faithfully, nor could he see Norfolk as other than self-centred and opportunist. Remembering Buckingham and the others, he retained something of the fear of feudal influence that had haunted his father and he had no wish, as a result of marriage to Anne Boleyn, to make the crown of England dependent on the house of Howard. But a cardinal legate might still be of use to him on the international stage, although perhaps not in promoting the divorce from Catherine, and could in domestic affairs be a counterweight to the Howard–Boleyn faction. There was still the chance of pardon and rehabilitation for the broken man confined to Esher.

Wolsey was by now desperately short of money to pay his diminished household staff and lacked linen, crockery and a host of everyday items. For a man who had lived in such style and had never needed to worry about finance this change of fortunes was humiliating. Winchester and St Alban's Abbey were taken from him and his foundations at Oxford and Ipswich were in danger of immediate dissolution. At the Council's suggestion the new gallery he had built at Esher was dismantled before his eyes and taken in sections to Westminster to be incorporated in Henry's 'Whitehall'. Chief Justice Shelley visited him to obtain the formal surrender of York House, since the King had asked the lawyers how he might lay hands on the residence. (Unlike Hampton Court, it was not a personal possession but the property of the archbishops of York.) The lawyers had ruled that the house could be legitimately surrendered if the Cardinal acknowledged the King's right to it by signing a deed in the presence of a judge. Hence Shelley's visit. But even though he was so vulnerable and was ready to clutch at any straw that might assist his return to favour, Wolsey was not to be browbeaten and he told the Chief Justice to inform the men 'to put no more into his [the King's] head than the law may stand with good conscience, for when you tell him, "This is the law", it were well done ye should tell him also that "although this be the law, yet this is conscience".' The residence was not his to bestow on His Majesty. But when Shelley showed him the royal commission he at last submitted, and asked the judge to report to Henry that while he would not disobey his commands, 'I most humbly desire His Highness to call to his most gracious remembrance that there is both heaven and hell.'

It was a notable outburst and one wonders whether the judge had the nerve to report it to the King.

Norfolk, who had come down with Shelley but had rested while they talked, paid another visit to Esher and maliciously treated Wolsey as if he had still been 'my good Lord Cardinal' and were more eminent than any duke. He was not left in peace, for each day messages were brought from court, together with rumours of fresh charges against him to 'persecute his mind'. 'This order of life he had continually,' wrote Cavendish, who was with him, 'that there was no one day or even he went to bed, that he had not an occasion greatly to chafe or fret the heart out of his belly.'

His greatest comfort throughout those difficult months was the loyal support of Thomas Cromwell, who in and out of Parliament stood up for his master, came down to Esher whenever he could and offered wise advice, even drafting letters for him to write. Stephen Gardiner, by contrast, though he owed even more to Wolsey, was icily polite and not to be trusted. Now that he was King's secretary he feared that his long service in the Cardinal's household might be both an embarrassment for discharging his present duties and a hindrance to his future. 'I think he will do little or nothing to my Lord's avail,' wrote someone who knew him well. When Wolsey reminded him that he now had only the revenues of York to meet his heavy expenditure, so that 'approaching death, I must begin this world again', he met with a blank refusal of help.

The elevation of Anne Boleyn's father to the earldom of Wiltshire just before Parliament was prorogued was an indication of the way the wind was blowing. With the new year Wolsey became seriously ill and one night he was so short of breath that death seemed certain and his doctor, the Italian Agostini, prayed that one of the King's physicians might be sent for. As soon as Henry learned how critical the Cardinal's condition was he blurted out, 'God forbid that he should die, for I would not lose him for £20,000.' He hastily despatched Dr Butts and three other doctors to treat him, ordering them to remain with him until he was out of danger. To cheer him up Henry sent a ring, engraved with his own portrait in a ruby, which the Cardinal had once given him. He also persuaded Anne to send him the 'tassel of gold hanging from her girdle'. There followed cartloads of furnishings, plate and other items, valued at £6,300. These tangible expressions of the King's favour certainly added to Wolsey's recovery. Some people even thought he had feigned sickness to tempt Henry into agreeing to visit him. It seems more likely that he was indeed seriously ill, but exaggerated his condition in the hope of favourable treatment. Early in February he was well enough to be moved. He had asked if he might have the use of the Lodge in Richmond Park, as the air at Esher was too damp. The change did him a great deal of good, though he was not to be allowed to remain there very long.

He had meanwhile been attempting to reach some degree of *rapprochement* with the Boleyns, whom he regarded as much more likely to influence the King than Norfolk. He had written to Cromwell: 'If the displeasure of my Lady Anne be somewhat assuaged, as I pray God the case may be, then should it be well that by some correct mean she be further laboured with, for this is the only help and remedy. All possible means must be employed for attaining of her favour.' It was not the slightest use. At the same time he was busy seeking possible support from such different quarters as the French and imperial courts, and even the Pope, to aid his restoration to power and favour. All this was grasping at straws. When he heard about these intrigues Norfolk told Sir John Russell amid curses that if Wolsey succeeded in making a come-back 'he would eat him up alive'. For the Duke it was imperative to have the Cardinal safely removed to the north away from the King and the court, even more than from foreign envoys.

But for the unremitting hostility of Norfolk, Suffolk and the Boleyns, Henry might possibly have relented and gone some way towards rehabilitating Wolsey. The Council now ruled that he must return to 'his benefice'. Cromwell sounded Norfolk out on whether this could be interpreted as Winchester, but the Duke was adamant that he must travel to York – and stay there. Wolsey delayed setting out, probably because he was short of ready money, but also partly because he still thought he had a fighting chance of not having to leave the south. On 12 February he had received a full pardon from the King and two days later was restored to the archbishopric of York. Norfolk said to Cromwell: 'Methinks that the Cardinal, thy master, maketh no haste to go northward. Tell him, if he go not away, but shall tarry, I shall tear him with my teeth.' At Richmond he had recently moved from the Lodge to the Charterhouse in the park, where Dean Colet had died, and appeared to be taking a great interest in the Carthusian rule, discussing theological problems with the brothers in their cells and even occasionally wearing a hair shirt they gave him. But his mind was by no means closed to practical matters. He was endeavouring to call in the arrears of the pensions due from France and Spain and was again pressing Gardiner to use his influence with the King to provide funds for the journey to York, though the secretary was blunt with the messenger, saying 'he had no such trade' and that if Wolsey had not enough to live on, it was his own fault. Cromwell was more successful in wheedling money out of the Council, and Henry added £1,000 of his own. With this sum assured, workmen were engaged to put in habitable condition the archiepiscopal residences at Southwell and Cawood: equipment and household stuff were loaded into coasting craft on the Thames for sending to Hull and arrangements were afoot for the retinue.

At last on 5 April Wolsey set out on his long journey, with as few as 160 attendants. He was at Peterborough for Holy Week and Easter, washing the feet of fifty-nine paupers on Maundy Thursday and celebrating the Easter high mass in the cathedral. After staying several days with Sir William Fitzwilliam at Milton he arrived at Southwell on the twenty-eighth of the month. This was the first time he had entered his province of York since his appointment as archbishop in 1514. He wrote to the King reporting his arrival: 'According to your pleasure, I have come into my diocese unfurnished, to my extreme heaviness, of everything that I and my poor folks should be entertained with.' It was ironic that the brethren of his province, deprived of his presence throughout the years of his power and glory, should be welcoming their Cardinal Archbishop in such reduced circumstances. Altogether Wolsey painted a gloomy picture of makeshift arrangements, of baggage undelivered and of being hounded by creditors. He was 'wrapped in misery and need on every side', and asked Henry to have 'compassion on your poor Cardinal who is, and ever shall be, his life during, your faithful and most obedient creature, daily beadsman and slave'.

Yet he had no intention of removing to York. His orders had been to 'repair to his diocese', not to go specifically to York, so he stayed on at Southwell for four months. He could not believe that there would not be a sudden turn of fortune, bringing a summons to attend the

King. 'The Cardinal has not yet gone to York,' wrote Chapuys to Charles v. 'Probably he does not wish to remove so far from the court, as he would then have less facility for watching his opportunity and returning to it.' Despite his frequent complaints of poverty he entertained lavishly at Southwell and even ordered rebuilding to proceed, for which Cromwell, when he heard of it, chided him: 'Some allege you keep too great a house and are continually building. I beseech you, as I have often done before, to consider the times and refrain all building more than necessity requires.' But the Cardinal refused to economize and still hankered after building on the scale of York House or Hampton Court.

In May 1530 Cromwell advised him to be much more circumspect in what he wrote and said, for the King knew he was trying to undermine Norfolk's position, and this was playing with fire. Wolsey was not content to serve in his diocese as Foxe and Wareham had done, but consistently planned a return to political life; he could not resist the temptation to meddle. It was natural that he should attempt to win over Catherine of Aragon, who like him had suffered so much at the hands of the Norfolk–Boleyn faction. He hoped that she might be the means of his achieving a reconciliation with the Emperor. By August he was writing frequently to Chapuys to learn how Catherine's cause was progressing and to complain that 'it is not more energetically pushed'. 'He disliked delay above all,' the ambassador wrote to Charles v, 'for he thinks that, this business settled, he has a good chance of returning to power.'

The rumours in London were disturbing and when the Cardinal suddenly left Southwell for York by easy stages on 1 September, the Council ordered the ports to be closed, though the chances of his fleeing abroad were remote. As he travelled further north into his diocese he was fêted by high and low, attaining within a few days a popularity he had never known in his years of power. From 6 to 30 September he stayed at his house at Scrooby, from which he visited neighbouring churches to say mass and 'ministered many deeds of charity'. Resuming his journey he spent the whole of one day, with only a short break for dinner, confirming children in Nostell Abbey. Then at last on 2 October he reached his palace at Cawood by the river Ouse, about 10 miles from the city of York. The Dean and canons of York came to welcome him and he answered their greeting by saying he had come not just to be with them for a time but 'to spend my life with you as a very father and mutual brother'. Dean Higden made clear to Wolsey, however, that by the ancient statutes of the cathedral an archbishop could not proceed beyond the choir door of the Minster until he had been enthroned – as the Cardinal should have known had he taken his earlier duties as Dean of York seriously. Accordingly he ordered plans to be made for his enthronement on 7 November and himself summoned a convocation of the northern province to meet at York on the same day. He knew perfectly well that not even a cardinal could do this without the royal mandate. Yet he seemed determined to go through with it, despite sundry warnings from Bishop Tunstall, who had been in the north since July, not only as Bishop of Durham but as President of the King's Council in the North, to keep an eye on the Cardinal's doings. Wolsey nevertheless sent out his summons to all peers, abbots, priors, knights and esquires of the diocese to attend on him at Cawood, to bring him to York 'with all manner of pomp and solemnity'.

Despite the presence of Tunstall in York, the Council was uneasy. There were wild rumours of Wolsey entering the city with eight hundred horsemen and 'returning to his ancient pomp and corrupting the people'. Even if York was a long way off, it was still the second city in the kingdom, still the spiritual home of the remnant of the white rose party, and the reports of the messengers coming from the Cardinal were extremely alarming. The arrival of a papal nuncio in England created further suspicion. And when one day the King lost his temper in the Council room he said in his fury that 'the Cardinal was a better man than any of them for managing matters,' wrote Chapuys. 'Repeating this twice, he flung himself out of the room. Since then the Duke [of Norfolk], the Lady Anne and her father have not ceased to plot against the Cardinal, especially the Lady.'

Norfolk, fearing that after just a year's disgrace Wolsey might yet be recalled, had Agostini, the Cardinal's Venetian physician, arrested and examined. The Italian had certainly been used to negotiate with the French ambassador and others and some letters of his in cipher had already been intercepted. A confession was therefore extracted from him to the effect that Wolsey had intrigued with the Pope and other potentates against the King. This evidence was not, however, obtained until *after* Henry had ordered the Cardinal's arrest. For the King the most telling fact was the report from Rome, which reached him on about 23 October, that a papal brief had been issued forbidding him to marry *pendente lite*. There were rumours that Clement was to excommunicate Henry and order him to send Anne away from court. Such news coming at the same time as the reports about the summoning of the northern convocation suggested that Wolsey intended to make his enthronement on 7 November a political occasion on which he might publish a papal excommunication. The King was readily persuaded that he was up to some underhand trick and in a panic declared that he must be guilty of 'presumptuous, sinister practices made to the court of Rome'. On 1 November he issued a commission for his arrest jointly to the Earl of Northumberland and to Walsh, a groom of the chamber, who at once left for York with the document.

Ever since his days as Wolsey's ward, when the Cardinal had made him break off his suit for Anne Boleyn's hand, Northumberland had harboured resentment and this had turned to hatred as a result of 'a sharp remonstrance discharged to him by Wolsey for real or imagined misconduct in the north'. Percies had been kings in their own domains for generations and the slight could never be forgotten. The Cardinal was taking his dessert after dinner in an upper chamber when the Earl and his train arrived at Cawood on 4 November. Northumberland took the keys from the porter, posted sentries and then came upstairs. Wolsey expressed dismay that he had not let him know he was coming. Had he known, they could have postponed dinner, and had him shown to his bedroom to change from his riding clothes. The Earl laid his hand on him and in a quiet voice said, 'My Lord, I arrest you of high treason.'

Wolsey was literally struck dumb. He eventually recovered himself sufficiently to demand a sight of the royal commission. When Northumberland refused to show it he said he would not obey his authority. Then Walsh, who had been arresting Agostini the doctor (and sent him on his way to London under guard to face Norfolk's interrogation), entered the room and shouted to Wolsey, 'Go in, traitor, or I shall make thee.' He, too, refused to show the commission. But Wolsey had recognized him and said he would accept that the lowliest official of the King's Chamber could, on the word of his sovereign, 'arrest the greatest peer of the realm'. He placed himself at Walsh's pleasure, no doubt taking delight in snubbing Northumberland, and surrendered the keys of his own coffers. On the Saturday he told Cavendish, 'I am left here bare and wretched, without help or succour, but in God alone.' He argued with his servant that these were feigned accusations, yet he knew this would be 'an occasion that I shall not have indifferent justice, but they will rather seek some other sinister ways to destroy me'.

Northumberland stayed on at Cawood, but Wolsey was taken by Sir Roger Lascelles under guard to Pontefract, with only five of his retainers. As he left his palace people from the neighbourhood assembled to show their grief and voice the hope that 'the foul fiend might catch' those who had taken away their cardinal, the great ecclesiastic whom they were to have seen enthroned in majesty in the Minster the following day. While Wolsey rested at Sheffield Park with the Earl of Shrewsbury, Sir William Kingston, the Keeper of the Tower of London, arrived with twenty-four men-at-arms, bearing instructions to take him to the Tower, though he told Wolsey that he was to be taken to the King's presence. Kingston tried to comfort him further by predicting that he would clear himself at his trial. But Wolsey was not to be taken in: 'I know what is promised for me,' he answered darkly, thinking perhaps of Buckingham.

He arrived at Leicester Abbey with Kingston late on Saturday night (26 November). Progress had been slow and on the way from Hardwick Hall 'he waxed so sick that he was divers times likely to have fallen from his mule'. When they were greeted with torches at the abbey gates, the Cardinal said to Abbot Pexall: 'Father Abbot I am come hither to leave my bones among you.' He was taken to bed – which he was destined not to leave. Ill though Wolsey was, on the Monday Kingston attempted to question him about the sum of £1,500, which, Northumberland had reported to the King, could not be found at Cawood. (Even though Wolsey was on his way to the Tower, Henry could not wait but had sent a messenger to Leicester to cross-question him!)

The Cardinal was now aware that life was ebbing from him and had a premonition that he would die at eight o'clock in the morning. When on Monday he was still alive beyond that hour he could scarcely believe it. The faithful Cavendish and Dr Palmes, his confessor, watched over him. When he stirred very early on Tuesday morning and asked for meat none was ready, so he was given some chicken broth, though he would not take much of it when he remembered it was a fast day. When Cavendish thought he was *in extremis* he sent for Sir William Kingston. He 'bade him be of good heart, and then he would surely recover', but Wolsey, who retained to the end his intense interest in the state of his health, told those standing round his bed that he had 'some experience in my disease'. It was a flux with a constant fever, he said, and he knew that if there were no improvement within eight days from its onset, death was inevitable.

Kingston told him he had no need to be apprehensive of the King's attitude, for groundless fears were making him worse, but the Cardinal replied:

Well, well, Master Kingston, I see the matter against me, how it is framed; but if I had served God so diligently as I have served my King, He would not have given me over in my grey hairs. Howbeit, this is the just reward that I must receive for my worldly diligence and pains that I have had to do him service. Commend me to his Majesty, beseeching him to call to his remembrance all that has passed between him and me to the present day, and most chiefly in his great matter; then shall his conscience declare whether I have offended him or no. He is a prince of royal courage, and hath a princely heart; and rather than he will miss or want part of his appetite he will hazard the loss of one half of his Kingdom. I assure you I have often kneeled before him in his privy chamber the space of an hour or two, to persuade him from his will and appetite, but I could never dissuade him.

He went on to tell Kingston that if he should one day become a Privy Councillor he must be most careful with any idea he put into the King's head, 'for ye shall never pull it out again'. He urged at some length that the King should rigorously suppress Lutheranism and other heresies, which otherwise would destroy his authority. It was a long deathbed speech and he had intended saying more, but instead concluded by saying farewell. With his last breath he asked his hearers to remember his words. The Abbot was summoned, and as the clock struck eight the Cardinal died. Later that day his corpse, dressed in his vestments, was placed with his mitre and cross in a simple wooden coffin which was carried to the Lady Chapel to lie in state through the night. At four in the morning on Wednesday a requiem was sung.

Wolsey had long ago planned to be buried in St George's Chapel, Windsor, as if he were a king, and had commissioned Benedetto da

Rovezzano of Florence to devise a tomb for him that should be no less superb than the one Torrigiano had made for Henry VII. On the sarcophagus of black marble there was to be a recumbent statue of himself in gilt bronze; the four corners of the platform on which it was to stand were to be four great pillars of bronze, 9 feet high, each supporting an angel bearing a candlestick, while four other angels were to kneel at the head and foot, supporting the legatine pillars, the archiepiscopal cross and the cardinal's hat. This magnificent monument had never been completed. Though Henry VIII intended to make use of it when his time should come, his coffin was instead laid to rest in Jane Seymour's grave. Centuries later a noble use was found for Wolsey's empty sarcophagus, for it was adapted to serve as Nelson's tomb in the crypt of St Paul's. The Cardinal was buried in the same grave at Leicester Abbey where Richard III's coffin had been placed – subsequently known as 'the tyrants' grave'.

Even Cavendish, who had chronicled the Cardinal's last days in the most moving way, could not bring himself to write a favourable obituary notice of his master:

> Here is the end and fall of pride and arrogance of such men exalted by fortune to honour and high dignities; for I assure you in his time of authority and glory he was the haughtiest man in all his proceedings that then lived, having more respect to the worldly honour of his person than he had to his spiritual profession, wherein should be all meekness, humility and charity. . . .

When Cavendish was summoned to Hampton Court to relate the events of his master's final hours, the King told him he would give £20,000 to have Wolsey still alive, and then ruined everything by questioning him about the whereabouts of the missing £1,500. Later Henry was said to have sighed, 'Every day I miss the Cardinal of York.' Yet he showed no grief, convinced as he was of his treacherous scheming. A timely death at Leicester Abbey had saved the fallen minister from a state trial – the verdict a foregone conclusion – and had saved Henry from another assault on his conscience similar to that produced by Buckingham's execution. A company of actors, promoted by Anne's father, played a farce, *Of the Descent of the Cardinal into Hell*, and the text was subsequently printed on Norfolk's order. Contemporaries preferred to forget his earlier striking diplomatic triumphs and his lofty ideals for European peace. His work in Chancery and his impartial administration of justice in poor men's causes were derided by men who vowed England must never again have a clerical Lord Chancellor. Sycophants who congratulated the King on the splendours of his new palaces at Whitehall and Hampton Court begrudged the Cardinal his due for being their builder. Few regretted that his educational schemes had been abandoned or appreciated how mild this powerful churchman had been in his dealings with heretics when the rest of Europe suffered violent persecution.

Later generations have been no more generous in their verdicts. Because of his central place in the Reformation Wolsey's reputation has been at the mercy of both Catholics and Protestants, and each camp has branded him as the villain. Those of the old faith have seen him as, at least the promoter, if not the author, of the King's divorce and the architect of the schism, a cardinal who brought down the entire Church with him by provoking a fury of anticlericalism. The Protestants have continued to see him as the embodiment of the evils of the unreformed Church, worldly, uncaring and with an exclusive priesthood, a proud prelate tied to Rome who, like the Pope, had encroached unwarrantably on temporal affairs, yet failed to rectify clerical abuse and had disastrously involved England in continental affairs. For all his faults there was undoubted grandeur about Thomas Wolsey and, despite his failure in the King's Great Matter, there was an unprecedented span of devoted service to the crown. His efforts at attempting to bring a permanent peace to Europe mark him out as an idealist in an age when rulers regarded warfare as the most effective arm of diplomacy. He was the one English statesman of the first rank before the Reformation to have risen from humble origins. His choice of servants was unerring and the training he gave them unique. The best of them would pass sooner or later to the King's service, headed by the man the Cardinal had selected as his solicitor, whom Henry would appoint as his chief minister.

6
Fortune's Wheel

Thomas Cromwell was Wolsey's junior by about a dozen years. As with the Cardinal, the exact year of his birth is unknown, though it was probably within a year either side of Henry Tudor's victory at Bosworth. If so, Cromwell was the contemporary of Zwingli, the Swiss reformer, of Cortez, the Spanish conqueror of Mexico, and of Arthur, Prince of Wales, whose early death was destined to have so remarkable an influence on English politics in Cromwell's lifetime. As Vicar-general Cromwell was to issue instructions in 1538 requiring every church to maintain a register for recording baptisms, marriages and burials, which (if properly kept) would enable every Englishman to prove his age and parentage. As it is we know neither the family of his mother, nor her Christian name, though according to tradition she had come from Derbyshire to live in the house of a lawyer at Putney in Surrey; Putney became her permanent home when she married Walter Cromwell, a blacksmith who also practised the trades of a fuller of cloth and a brewer. The multiplicity of his trades indicates the small extent of his business and the Cromwells' house in Putney was no more affluent than the Wolseys' in Ipswich. Walter's eldest surviving child was a daughter, Katherine, who in due course married Morgan Williams, a native of Glamorganshire, but by then a brewer of ale in Putney. Their son was to change his name to Cromwell, after his distinguished uncle, and to settle in Hinchinbrook near Huntingdon, where his famous great-grandson, Oliver, would be born. Thomas also had another sister, Elizabeth, who survived infancy, but beyond this we know nothing. The chronology of the events in the first half of his life remains uncertain and the information set down long afterwards by such writers as Cardinal Pole and John Foxe is far from reliable.

Unlike the Cardinal he had no formal schooling and never went to a university, which was the normal way for one of humble parentage to reach office. Yet rarely can a self-taught man have acquired such a range of knowledge or been more at home in the company of learned men. Books were among his most prized possessions, especially volumes concerned with history, law, politics and economics, and he became an omnivorous reader. He acquired a sound grasp of Latin, a little Greek if no more than a smattering, and was able to read both Italian and French with some facility. This was a surprising achievement for a person who had so poor a start in life and indicates tremendous personal discipline and ordered effort. Cromwell taught himself to memorize a host of passages and his brilliant use of his mother tongue in speeches and letters is comparable in its way with Winston Churchill's, whose own formal education meant so little to him. Pragmatism and opportunity were Thomas Cromwell's teachers and he sat under them until the end, whereas Wolsey, the boy bachelor, had ceased to read widely or deeply much beyond his precocious graduation. Cromwell remained extremely receptive to new ideas and had the intellectual equipment to test them effectively, for he could not easily be swayed by novelties. As Gabriel Harvey, the Elizabethan scholar, put it in his jottings: 'The Lord Cromwell, of a Roman disposition, in his kind a Marius or Sylla. Small learning, but nobly minded and industrious, with sufficiency of common wit, utterance and experience.' Wit and pragmatical dexterity made him, in spite of himself, an intellectual, so that he 'obscured even our greatest clerks'.

As a youth Cromwell seems to have quarrelled with his father and he left Putney to become a soldier of fortune in Italy. He served in the French Army, and some authorities say (though the matter is in doubt) that he was in action in the last days of 1503 at the battle of Garigliano, which completed the Spanish conquest of Naples and assured Spanish control of southern Italy. The imperialist Chapuys noted that when he was young Cromwell had been ill-behaved (*'assez mal condicionner'*) and Foxe mentions that he had himself told Archbishop Cranmer, with whom he was intimate, 'what a ruffian he was in his younger days'. At that time Italy was certainly the stage on which the main political drama was being enacted. Cromwell would have been nearby at the fall of Cesare Borgia and at the meetings between Ferdinand I and Louis XII at Savonna (1507). He would have heard about Bramante's commission to rebuild St Peter's and about Machiavelli's foundation of the Florentine militia, Italy's first standing army.

At some stage Cromwell gave up active soldiering to settle in Florence as accountant to a merchant, and also to trade himself. This opened his eyes to economic problems and gave him first-hand knowledge of the essential points of international commercial law. This represented invaluable experience. He left Florence before 1512 for the Netherlands, which had become the hub of international trading. Here he served as clerk to an English merchant adventurer, also operating on his own account as a middleman in the English cloth trade. Perhaps, too, he came to hold some semi-official position with the Fellowship of Merchant Adventurers in Antwerp. But before long he was in London, where he continued his business enterprises, dealing in cloth and also lending money, besides founding his own legal practice as a solicitor. About this time (1513) he married Elizabeth Wykys, a widow of means, whose father had been a shearman before he extended his fortunes through service as a gentleman usher in Henry VII's household; her first husband had been a yeoman of the guard. Cromwell took over his father-in-law's interests in the clothing trade, which accounted for so much of England's total exports to the continent, and developed them through shrewd assessment of the market. He now had a first-hand knowledge of European affairs, through his service in Italy and his period of residence in the Low Countries and, like his father, had shown considerable versatility in earning his living as scrivener, money-lender and trader. These first-hand experiences, no less than the contacts he had built up, were to be of great benefit to him as a man of affairs. Sometimes business took him further afield and he was in Rome in 1514, where he stayed in the English Hospice at about the time Cardinal Bainbridge was buried in its church.

John Foxe tells a story, which has been confirmed from other sources, that Cromwell returned to Italy as one of the special envoys of the town of Boston in Lincolnshire. His task was to solicit the Pope to grant special privileges to a guild in St Botolph's Church, so that the strict rules of Lenten observance might be relaxed for its members. Foxe, as a native of Boston, would scarcely have fabricated the tale.

Accordingly Cromwell accompanied Geoffrey Chambers of Boston to Rome, where they won the Pope's heart by presenting him with some delicious sweetmeats and jellies (concocted from an English recipe), which were unknown in Italy. This journey, it has now been established, took place in 1517 or 1518, not in 1510 as Foxe thought, so the pontiff in question was Leo x, not Julius II. However, the point of Foxe introducing the story was to make plain Cromwell's love and knowledge of the scriptures, for he said that on his journeys to Rome and back he had learnt by heart Erasmus's Latin version of the entire New Testament. It is not surprising that a man who had become intimately acquainted with holy writ the hard way should some twenty years later have ordered the English bible to be set up in every parish church.

Religion was a very real and pressing aspect of Cromwell's life. Like many laymen and clerics, he regretted that while he was legate his master, Wolsey, had not grasped the opportunities for leading a reform of the Church along the paths Erasmus had indicated. Being essentially in the Erasmian tradition, he was not knowingly an innovator in matters of doctrine. When there was a rumour in May 1530 that Luther was dead, he wrote to Wolsey: 'I would he had never been born.' In due course we shall trace the development of his religious views under the impact of political strife, but it is important to note that he always stressed the *via media*. He was never an iconoclast, but had a very genuine sense of mission to reform the commonwealth on Christian principles: 'My prayer is that God give me no longer life than I shall be glad to use mine office in edification, and not in destruction.'

Much ink has been spilled over Cromwell's knowledge of Machiavelli's writings. The label 'Machiavellian' was bestowed on him by Cardinal Pole in his vituperative and unreliable *Apologia*, written in the aftermath of the King's destruction of his family. Pole recalled a conversation with Cromwell in 1528 that concluded by the latter recommending to him a book that he later discovered was *The Prince*, although in fact the treatise was not to be printed until 1532. It is of course possible that Cromwell had met Machiavelli during his sojourn in Italy, subsequently read the tract and even owned a copy. Indeed for a man with his interests in Italy this is quite likely, though the evidence is inconclusive. Yet if he had read *The Prince* he would never have regarded it as a blueprint for Henrician England, and if his reading of it had been blind and unimaginative Lord Morley would hardly (in the last year of Cromwell's life) have recommended the work as 'a very good thing for your Lordship . . . to look upon for many causes, as I suppose yourself shall judge when ye have seen the same'. Cromwell was too realistic a politician and far too sensible to imagine that a treatise concerning royal power in an Italian state could be translated into English practice.

It is unlikely, as some authorities have said, that Cromwell entered Wolsey's service early in 1514. Of course he turned his abilities to every opportunity that presented itself and as a practising lawyer would have been reluctant to turn down any business that came his way. This could well have included suits involving the Cardinal and his household, and work in connection with the administration of the vast ecclesiastical property, and its revenues, that Wolsey had acquired. We do know, however, that by 1522 he was described as 'a servant' of the Marquess of Dorset – the same man whose brothers had been Wolsey's pupils at Madgalen College School. Perhaps it was through Dorset that Cromwell began very soon after this to be much more closely connected with the Cardinal's legal matters, so that by 1525 he had become his principal man of affairs.

Undoubtedly, too, his membership of the Commons in 1523 brought him to the fore. Even if he did not actually deliver the forceful speech he had prepared against the policy for waging the French war and the heavy taxation proposed to meet it, fellow members would have been aware of his forthright views. He began by a fulsome display of loyalty, flattering the crown and identifying himself with its interests, for there was not a man among them who would not readily offer his goods and his life ten times over to ensure the recovery of England's French dominions. He then, like any modest maiden speaker, apologized to his hearers for addressing them. This was, in his view, no time for peace, but the methods by which the Cardinal proposed waging the war troubled him. Siege warfare on the continent was incredibly expensive, as the last campaign had shown, 'when the winning of Thérouanne cost his Highness more than twenty such ungracious dogholes could be worth unto him'. Worse, he understood from Wolsey that the King would himself lead the invading force, 'which thing I pray God for my part I never live to see'. The King should not risk his life, leaving the succession to the throne uncertain, as this might plunge the country into civil war. Well versed in financial problems, Cromwell regarded the size of the proposed subsidy as excessive: were such sums to be granted and collected a great store of bullion would be wasted; the King would be reduced 'to coin leather again' and the Flemings would exploit England's financial difficulties.

There was much close argument in pithy sentences in this speech, which ran to over five thousand words before the loyal peroration – 'in which enterprises I beseech God send our most dear and most redoubted Sovereign prosperous succession and fortunate achieving of all this his noble enterprise'. The draft he prepared is a little master-piece of oratory, yet even if he never delivered the speech in the Chamber there would still have been other opportunities during the session for him to impress Speaker More, and the men who counted in the court and with the Cardinal, with his independent cast of mind and his ability to get to the heart of a problem. With his tongue in his cheek, Cromwell wrote to his friend John Creke in Bilbao in August:

I amongst others have endured a Parliament, which continued by the space of seventeen whole weeks, where we communed of war, peace, strife, conten-tion, debate, murmur, grudge, riches, poverty, penury, truth, falsehood, jus-tice, equity, deceit, oppression, magnanimity, activity, force, temperance, treason, murder, felony, conciliation and also how a commonwealth might be edified and also continued within our realm.

He did not despise Parliament for being a talking shop, for the renewal of the commonwealth involved discussions about justice, equity, magnanimity and conciliation no less than the framing of laws for ending poverty, oppression and treason. Those seventeen weeks at the hub of affairs, when the Cardinal had come to demand the entire subsidy, was an experience Cromwell never forgot. It made him a Parliamentarian and, unlike Wolsey, he would in the days of power work through Parliament.

The next year Cromwell became a member of Gray's Inn in recogni-tion of his status in the legal profession. A generation later the Inns of Court included among their members peers, administrators and landowners who had no intention of acquiring any expertise in the law, but treated their Inn rather as a London club. In 1524, however, the Inns were still exclusively concerned with legal education and the organization of the profession, though they provided an admirable opportunity for informal discussions with men of informed opinions. To a self-taught man like Cromwell membership of Gray's Inn gave a broader basis to his knowledge and a greater assurance, so that he became less rough-mannered and was accepted as an equal. (He was in fact destined to be the first member of Gray's Inn to be elevated to the peerage.) He was now described as 'Councillor to my Lord Legate'. His new master was impressed by his enormous capacity for business, that quality which mirrored in others his own unwearying mental activity.

At the very beginning of 1525 Wolsey regarded him as the obvious choice to take charge of the intricate problem, so dear to his heart, of dissolving a score of religious houses to endow the new colleges he was founding in Oxford and Ipswich. As the agent of dispossession and appropriation Cromwell inevitably became unpopular, especially in country districts. His undisguised zeal for the work, together with the harsh way in which he and his underlings went about it, made him many enemies. He was identified with the plundering of sacred shrines and the destruction of hallowed places. He had to survey the entire property of each of the monasteries concerned, arrive at a careful valuation, prepare inventories of their goods and arrange for all the moveables to be taken away for sale. There were complicated deeds to be drawn up and executed for the leasing or sale of the lands, these transfers of property involving settlements with tenants and the adjudication of conflicting claims. Arrangements also had to be made for the pensions of the monks and nuns who were losing their homes. The amount of paperwork was enormous, even though Cromwell was aided by Sir William Gascoigne and Dr Allen. The work sharpened his administrative skill, and whereas before 1525 his reputation was chiefly that of a skilled conveyancer, he now became the most powerful of the Cardinal's servants.

Wolsey was full of praise for his thoroughness and his exemplary industry. Once the dissolutions proper were completed, Cromwell was busy with the new foundations that these would finance and himself supervised the extensive building programmes. It was with evident pride that he could report to the Cardinal from Oxford in April 1528:

The buildings of your noble college most prosperously and magnificently doth arise in such wise that, to every man's judgement, the like thereof was never seen nor imagined, having consideration to the largeness, beauty, sumptuous, curious and most substantial building of the same. Your chapel within the said college [is] most devotedly and virtuously ordered, and the ministers within the same not only diligent in the service of God, but also the service daily done . . . so devout, solemn and full of harmony that in mine opinion it hath few peers.

This was indeed music to Wolsey's ears. A little later Cromwell is asking him to decide on the name chosen for the dedication of the college at Ipswich, to enable the various foundation deeds to be engrossed 'that no time should be lost'. Cromwell always felt an urgency about the work in hand and no man was less of a procrastinator. He spent hours in the saddle on muddy roads visiting distant manors, scenting evasions, unravelling knotty problems of tenures, writing detailed reports – the epitome of the active, efficient man of business. Wolsey was content to leave the mass of detail to him for four and a half years, giving him *carte blanche* to proceed in his own way. There were, of course, opportunities for bribes, particularly in the new leases for farms, and for taking a cut in the underhand profits from concealment of monastic goods and the purchase of immunities. Cromwell obviously did well for himself out of the operation – as by the practice of the day he was expected to. There were outcries about his embezzlement, and tales of 'incredible things' reached the King's ears; it was even said that some people were lying in wait to kill him. Yet he still found time to conduct his own legal practice, one of his clients being Anne Boleyn's aunt, Lady Clare, whom he defended in an action for debt. His advice on property values, the law merchant and interest rates was expert and he continued to do brisk business as a moneylender.

In 1527 his wife had died, leaving him a son, Gregory, whose lack of application as a scholar was a disappointment, and two little daughters, Anne and Grace, who did not reach maturity. He never remarried, but even without a hostess his house at the Austin Friars in the City – his principal home until he moved to Stepney in 1533 – remained a lively centre for his growing circle of friends, many of them in the Erasmian tradition. Cromwell was basically a companionable man, who cared deeply for his friends, as is clear from the correspondence with Stephen Vaughan. The table-talk at the Austin Friars was excellent. One frequent guest, the lawyer John Oliver, looked back with affection to the 'dinners and suppers, where I indeed did hear such communications which were the very cause of the beginning of my conversion' to the truth of the gospel. Thomas Starkey, too, recalled his many talks with Cromwell 'of God, of nature and of other politic and wordly things', which enabled him to gather 'more fruit of truth than I have done of any man living, since I came here' – a rich compliment. He was generous in lending his books, helpful in finding niches for indigent scholars and determined to make a positive contribution to the problem of higher education. This underlines his zeal for working as Wolsey's 'architect' of the colleges in Oxford and Ipswich.

Cromwell was a good listener, who brought out the best in those gathered round his 'honourable board' as they discussed the perennial problems of philosophy, the meaning of the gospels and the practical ways of reforming Church and state to inaugurate a new commonwealth. He shared the idealists' visions of a glorious future if the foundation-stone of a new Jerusalem could be laid aright, yet his feet were fixed too firmly on the ground to be content with ivory-towered generalities and mere intellectual talk. The Cardinal had never had a plan beyond saving the old order, so that the Church might retain its primacy, and even his new colleges were for him buttresses of the established regime. The insistent questioning of doctrine – and of so much more than doctrine in those years when opinions were in ferment – was alien to Wolsey and he was too preoccupied to give a sympathetic hearing to the prophets concerned with the morrow. Cromwell was the opposite, groping towards a new order, jealous of reserving time for discussion and reflection, surer each day that he had a mission to play a significant role in bringing it all about. One historian depicts him as 'swift, ruthless, accurate, corrupt, a master of detail and inaccessible to sentiment', but this is but a partial portrait. Only a man with a sense of mission could have driven himself so hard in the fifteen years from 1525. Throughout he was a man of the gospel, and however impassive his outward appearance there burned within him, no less than in Cranmer, the fierce fire of belief.

Holbein's portrait, painted when he was at the peak of his power, shows a massive, seated figure, soberly dressed in a black cap and coat, trimmed with a fur collar, like a city father, but without ostentation. Clean-shaven, he wears his hair close-cropped, and by now he has a double chin. He is a formidable man, but it is hard to detect in the painting (as R. B. Merriman did) a 'cruel' mouth or to infer from it that his searching grey eyes, set too close together, 'moved restlessly'. The portrait in fact gives very little away and we learn more about Cromwell from the objects on the table in the foregound, covered with a green baize cloth – a quill pen, letters, a sealed deed and a finely bound volume that was perhaps a bible. Those items and the paper clasped in his left hand help the artist to present a person of singular authority, a serious man, hard to move, a busy administrator pausing to reflect on something he had written or to listen attentively to someone's opinions. The ambassador Chapuys, who came to know Cromwell well, remarked that during a conversation his face would suddenly light up and the dull exterior be transformed with unexpected animation; at the same time he would liven a discussion with witty comments and pointed glances. Another contemporary commented on his awkward gait; he was overweight, no doubt, and perhaps had one foot longer than the other, but his odd manner of walking never became clownish. He was formal, often serious, but never pompous, as the Cardinal had always been.

Cromwell cannot have been ignorant of the extreme difficulties that Wolsey faced at home and abroad over the King's Great Matter. A day or so after Campeggio's adjournment of the legatine court, he was asked to look out all the papal bulls concerned with Wolsey's legacy, which were to be shown without delay to the King's attorney – an ominous request. In the following weeks the situation rapidly deteriorated. Though the writs were issued for the return of members for a new Parliament, and although he had sat in the last, six years before, he took no steps to seek election until, as it happened, the very last minute.

Throughout those weeks, as he continued with his work for the colleges, he must have felt the future was uncertain. In the autumn, as the law term opened, he seemed very likely to be compromised by the Cardinal's fall, for to many people it appeared that the man who held so responsible a position in Wolsey's service could not possibly escape the heavy fire aimed from all sides at his master. In London there were rumours that he had been sent to the Tower and his friend Stephen Vaughan in Flanders was greatly alarmed, fearing he had been affected 'in this sudden overthrow of my Lord your master. I never longed so sore to hear from you as now.' He implored him to be patient, 'not doubting' that he would escape danger, yet making it rather obvious that he was very doubtful of the outcome.

At Esher on the morning of 1 November, two days before Parliament assembled, Cavendish saw him in the great chamber. Both the scene and the conversation he related have an authentic ring. Master Cromwell was:

... leaning in the great window with a primer in his hand, saying Our Lady Mattins (which had been since a very strange sight). He prayed not more earnestly than the tears distilled from his eyes. [After greeting him Cavendish asked] 'Why, Master Cromwell, what meaneth all this your sorrow? Is my lord in any danger for whom ye lament thus, or is it for any loss that ye have sustained by any misadventure?' 'Nay,' quoth he, 'it is my unhappy adventure which I am like to lose all that I have travailed for all the days of my life, for doing of my master true and diligent service.' 'Oh Sir,' quoth I, 'I trust ye be too wise to commit any thing but my lord's commandment otherwise than ye ought to do of right, whereof if ye have any cause to doubt of loss of your goods.' 'Well, well,' quoth he, 'I cannot tell, but all things (I see before mine eyes) is as it is taken. And this I understand right well, that I am in disdain with most men for my master's sake and surely without first cause. Howbeit, an ill name once gotten will not lightly be put away. I never had promotion by my lord to the increase of my living; and this much will I say to you, that I intend, God willing, this afternoon when my lord hath dined to ride to London and so to the Court, where I will either make or marr; or I come again I will put myself in the press to see what any man is able to lay to my charge or misdemeanour.'

Cromwell assisted the Cardinal after dinner in drastically reducing his household servants and then, with his permission, set out for the court with Ralph Sadler, his clerk, promising to return within a couple of days if matters went well. He had crossed his Rubicon.

Cromwell's immediate plan was to find a seat in the new Parliament, for he already knew that some of the Cardinal's lay officials had succeeded in being elected. Before the day was out, through Sadler's prompting, Sir John Gage, Vice-chamberlain of the royal household, had spoken about this to the Duke of Norfolk, who himself consulted the King. Henry was 'very well contented ye should be a burgess', Sadler wrote that evening to Cromwell, advising him to discuss the matter next day in London with the Duke and others. Mr Rush, who had been connected with Cromwell over the college at Ipswich, would try to get him returned for Orford in Suffolk; if he were unsuccessful there William Paulet might be able to find him a seat for one of the boroughs of the bishopric of Winchester. The latter was indeed much less of a long shot, since as Bishop of Winchester – even if his temporalities had been surrendered to the King – Wolsey's influence would count for much. As it happened there was by now no vacancy at Orford, but Paulet secured Cromwell the second seat for the borough of Taunton, one of the most prominent of the corporate towns under his master's sway. Paulet, with strong personal connections with the borough, had clearly been empowered by the mayor to make a last-minute appointment to fill the vacancy. Accordingly, though Cromwell came into the Commons with royal approval and with the agreement of the Lord Treasurer, his old master's principal enemy, he did not achieve his seat through the patronage of either King or Duke. His profession when he entered the House was still that of Wolsey's solicitor and when he left Esher for Westminster he had not deserted the Cardinal for the Duke, nor had he entered the royal service. This was none the less the turning-point in his career, just as the assembly of the 1529 Parliament was itself a watershed in England's political development. Cromwell returned to Esher 'with a much pleasanter countenance', told the eager Cavendish he had 'adventured to put in his foot where he trusted shortly to be better regarded' and had a long private discussion with Wolsey. We can surmise that their earnest conversation largely concerned the role Cromwell would play in opposing a Bill of Attainder.

He realized that the foregathering of Parliament at so critical a time would give him the chance of impressing the King with his abilities. His seventeen weeks in the House in 1523 had provided him with experience of work in the Commons and, perhaps, had given him a taste for it; he would have an advantage over most Members who were sitting for the first time. He would, moreover, be able to speak with authority on the topic that dominated the opening session – the problem of the Cardinal. Though he would forcibly speak up for

Wolsey, passionately so, he knew that he must hitch his waggon to another star, for his master had been ousted from the Chancellorship and deprived of his ecclesiastical appointments. Even if he was partially restored to favour, he would never wield the same power again. Of Cromwell's ambition there is no question, for he aimed at entering not Norfolk's service but the King's, and he realized more than anyone else that Wolsey's removal had left a great void. No one would have had much regard for a turncoat, least of all the King, and few would have thought it laudable for him to have sat passive and silent when the Cardinal's fate was being debated.

Cromwell rose to the occasion. It is not a fair interpretation of the evidence to conclude (as, for instance, the author of the biographical article in *The Complete Peerage* has done) that 'self interest alone seems to have been Cromwell's ruling star and his defence of Wolsey was limited accordingly'. Cavendish gives quite a different view: 'There could nothing be spoken against my Lord in the Parliament House, but he would answer it incontinent, or else take unto the next day, against which time he would resort to my Lord to know what answer he should make on his behalf' – almost as if he were appearing for him as his solicitor in court. To every charge made 'he was ever ready furnished with a sufficient answer, so that at length, for his honest behaviour in his master's cause, he grew into such estimation in every man's opinion, that he was esteemed to be the most faithful servant of his master, of all the others, wherein he was of all men greatly commended'.

Universal commendation was one thing, and Cromwell prized it, but his heart was in the cause for which he received such praise. In the absence of Parliamentary debates and draft speeches (such as the one in 1523) Cavendish's account is of prime importance and it is confirmed by the whole tone of Cromwell's correspondence with Wolsey, almost to the latter's death. Thanks to his skilful advocacy the Commons dropped the articles of attainder in December 1529 and, as we have seen, Henry VIII, for his own reasons, let the matter lie.

Wolsey had put all his faith in Cromwell for his 'discreet advice and counsel'. He addressed him in the warmest terms as 'mine own entirely beloved Cromwell' and 'mine own good, trusty and most assured refuge in this my calamity', and signed himself 'your assured lover' – the most affectionate valediction in his extensive formulary of letter-writing. His solicitor's letters are a tonic for him, he writes, but his presence would be greater and he is distraught if he cannot come and see him regularly. Cromwell came to Esher whenever he could to confer on matters that could not be trusted to writing and to go over the lengthy list of charges in the bill against him. As to his defence, Wolsey wrote: 'I have no doubt but that which on my part lacketh, shall be on your part supplied.' When Parliament was prorogued a week before Christmas Wolsey was imploring Cromwell to use all his influence to obtain a satisfactory financial provision, for himself and his household, from Henry, and was grateful for his readiness to draft appropriate letters to the King. It was through Cromwell's agency that the Cardinal received his full pardon on 12 February 1530; it was Cromwell who sent him medicines; Cromwell who tried to persuade Norfolk that he should be allowed to move to Winchester and, when this was impossible, arranged funds for his journey to York and well-wishers to entertain him and his entourage *en route*. The two men probably met for the last time on 5 April 1530, as Wolsey left Richmond.

At the beginning of February Vaughan wrote to Cromwell from the Low Countries, delighted to learn that his friend was now sailing 'in a sure haven', the immediate danger over. He warned him somewhat gratuitously that 'a merry semblance of weather often thrusteth men into the dangerous seas, not thinking to be suddenly oppressed with tempest, when unawares they may be prevented and brought in great jeopardy'. Cromwell had indeed launched himself into dangerous waters when, in the first session of the Reformation Parliament, besides defending Wolsey, he had been in the forefront of the vigorous movement against the ecclesiastical courts, guiding anticlericalism towards a constructive goal, and he had begun drafting the paper that was to become known as the Supplication against the Ordinaries. In the discussions here, no less than in his actions to save Wolsey, Cromwell showed his growing mastery and went far in establishing his ascendancy.

Though it is impossible to date his altered status with certainty it must have been in the first weeks of 1530 that Cromwell entered the King's service. He was *not* appointed to a specific office at that time (as had been the case with Stephen Gardiner, who in the previous September had left the Cardinal's secretariat to become the King's

Secretary). Yet he began to wear the royal livery and to be under the King's special protection as a servant of the crown. The chronicler Edward Hall put Cromwell's change of master in early April, but a correspondent in Norwich wrote to him on 6 February: 'I hear that you be the King's servant.' Moreover in the letter of 3 February quoted above Stephen Vaughan goes on to say that he understands that Cromwell is to accompany Lord Rochford on his embassy to France. The report in the Netherlands was incorrect, as it happened, but it can scarcely have gained credence if Cromwell had not already been in Henry's service.

In later years some felt there was a need to explain Cromwell's rise in the King's favour by a single occurrence – a decisive audience with his sovereign – just as others were to invent Walter Raleigh's throwing his cloak in the mire for Queen Elizabeth to walk upon as the necessary explanation for his meteoric rise. The ambassador Chapuys, writing at the end of 1535, mentions that not long after Wolsey's death Cromwell obtained an audience of the King in which he promised to make him the richest monarch England had ever seen – yet we know that throughout 1530 Cromwell was regularly discussing matters with Henry. Cardinal Pole, writing his *Apologia* three years after Chapuys's despatch was sent, also describes a dramatic interview, in this case in 1529, during which Cromwell is made to produce a blueprint for the entire legislation of the Reformation Parliament. Later on John Foxe, in his *Acts and Monuments*, has Cromwell introduced to the King by Sir John Russell (with whom he is wrongly said to have served in Italy four years before), and in the royal presence giving documentary proof of the entire clergy's guilt of *praemunire*. These are not trustworthy accounts, though they still have their followers. The only contemporary author who was in a position to be knowledgeable about Cromwell at this time was George Cavendish. He wrote of the King's growing confidence in him over a series of audiences, which caused Henry 'to repute him to be a very wise man and a meet instrument to serve his Grace'. The issue of Wolsey's pardon and the decision that, when well enough to travel, he should leave for his northern diocese, emphasized a break with Cromwell that had already taken place. Cromwell's letters to the Cardinal at Southwell are more businesslike in tone and he is not writing any longer as a loving servant, but as a friend at court.

Henry had certainly appreciated Cromwell's worth in view of what he had achieved in the Commons. But there was another factor. The upheaval caused by Wolsey's surrender of York House and his other temporalities involved Cromwell in much legal and financial business. With a view to gaining some measure of restoration he advised the Cardinal to make grants of land and pensions to the most influential courtiers; Anne Boleyn's brother George, for instance, received an annuity of £200 from the revenues of the bishopric of Winchester and 200 marks from the lands of St Alban's Abbey. Among other beneficiaries were Lord Sandes, controller of the royal household, Sir William Fitzwilliam, the King's treasurer, and Henry's favourite courtier, Sir Henry Norris. Cromwell thus became in effect a patronage secretary and as such strengthened his own favour and protection at court.

In these complicated dealings his legal expertise was much in evidence and with the negotiations in his hands alone some of the money naturally stuck. In the tangle of title to lands and annuities granted out of Wolsey's temporalities that had come to the crown through the *praemunire* proceedings, there was much uncertainty as to whether such grants would be valid only so long as the Cardinal lived. Accordingly the grantees looked to Cromwell to obtain confirmations from Wolsey that would not be challenged. 'Then began both noblemen and others who had any patents of the King ... to make earnest suit to Master Cromwell for to solicit their cases, and for his pains therein they promised not only to reward him but show such pleasures as should be at all times in their small powers.' In completing this business the Cardinal's solicitor needed (adds Cavendish) 'continual access to the King, by means whereof and through his witty demeanour he grew continually into his Majesty's favour'. When, for instance, Henry wanted to reward Lord Sandes with an office in Wolsey's gift, the matter necessarily had to pass through Cromwell and we find the King asking him to draft a letter for him to send to the Cardinal for his consent. He was in and out of the palace, a man whom courtiers now treated with deference, for they knew how influential he had become. 'After your departure, the King his Grace had very good commendation of you,' Sir John Russell wrote to Cromwell – a piece of information that reveals how a man of Russell's status at court felt it important to flatter the newcomer. Cromwell continued to supervise the affairs of Wolsey's colleges most closely and when, in the middle of 1530, the King decided to dissolve them, his detailed knowledge of all the earlier transactions made his expertise invaluable. He still found some time for his private legal practice, especially in arbitrating in disputes concerning title to lands, and his trading activities with the Netherlands continued.

With Wolsey first in Southwell and then, at last, in York, Cromwell felt under less pressure, though the Cardinal still wrote to him frequently to enlist his aid in matters great and small, from seeking an understanding with the Boleyn faction to sending him some quails. Cromwell reported in May that Anne Boleyn had received his letters: 'She gave me kind words, but will not promise to speak to the King for you' – surely the last thing that Anne would have done! Two developments during the summer particularly shook Wolsey. The first was Henry's decision to dissolve his collegiate foundations. When Cromwell imparted the news to him he still did not know whether the King intended subsequently to refound them in his own name. Argument was useless and he firmly told Wolsey 'to be content and let your Prince execute his pleasure'. No less alarming was the news that there was to be a series of inquisitions into the lands belonging to the see of York. In a long letter of mid-August Cromwell did his best to calm him, reassuring him that there were legal technicalities to be settled and that what was being done should effectively safeguard his property as archbishop. After warning him against having too great a retinue and indulging in extensive and extravagant building operations – his usual besetting sins – which would inevitably be exploited by his enemies at court, Cromwell attempted to comfort the Cardinal by hoping that he would come to terms with his lot. Some have regarded this as an arrogant piece of sermonizing, yet Cromwell, who knew his Wolsey, meant what he said in the most sincere way and quite clearly expected what he wrote to be taken as words of comfort:

I do reckon your Grace right happy that ye be now at liberty to serve God and to learn the vain desires of this unstable world, which undoubtedly doth nothing else but allure every person therein and specially such as Our Lord hath most endowed with his gifts, to desire the affections of their mind to be satisfied; in studying and seeking whereof, most persons, besides the great travails and afflictions that men suffer daily, been driven to extreme repentance, and searching for pleasure and felicity find nothing but trouble, sorrow, anxiety and adversity. Wherefore, in mine opinion, your Grace, being as ye are, I suppose ye would not be as ye were to win a hundred times as much as even ye were possessed of.

This was a timely reminder and exhortation, which Cromwell devoutly hoped would not fall on deaf ears.

As a result Cromwell must have been particularly disturbed when the news reached London that Wolsey was summoning a northern convocation to coincide with his enthronement as archbishop in York Minster. He was no less troubled over the reports of his alleged intrigues with France and the Empire, since he can hardly have been ignorant of what was being discussed at court. What hurt him most, just before the final storm broke, was that he learnt that the Cardinal had been spreading false tales about him. In his last surviving letter, written on 18 October 1530, Cromwell does not hide his feelings, nor pull his punches:

I am informed your Grace hath in me some diffidence, as if I did dissemble with you, or procure anything contrary to your profit and honour. I much muse that your Grace should so think or repeat it secretly, considering the pains I have taken . . . I beseech you to speak without feigning, if you have such conceit, that I may clear myself. I reckoned that your Grace would have written plainly unto me of such thing, rather than secretly to have misrepresented me. But I shall bear your Grace no less good will. Let God judge between us. Truly, your Grace in some things over shooteth yourself. There is regard to be given what things ye utter, and to whom. . . .

The rest is silence. When Wolsey was arrested Cromwell must have known that his old master would be unlikely to emerge from the Tower – except for a state trial with no hope of acquittal. As a servant of the crown he would on this occasion be under no obligation to attempt an impossible defence. Wolsey's death in Leicester was accordingly a timely relief from a burden. It freed Cromwell from his past and from any lingering suspicion that he remained a partisan of the Cardinal. A friend, who had feared that Cromwell would be 'in great trouble for my Lord Cardinal causes', was overjoyed that he was 'in favour highly with the King's Grace . . .'. Within a few days of Wolsey's end he was sworn as a Privy Councillor.

7
Master Secretary

Recognized by Henry as a man of unusual ability, Cromwell rose steadily in royal favour from the last days of 1530 onwards. Within twenty-five months he was considered by Chapuys to be the individual who had chief influence with the King, ousting a reluctant More, a disgruntled Norfolk and a pushing Gardiner. For little short of ten years he was to bestride English politics, a seemingly indispensable partner of the King in framing and executing policy. Although he was allowed a measure of independence and personal power such as no other royal servant enjoyed, he never became the rival to the monarch that the Cardinal had been. With wide-ranging interests, as his series of remembrances or personal memoranda show, and an appetite for detailed work, he became omnicompetent and shaped the office of Principal Secretary so that it dealt with virtually every aspect of domestic affairs as well as foreign policy.

It was the character of the man, however, not the particular appointments he held that counted, and these grew in importance as Cromwell became master of the political and administrative scene and saw more clearly how he might put into practice his vision of a national, sovereign state. His legacy was not merely the subjugation of the Church to the state and the curtailment of feudal power, but the establishment of the 'King in Council' as the supreme executive and the 'King in Parliament' as the sole legislative authority. Cromwell's visit to Thomas More in Chelsea, recorded in Roper's *Life*, probably belongs to the period about Christmas 1530. The Lord Chancellor from personal experience offered the new Privy Councillor friendly guidance: 'Master Cromwell, you are now entered into the service of

a most noble, wise and liberal prince. If you will follow my poor
advice, you shall, in your counsel giving unto His Grace, ever tell him
what he ought to do, but never what he is able to do. So shall you shew
yourself a true faithful servant and a right worthy Councillor. For if a
lion knew his own strength, hard were it for any man to rule him.'
The law of the jungle was to prevail, however, for Cromwell no less
than More was to be torn asunder.

Almost at once Stephen Vaughan, Cromwell's friend in Antwerp,
attempted to persuade him to use his influence to secure the return to
England of William Tyndale, whom the King was convinced was a
heretic. Could not the reformer be granted a safe conduct, the earnest
and naïve Vaughan asked, on the understanding that he would
employ his literary talents in writing in favour of the King's divorce?
Cromwell acted warily. While he shared some of Tyndale's views, for
instance on clerical reform, he recognized him as too unpredictable a
man to back. It was a shrewd appraisal, for a close involvement with
Tyndale or the other English refugees in the Netherlands could have
jeopardized his future. Henry let the Tyndale affair take its course,
partly in order to wait until he had perused his latest tract, *The Answer*,
but partly, one suspects, to see how far the untried Councillor had
committed himself. By May 1531 Cromwell knew the extent of the
King's displeasure with Tyndale and, at one remove, with Vaughan
for making the proposal; he was indeed thankful that he had not
compromised himself. Henry had found *The Answer* 'filled with
seditious, slanderous lies and fanatical opinions', so Cromwell warned
Vaughan to have no further truck with him, for Tyndale was a man
'replete with venomous envy, rancour and malice'. Vaughan did not
give up hope of his friend at court being able to forward the true
gospel and he was not above chiding him for indifference to religion and
for resting on his laurels, yet Cromwell took these lectures on his duty
in a friendly enough spirit, concluding how little Stephen Vaughan
knew of King and court.

Though given the status of a councillor, Cromwell remained
without an office for some little while and had to rely on the income
from his private legal practice and, to a lesser degree, from his business
activities. But because he was at the hub of affairs he was being
constantly sought by men great and small, who looked to him for
favours at court. In consequence he was the recipient of the customary

gifts suitors proffered. During 1531 he was increasingly immersed in legal administration, civil and criminal, hearing appeals and acting for the King in exchanges of property; yet until the very end of that year he was still only on the fringe of policy-making.

Freed from Wolsey, Henry hoped for quick results in his negotiations. Yet in his dealings with Rome he had been floundering and found progress as hard to achieve as had the Cardinal. In the twelve months following the ending of the legatine court at Blackfriars, the King's policy had been remarkable only for the uncertainty of strategy and tactics. The only new development was a commission to Thomas Cranmer of Cambridge to sound the universities of Europe on the question of the divorce. Early in 1530 Pope and Emperor at last met and their *entente* was completed, yet strangely the King decided the time was ripe for a personal approach to Charles V and furthermore he chose as his chief emissary Anne's brother, Lord Rochford. In June, when his case had already formally opened in Rome, Henry summoned his leading subjects to court to give speedy judgement on his behalf, since informed opinion in England and beyond (he said) was in no doubt of the strength of his case. At this very time, however, he urged William Bennet and his colleagues in Rome to procrastinate. By August 1530 Henry had completely changed his tune, for he now maintained he had no case to answer before the Pope, that he was not subject to papal authority and the jurisdiction of the papal courts. He had shifted his whole argument for a divorce from scriptural grounds, the validity of papal dispensations, and the fact that learned men throughout Europe said a divorce was his due, to the area of political philosophy. No Englishman, he stated, could by ancient custom be cited to appear in a foreign court. This novel doctrine of *Privilegium Angliae*, to the effect that in his realm the King of England is above both Emperor and Pope, so astounded Bennet and Carne in Rome that they declined to convey even the gist of it to the Pope for several months. Such was the origin of the concept of the royal supremacy that was to be refined and defined over the next few years.

All the evidence suggests that the germ of the idea of the royal supremacy was Henry's own. Had Cromwell been consulted at this stage it would have been most unlikely for there to be no evidence of it among his voluminous papers. There would surely have been, after many drafts, a forceful memorandum, providing references from his reading in law, history and scripture, which could be presented as an arguable case. This was not Henry's case in the summer of 1530. The idea owed something to his fascination with the imperial ideal, to his disappointment at failing in the 1519 election and to his subsequent disenchantment with Charles v. As long ago as the end of October 1529 in a lengthy conversation with Eustace Chapuys, the imperial ambassador, Henry had dwelt on the vanity of popes and cardinals and the need for Church reform, adding that the powers of the clergy over laymen – even the power of the Pope himself – should be severely limited. He regretted his youthful, overzealous book against Luther in which, he now feared, he had sold his birthright for a papal title. Now, looking for urgently needed facts to bolster his thesis, he set Bennet and Carne on an impossible piece of historical research – no less than to read *all* the Vatican Registers to abstract entries that would support his claim to an 'authority imperial', as well as the general problem of whether popes had ever had ultimate jurisdiction in matrimonial causes from the earliest times. Their researches, thwarted at every turn by the cardinal librarian, yielded not a scrap of help. Next Henry tried ancient British mythology, hoping that an imperial dignity could be grounded on the shifting sands of Geoffrey of Monmouth's chronicle, the stories of Brutus, King Arthur and the rest, which had already been exposed by the critical approach of Polydore Vergil and found wanting as historical evidence. Finally there was Old Testament kingship, exemplified in an anointed Solomon, to which in the long history of monarchy first Constantine then Charlemagne added their own mystique. Soon Henry's concept of Caesaropapism was to be given an intellectual basis by Cromwell, but as yet he was grasping at straws.

Some have detected Cromwell's hand in the King's campaign against the English Church early in 1531, but this is rather unlikely: there are too many loose ends in it, too many inconsistencies, and the relations between crown and Church, at home as in Rome, were for months characterized by conflicting policies. The convocation of Canterbury submitted to the charge of *praemunire* – not just as guilty parties in Wolsey's usurped jurisdiction, but for exercising their own jurisdiction in their respective ecclesiastical courts, which was deemed to be prejudicial to the laws of England 'and specially contrary to the form of the statutes of provisors, provisions and *praemunire*'. The clergy sued for pardon and were fined £100,000 for the province of Canterbury, £18,840 for the province of York, yet their statutory pardon left their powers undiminished, and their fines could be paid over five years. Almost at once, however, Henry returned to the attack. Convocation must acknowledge the King's right to be called 'Protector and Supreme Head of the English Church and Clergy', and after private heart-searching but no discussion the royal claim was conceded – 'so far as the law of Christ allows'. The King's policy towards Rome was both temporizing and threatening, for he was still hopeful of success. Chapuys did not exaggerate when he reported: 'Parliament is prorogued from time to time, as if they do not know their own minds about the measures to be proposed therein.'

When the Commons considered the bill for the pardon of the clergy there was a determined move to prevent its passage unless the laity also were included in the pardon, which Speaker Audley conveyed to the King. Henry apparently had learnt something of the speeches in the Chamber from Cromwell, who was accused of disclosing Parliamentary secrets to the King. In the end the Commons got their way.

With the opening of the third session of the Reformation Parliament in January 1532 Cromwell emerges as the manager of government business. In the preceding few months he had entered the 'inner circle' of Councillors who were concerned with matters of high policy and had prepared memoranda about bills dealing with treason, wards and feudal incidents, the corn supply, wines and the woollen industry. It was not to be a straightforward session, for the Commons began by throwing out the bill Cromwell had drafted on feudal incidents (for regulating primer seisin and uses). With Audley's help he had a draft bill ready for abolishing the Archbishop of Canterbury's jurisdiction over bishops and transferring it to Convocation (this was devised to nullify Warham's refusal to grant Henry a divorce, and plans were afoot to secure a decree from Convocation that Parliament would speedily ratify). But on the King's instructions the measure was shelved as being too revolutionary and instead he decided to twist the Pope's arm by mounting an attack on annates – the first fruits paid to Rome by archbishops and bishops. Cromwell was dubious about its success in passing the House of Lords, let alone of its having any effect on Henry's cause: 'To what end or effect it will succeed, surely I know not.' The King then changed tack and required Cromwell to add a fresh clause that would delay the introduction of the Annates Act until it should be confirmed by royal letters patent. This showed that even now, in March 1532, Henry was hopeful that negotiations with Rome would succeed and so preserve England's links with the papacy. Even with this delaying clause it was only the King's personal appearance in the Upper House that secured its passage. But before then a much more significant move was afoot.

On the last day of February Norfolk wrote of the 'infinite clamour of the temporality here in Parliament against the misusing of the spiritual jurisdiction', and he added that no previous Parliament had complained a tenth as much about the abuses of churchmen. There was a fresh wave of anticlericalism in the Commons (as fierce as anything seen since the affair of Richard Hunne in 1515), which was to lead to the presentation to the King of the 'Supplication of the Commons against the Ordinaries' on 18 March. Archbishop Warham seemed spoiling for a fight, for on 24 February he issued a formal protest, dissociating himself from any statutes Parliament might pass that affected papal power or the liberties of the Church. A fortnight later he cited Hugh Latimer, a preacher popular at Court, to appear before Convocation to answer charges of heresy, for which he was to be excommunicated.

The 'Supplication' poses many questions. In recent years much detailed research has been undertaken on this crucial episode of the Reformation, which was to provoke the 'Submission of the Clergy' to Henry VIII, and it is unlikely that uncertainties about it can ever be satisfactorily resolved. It seems most likely however that Cromwell, who had as a private member in 1529 drafted and re-drafted the complaints against the clergy, which had then been put aside, now turned to them again and used them as a basis for attacking the Church, or rather English churchmen, for the 'Supplication', even in its revised and strengthened form, was never envisaged as a bargaining counter in Rome over the divorce, as was the case with the First Annates Act. Despite lack of evidence, it is hard to resist the conclusion that Cromwell, the minister in charge of government business in the House, who had been thwarted by an irate and unco-operative Commons that disliked the crown's fresh financial demands and had been in no mood to give an impartial hearing to his bills for reforming Wills and Uses, saw the possibility of a manoeuvre that would win for the government a popularity it badly needed. From a new *rapport* between crown and Commons much might stem, though it would be stretching credibility to suggest that at the start of the affair the minister envisaged that the clergy would formally submit. At the very least, even if Cromwell had not himself taken the initiative in renewing the campaign against ecclesiastical privilege and power, he saw how it could be turned to advantage.

The primary intention of the 'Supplication' was to check the activities of the ecclesiastical courts. The document drew attention to 'the extreme and uncharitable behaviour and dealing of divers ordinaries, who have the right to examine . . . heresies', and it dwelt on the 'subtle interrogatories concerning the high mysteries of the faith', which trapped the unwary into trials for heresy. It underlined the vexatious delays that made proceedings in the ecclesiastical courts a byword, especially in testamentary affairs, the great costs and inconveniences to laymen in being cited to appear in courts outside the dioceses in which they resided, and the heavy fees of litigation. Among the other clerical abuses noted was the independent power of Convocation to frame laws – most topical for at the very time fresh canons were being framed. Nepotism, the number of secular posts held by clerics and the free use of the weapon of excommunication were also roundly attacked. The Commons, protesting their 'marvellous, fervent love' towards their sovereign, asked him for redress of their grievances; instead of a united people, his subjects had become two nations, and this division between clergy and laymen provoked 'breach of your peace within your most Catholic realm'.

Speaker Audley, who led the delegation to the King on 18 March, mentioned the hopes of members that Parliament might soon be over so that they could return home. Henry in his reply fastened on to this inconsistency: 'You require to have the Parliament dissolved . . . yet you would have a reformation of your griefs with all diligence.' The remedy, he said, lay in their hands, and he chided them for their stubbornness over various bills. The Commons in consequence now discussed measures to prevent bishops from citing laymen out of their dioceses and for limiting benefit of clergy.

After the Easter recess the King asked Warham for a formal reply to the Commons' Supplication. This was prepared by Gardiner, who maintained that the laity had much exaggerated their grievances, though reforms were even now being implemented. More important, Convocation's power to legislate in ecclesiastical affairs was, he said, of divine origin, thus the clergy 'may not submit the execution of our charge and duty, certainly prescribed by God, to your Highness' assent'. This was a high-flown and tactless answer, which nearly cost Gardiner the secretaryship, and most certainly ended his chances of succeeding Warham as archbishop. The humble plea for royal protection that Convocation added as an afterthought seems in the context bizarre. The King conveyed Convocation's answer to the Commons with a characteristic note: 'We think their answer will smally please you, for it seemeth to us very slender. You be a great sort of wise men; I doubt not but you will look circumspectly on the matter, and we will be indifferent between you.'

Cromwell now saw his chance and, with Audley and probably others, drafted for the King a comprehensive document for Convocation to submit all its legislation, past and present, for his consent. Their canons would be scrutinized by thirty-two experts appointed by him, half from Parliament, half from the clergy, and any found repugnant to the laws of the realm would be abrogated. Before Convocation could consider this, Henry delivered another broadside. On 11 May he sent for Audley and twelve members and, flanked by his chief councillors, told them:

Welbeloved subjects – we thought that the clergie of our realme had been our subjectes wholy, but now wee have well perceived that they bee but halfe our subjectes, yea, and scarce our subjects: for all the prelates at their consecration make an othe to the pope, clene contrary to the othe that they make to us, so that they seme to be his subjectes, and not ours. The copie of bothe the othes I deliver here to you, requirying you to invent some ordre, that we bee not thus deluded of our spirituall subjectes.

Tradition going back to Cardinal Pole and John Foxe has it that it was Thomas Cromwell who suggested this approach to the King and it tallies with the idea of the royal supremacy that he developed. Four days later Convocation submitted and on 16 May presented Henry with the 'Submission of the Clergy', in which they conceded all his demands. England had become Erastian. As Chapuys put it, the churchmen were now of less account than cobblers, for such tradesmen could still assemble and make their own rules for their craft guild, which the clergy no longer could. The next day Sir Thomas More resigned the Chancellorship and his successor was to be Audley, Cromwell's close friend.

Cromwell's service to Henry in the Parliamentary sessions of 1532 at last led to a royal appointment – the Mastership of the King's Jewels – in April with a salary of £50 a year. This was, as its name implied, a post in the royal household concerned with the custody of the jewels and plate, including the chested treasure kept aside as reserve funds; his predecessor had been a London goldsmith. We see Cromwell writing to the King about his approval of the pattern the goldsmith had made for his new collar and later, when Catherine of Aragon had become reduced to the status of Dowager Princess of Wales, calling in the plate engraved with her arms as Queen. Three months later Cromwell also acquired the post of Clerk of the Hanaper, which was the financial department of Chancery. This brought in rather modest fees, principally from sealing patents, which rarely amounted to more than £60 a year. The following April he added a third to these two minor offices, that of Chancellor of the Exchequer, which was in those days scarcely more important than his posts in the Jewel House and the Hanaper. The status that the Chancellor was to acquire in Hanoverian days was undreamt of, for in 1533 he was no higher in seniority in the Exchequer than fourth place beneath the Lord Treasurer. Soon Cromwell would achieve appointments of much greater weight and with very much larger stipends, yet he never parted with his earliest preferments. Like Wolsey he clung to whatever he gained.

His three earliest posts gave Cromwell the opportunity of acquiring a clear view of financial affairs in the Household, the Exchequer and the Chancery. He made good use of this experience, which enabled him to become to some degree a 'minister of finance'. He had a much wider appreciation of problems than Lord Treasurer Norfolk, whose knowledge was confined to one department only, in which he played a mainly titular role. By contrast Cromwell had an enquiring mind and was never satisfied with being a mere figurehead. His next posts, those of Principal Secretary (1534–40), Master of the Rolls (1534–6) and Lord Privy Seal (1536–40), brought under his personal control the main government secretariat, for the clerks respectively of the Signet, the Chancery and the Privy Seal were responsible to him.

From September 1532 he acted as Secretary, since Stephen Gardiner was abroad, and the signet was transferred to his custody. But already much earlier he had been arranging for foreign news letters to be translated for the King and, since ambassadors taking up appointments were issued with plate from the Jewel House, he had taken a close personal interest in diplomatic representation. But now as he stood in for Gardiner he saw the possibilities of the office of secretary. Much of the routine work of his temporary Secretaryship Cromwell left to Ralph Sadler, an able clerk in his private service who was destined to have a distinguished career in administration, but the less straight-forward business he found time to carry out himself. He greatly valued this experience, for it brought him into much more frequent contact with the King than hitherto. He was determined to unseat the Bishop – since Gardiner had been provided to Winchester at about the same time that Cromwell had become a Councillor – and he could not easily forgive him for achieving the Secretaryship in the summer of 1529, swiftly changing his allegiance from Cardinal to King. When Gardiner returned from his diplomatic mission at the beginning of 1534 he was in disgrace with Henry for opposing the Act of Supremacy and was ultimately banished from court. By April Cromwell had ousted him. He rubbed in his victory by writing almost at once to Gardiner asking for the advowson of a Hampshire parsonage for a friend.

Unlike Gardiner and his predecessors Cromwell remained at home, for the post, as it developed under him, was far too demanding to allow for absences; henceforward ambassadors were to be largely his choice. While Wolsey had been principal minister through holding the Lord Chancellorship, Cromwell transformed the Secretaryship of State into the office that really mattered. No longer was it an appendage of the royal household – a writing-office for royal letters – but 'a ministry of all affairs', as has been said. All Secretaryships of State in the modern British Cabinet indeed stem from Cromwell's constructive tenure of a singleton post. Simply because of his extensive interests and his enormous drive, he made the Secretaryship, with the custody of the signet, the keystone in administration. This gave him a unique authority and his personal achievement in raising the post to such an importance was recognized in an Act of Parliament of 1539 dealing with precedence, where the Secretary of State is acknowledged as one of the great officers of state.

From the opening of the Reformation Parliament until his death Cromwell remained predominantly in London, though from July 1535 he generally accompanied the King for much of his summer progress. But he was no lover of the court and, apart from the chances it afforded of hunting and hawking, he disliked the inconvenience and interruptions of progresses. Unlike Wolsey, Norfolk or Gardiner he never left England, for he knew the importance of staying close to Henry. An absentee was vulnerable to the intrigues of enemies and for this reason Cromwell contrived wherever possible to have his chief rivals sent away on business. Gardiner was appointed to another long embassy in France from October 1535, while Norfolk, who did not have the temperament to play second fiddle to him for long at a time, became 'wonderfully sick of the court' and spent as much of the year as he could at Kenninghall.

The evidence for the Secretary's activities is his surviving cor-respondence – an enormous archive, with a very considerable range of subject matter. In addition to the domestic front, where finance, law and order, and problems of central and local administration were of prime importance, he took special interest in England's outpost at Calais, and in the new status of the Principality of Wales. There was, too, a regular flow of instructions to ambassadors abroad and less frequent letters to resident envoys at Henry's court, for where Wolsey would have given an audience Cromwell would write a letter. No surviving letter appears to have been penned unnecessarily and there are very few superfluous sentences. Cromwell's direct style breathes a sense of urgency and there is no time for frills. His passion for detail is apparent, but it is always relevant detail. Most of what he wrote are instructions: the question of the lease has still to be answered; audited accounts are to be sent forthwith; the abbot is to report about the pension, or the mayor about the prisoner's examination; my lord must repair to court, or the bishop must peruse the statute. Even with his most important correspondents, after conveying his 'right hearty commendations', Cromwell at once gets down to business but, much to our loss, conveys nothing of the gossip of court. Only rarely, when writing to Bishop Gardiner or to Sir Thomas Wyatt abroad, does he relate in his own words some momentous event, such as the fall of Anne Boleyn. Indeed, only with those two correspondents does he now and again betray personal feelings, for he was ever anxious to show the absent Gardiner that he continued to respect his abilities and desired to remain 'his loving friend', while in his letters to 'gentle Master Wyatt' Cromwell cannot conceal his real affection, even when administering a reproof: 'I think your gentle, frank heart doth much impoverish you; when ye have money ye are content to depart with it and lend it, as ye did lately 200 ducats to Mr. Hobby', a colleague in the diplomatic service who had an ample allowance when he was sent to Milan. 'We accustom not to send men disprovided so far. Take heed therefore how ye depart of such portion as ye need. And forsee, rather, to be provided yourself than for the provision of other to leave yourself naked. Politic charity proceedeth not that way. . . .' Cromwell's earlier letters to Wolsey often contained descriptions and an element of chattiness. As Principal Secretary he is businesslike, precise and is no longer considering the whims of a patron. Though Latin remained the language of the formal records of the ancient courts of law, and would so continue for two centuries, it was through Cromwell that English became established as the normal language of public administration.

As a lawyer by training and a man to whom the making and the execution of laws was of paramount importance, Cromwell took special pride in his appointment as Master of the Rolls in October 1534. Usually held by clerics this post had become the equivalent of deputy to the Chancellor. It was a lucrative post and besides rich pickings from fees the Master had an official residence at Rolls House, of which Cromwell made frequent use. It was the ordering of the Chancery clerks, whose work he had seen from his post in the Hanaper, that principally interested him, not the niceties of law. He was to vacate the office a month after being appointed Lord Privy Seal in July 1536. His final post, that of Lord Great Chamberlain which he held from April 1540, was one of considerable dignity but little administrative significance. All in all, these various offices afforded Cromwell a unique position at the centre of administration, from which he could see the existing system as a whole, compare anomalies, understand procedures and documentation and reach sensible conclusions about the measures of reform required. No one without his intricate knowledge of specialized departments could have proposed reforms that were feasible or made a comprehensive plan for efficient government. These indeed were problems that Wolsey had recognized, but the Cardinal had neither the talent nor the interest to transform the medieval system into an administrative machine suited to the modern nation state.

Stephen Vaughan was anxious about the burden Cromwell bore and in December 1534 warned him of the danger both to his health and to his powers of judgement if he tried to do everything himself. Just as the Venetian ambassador eighteen years back had compared the weight of Wolsey's duties with the much lighter loads of Italian officials, so Vaughan contrasted Cromwell's taxing role with that of a chief councillor in the Netherlands, such as the Bishop of Palermo, who had not 'half the business, no not the tenth part, that you have'. But, as always, the English merchant in Antwerp went on to point a moral: 'Constant travail of common causes', he wrote, would inevitably numb his critical faculties; and a councillor who went on like this 'by overmuch paining his body and cumbering his wits . . . hasteth his death before him time'. He must, Vaughan said, be more prudent in the stewardship of those great talents that God had given him. 'Half your years be spent,' he went on – though Cromwell was by now in his fiftieth year. 'Look therefore upwards and weary not yourself so much in the work as though it should ever endure.' Cromwell needed to get his priorities right, urged Vaughan, the eager evangelical, and then in a self-effacing way mocked himself for his 'presumptuous counsels'.

Cromwell had great stamina and was blessed not only with a sound constitution but with a robust attitude to his health, whereas the King (like the Cardinal) worried overmuch about illness and the risks of infection. He was also fortunate in the servants he selected to work for him in his private offices, men such as Ralph Sadler and Thomas Wriothesley, whom he could trust to discharge delegated duties. He undoubtedly drove himself hard, but he was physically and mentally equal to the challenge, so the risk of overwork was much less serious than Vaughan realized. When vacation came round, bishops went home to their dioceses, peers to their country estates and lawyers enjoyed a respite from the courts, yet rarely do we hear of Cromwell taking more than a few days' rest from public service. It was his life.

Did he never relax from the cares of state? Cromwell was no dryasdust and no recluse. We know that he especially enjoyed hawking and was delighted to receive presents of hawks. He also hunted in the summer with the King and kept his own greyhounds. He could shoot well with a longbow and sometimes played bowls. At court he would join in card games, such as mumchance, and throw dice, sometimes for high stakes. At home he would read from his considerable library, amuse himself with his singing birds and enjoy listening to music, for among his servants there were a few musicians, though there is no hint that he played any instrument himself. He owned a number of pictures, mostly portraits and scenes from classical mythology. With his wife's death he might have withdrawn from social life, yet he went out of his way to entertain in some style and was happiest when friends of scholarly tastes came to dine. Out-of-hours he was a convivial man, he kept a good table and would generally have his wine bought in Calais by Lord Lisle.

He favoured most the house near the Austin Friars that he had bought from Anthony Vivaldi. Though not so large as the London residences of bishops or temporal peers, it was of a comfortable size, with its own gate tower, a well-proportioned dining hall and extensive stables. Cromwell felt more at home in the City than in the now fashionable area of Westminster, as courtiers became attracted to houses in the vicinity of Whitehall Palace. He knew his place and never contemplated giving banquets at the Austin Friars for ambassadors, let alone entertaining his sovereign there. Compared with York Place it was an insignificant residence, but it sufficed for him and he furnished it with great care. His friends in the Netherlands were always having commissions from him to purchase particular items and he waited long to acquire a carved table for his dining hall 'of such size as there are few in England'. Like Louis XI of France Cromwell had a passion for facts. He possessed a globe and was the first English minister to appreciate the importance of statistics, though unlike Louis he did not despise opinions.

The practical man of politics displayed some interest in political theory. He had read Aristotle's *Politics* and studied Marsiglio of Padua's *Defensor Pacis*. Thomas Starkey mentions his conversation with Cromwell, 'of God, of nature and of other politic and worldly things', and he was to sponsor some of Starkey's political tracts. His ideas

about national sovereignty grew from notes he added to the 'Supplication of the Ordinaries' in 1529 and were the fruit of his abiding interest
in common law. It was natural that he should find canon law so
repugnant and that, as a firm believer in Parliamentary processes, he
should extol the legislative supremacy of the King in Parliament.
This received its first proper definition in the preamble that he drafted
for the 1534 Act of Dispensations:

In all and everey suche lawes humayne made within this Realme . . . your
Royall Majestie and your Lordes Spirituall and temporall and Commons,
representyng the holle state of your Realme in this your most high Courte of
Parliament, have full power and auctoritie . . . the seid lawes . . . to abrogate
adnull amplyfie or dymynyshe . . .

Parliament had been prorogued in May 1532 and was not in fact to
reassemble until February 1533. That interval was the crucial period
of Cromwell's career, for he was bent on providing a solution to the
problem that had eluded Henry — as it had earlier defeated Wolsey.
The Church at home had been cowed into submission, yet there
seemed no likelihood of the Pope taking a fresh look at the King's need
for a divorce; the conditional Restraint of Annates appeared no more
than shadow boxing. It was all very well for Francis I to advise Henry
to marry Anne Boleyn and present the world with a *fait accompli*, but
the imperious Anne wanted a lawful marriage and a public coronation
no less than Henry wanted an heir born in wedlock; for the sake of the
succession the child of their union must be above suspicion. Others
advised Henry to appeal to a general council of the Church, which
would surely vote as overwhelmingly in his favour as the universities
had done, but he knew that Charles v would never allow Pope
Clement to summon such an assembly.

More's resignation had removed an implacable foe to Henry's re-
marriage. He had accepted the Woolsack as Wolsey's successor on the
understanding that he would be absolved from playing an active role
in the King's matrimonial problems, yet this issue had come to
dominate all others and it was illogical that the Lord Chancellor
should be a committed supporter of Queen Catherine. Warham's death
in August removed an archbishop who for the last three years had
obstructed Henry at every turn; there was now at least the possibility
of the King referring his cause to a successor who was sympathetic. In

retrospect there seemed much merit in making the Restraint of Annates 'conditional', for it enabled Thomas Cranmer, Warham's successor, to obtain the bulls from Rome, providing him to Canterbury as a primate fully approved by the Pope, without difficulty. Awkwardness of timing could have called in question the validity of Cranmer's orders and nullified Cromwell's efforts to show the historic continuity of the Church in England. An amenable archbishop, however, could never prove of service to the King while England remained subject to the papacy. It was Cromwell who had seen most clearly that the Pope had to be expelled from England as firmly as Catherine of Aragon had been excluded from the palace, though this had to be achieved in a lawful manner.

This was the conundrum to which he directed all his legal skill and ingenuity. He needed to frame a compelling formula in legal terms, the result of a closely reasoned argument, that would at one and the same time satisfy the King, appeal to the vast majority of members of the Commons and the temporal peers, gain the backing of the moderate bishops and, outside England – the papacy apart – receive recognition as a statesmanlike solution to an intractable domestic problem that had hitherto baffled everyone who had grappled with it. The case had to be self-evident and not appear as an argument based on special pleading. There was no point in reiterating moral platitudes when both Houses of Parliament were more concerned with the constitutional implications. All Cromwell's expertise as a lawyer and a manager of Parliamentary business would be needed to carry his plans into effect. He had to deny the validity of papal claims and show that the body of the clergy in England possessed no jurisdiction, nor a coercive authority, except that which came to it from the crown. He had to argue that it was the intention of the Almighty that a national monarch should rule over a national church. Though effective proof would have been impossible, he knew many Englishmen would be disposed to accept this as a self-evident proposition if it were properly presented. The climate was favourable, since the moral authority of the unreformed papacy had sunk to a low ebb and – however widespread Catholic sympathies were – papal pretensions could be shown as the enemy of rising national aspirations and interests.

The heart of the matter was to be the Act in Restraint of Appeals, and the earliest of several surviving drafts was made during September

1532. In that month Cromwell had sufficiently impressed the King with what he was about that Henry could at last see light at the end of the tunnel. After five anguished years, marriage with Anne Boleyn was becoming almost a certainty and in September, as if to signalize his intentions, he created her Marquess of Pembroke. Parliament had been due to reassemble in November, but there remained much detailed work to be done on the drafting and for most of October Henry, accompanied by Anne, was on a state visit to Francis 1; accordingly the prorogation was continued until February. By the end of the year, however, Cromwell and Audley were so convinced that they had achieved a watertight case that Henry secretly married Anne, who was soon found to be carrying his child. It is usual for historians to comment that Anne's marriage and pregnancy increased the urgency for Cromwell to finalize his plans, but it is much more likely that Henry could throw caution to the winds, with Anne's ready acceptance, now that the way ahead was clear for her to become undisputed Queen and wife in Catherine's stead.

The Act in Restraint of Appeals opened with a fulsome preamble that firmly denied there was any novelty about the foundations of the New Monarchy.

Where by diverse, sundry, old, authentic histories and chronicles it is manifestly declared and explained that this realm of England is an empire, and so hath been accepted in the world, governed by one supreme head and King, having the dignity and royal estate of the imperial Crown of the same, unto whom a body politic, compact of all sort and degrees of people divided in terms and by names of spirituality and temporality, be bounden and owe next to God a natural and humble obedience. . . .

This 'empire', the Act emphasized, was 'governed by one supreme head', having equal sway over clergy and laity. The theory of monarchial power as expressed in this preamble was deftly constructed on the basis of the clergy's recent acknowledgement that Henry was 'supreme head' of the Church (though the proviso 'so far as the law of Christ allows' was here changed to 'next to God'), and the assertion by the Commons of a division between clerics and laymen. The theory owed perhaps more than Cromwell would have been prepared to admit to his reading of Marsiglio of Padua. Historical prolegomena were most necessary to show the historical continuity of the new Erastian

Church with the old medieval Church. From these introductory sentences Cromwell went on to reason that all jurisdictions within the realm, whether temporal or spiritual, derived from the King. Various monarchs, from Edward I onwards, had in partnership with Parliament erected statutes to prevent the papacy – and, indeed, other foreign powers – from interfering in English ecclesiastical affairs, notably by the statutes of provisions and *praemunire*, yet appeals to Rome were continuing to vex Englishmen. In one early draft there is a lengthy harangue on the ambitions of the see apostolic 'to be supreme lords of all the world', followed with instances of papal assumptions of power in appointing foreigners to English benefices, through collecting annates, by enforcing the taking of oaths which contravened Englishmen's natural obedience to their King and finally by assuming the 'authority to declare and adjudge when marriages of this realm shall be lawful and unlawful'. Successive popes had not been ashamed 'to declare and adjudge the succession and procreation, as well of princes and potentates as of all other subjects of the world'. In subsequent versions this strong anti-papal language was much toned down.

From the high flights of the preamble, the draftsmen had to descend to the practical details of enactment. Early drafts of the Bill, after noting how in the past civil wars had arisen in England from 'uncertainty of the posterity and succession', stated that the see of Rome must not be allowed to consider the legitimacy of any child of Henry's, and, in consequence, no summons to or sentence from a papal court concerning the King, or any of his subjects, should be obeyed. All causes, spiritual and temporal, were to be determined henceforth at home according to 'the ancient customs of this realm'. Interdicts and citations from Rome were nullified and any subject attempting to procure a judgement outside the realm in any cause was to be liable to the penalties of high treason. This attempt at directing appeals, hitherto heard in Rome, to English courts lacked precision, and lawyers would need to have a specific procedure stated in the Act. After considerable revision it was laid down that subjects' appeals should go from the archdeacon's court to the diocesan bishop and from him to the archbishop of the province, while for the King, or a case touching the whole realm, there would be an appeal from the court of the Archbishop of Canterbury (which would initially have heard the cause) to the upper house of Convocation. Much discussion had taken place among councillors and lawyers before a final draft was ready for the King's scrutiny. He made a few minor amendments to the wording – for instance, adding the phrase that foreign appeals had occurred in past times 'only by negligence or usurpation, as we take it and esteem'. But before Cromwell introduced the Bill in Parliament he took the precaution of showing it to a number of bishops, abbots and leading canon lawyers, meeting them for a conference, most probably on 5 February. As a result further changes were made to the text, notably in moderating the highflown claims for the monarchical origins of spiritual jurisdiction and allowing no appeal for a subject from the archbishop's court to a body of royal commissioners, as had until then been envisaged. By accepting these alterations, now incorporated in the Bill brought into the Commons, Cromwell purchased a good deal of clerical support, though we know that Archbishop Lee of York as well as Gardiner of Winchester remained opposed. Thanks to this careful process of consultation the Act in Restraint of Appeals was to pass both Houses of Parliament without significant change.

Cromwell was taking no chances about the passage of this and subsidiary legislation. He worked hard to secure appropriate candidates for by-elections to fill vacancies caused by death and by Audley's creation to the peerage. He also urged all members favourable to the King's cause to make special efforts to be in their seats, so that one of the members from Southwark, Robert Acton, who was a sick man, wrote to him: 'If your mastership do send me word to come to the Parliament, I will surely come, whatsoever become of me.' Temporal peers were also reminded of their duty and perhaps even now, as later in the year and more generally in 1536, Cromwell went so far as to discourage those hostile to the King from attendance. Sir George Throckmorton, a fervent supporter of Queen Catherine, was to write to Cromwell accepting his advice to stay at home and eschew politics. Even so, when the Appeals Bill was introduced in the Commons on 14 March it had a stormy reception, those with mercantile interests fearing retaliation by Catholic powers which would hamper England's overseas trade, especially with the Netherlands. But at the end of the debates in both Houses there was significant support for the measure.

The Act was effective. Convocation speedily declared that it was against the law of God for a man to marry his deceased brother's wife, that papal dispensations in such matters were void and that the con-summation of the marriage between Catherine of Aragon and Prince Arthur had been proved beyond doubt. Thomas Cranmer, formerly the Boleyn family chaplain, had been consecrated Archbishop on Passion Sunday, when he made his historic protestation – drafted with Cromwell's help – that his oath to the Pope could not bind him to violate God's laws or the King of England's prerogative, and on 23 May he delivered his verdict at the end of the trial of Dunstable on the validity of Henry's marriage – that this union had been invalid from its beginnings. Cranmer subsequently declared the King's marriage to Anne lawful and on Whit Sunday, 1 June, she was crowned. This was Cromwell's triumph, no less than Anne's, and he was now universally regarded as Henry's chief minister.

Further government measures were prepared for the fifth session, which opened in mid-January 1534. A fresh Annates Act confirmed that these dues would no longer be paid to Rome and made detailed provision for the election of bishops, for cathedral chapters were now legally bound to accept the candidate nominated by the crown. Peter's Pence were abolished and the relevant statute emphasized that the cutting off of this customary revenue was not to be taken as implying that Englishmen were departing from the 'very articles of the catholic faith of Christendom', and – almost as an aside – the crown was empowered to visit the monasteries. There was now statutory con-firmation of the Submission of the Clergy, achieved after a conference between representatives of both Houses of Parliament and both Houses of Convocation with the King as chairman. Italians who had been appointed by the Pope to English sees were formally deprived, for such preferment made nonsense of the royal supremacy (they included Lorenzo Campeggio, Bishop of Salisbury, who would be succeeded by Hugh Latimer). Catherine of Aragon was degraded to the status of Dowager Princess of Wales, and the succession was settled on the King's male heirs by Queen Anne or, in default of them, on those by a subsequent wife. Any subject could be called upon to swear an oath affirming the 'whole effects and contents' of the Act of Succession, under pain of penalties of high treason. Fisher of Rochester and Sir Thomas More, the two subjects whose support Henry needed most, were required to take the oath but while they agreed to swear to the succession itself neither could in conscience subscribe to the preamble to the Succession Act, which would mean giving personal approval to the repudiation of papal authority and the invalidity of the King's marriage to Catherine. Each had been caught up in the affair of Elizabeth Barton, the Nun of Kent, who had been voicing popular protest in favour of Catherine, and although Cromwell soon realized More had no case to answer, compared with the Friars Observant, who were dissolved, the oath was a very different matter, as is made plain later (pages 182–5).

To round off the legislation in the sixth session of the Reformation Parliament, extending from 3 November to 18 December 1534, acts were passed ratifying the royal supremacy, remedying a technical defect in the act of the previous session by prescribing a definite oath of succession, extending the treasons law and granting first fruits and tenths to the crown. The Act of Supremacy gave statutory expression to Henry's powers as head of the Church, but also included a clause authorizing royal visitations of religious foundations. The Treasons Act made attacks by speech or in writing on the King, Queen Anne or the succession treasonable, if made 'maliciously'. Fresh ground was covered by the highly technical Bill annexing first fruits and tenths to the crown. Not so long ago Parliament had described the first fruits paid to Rome as 'intolerable and importable', so it was most necessary to justify their collection by lauding the sovereign who had governed his realm in peace and unity and who by virtue of this work had been at 'excessive and inestimable charges'. As part of the new system royal commissioners were to value all benefices, monastic and collegiate foundations and their work became enshrined in the *Valor Ecclesiasticus*. The complicated First Fruits and Tenths Bill had involved Cromwell and Audley in much drafting, yet equally important was the batch of statutes that began the process of bringing English law and administration to Wales. Cromwell had hoped that 'some reasonable ways may be devised' for wardships and the related problem of uses, which had proved a sticking-point in 1532, but it had to be postponed yet again. An outbreak of the plague prevented the holding of the anticipated sessions in 1535 – the year that the Carthusians, Fisher and More, were executed – and there was much discontent in the land. Despite the prorogation, Cromwell was as busy as ever and towards the end of the year Chapuys reckoned he was more powerful than Wolsey had ever been.

Once again in preparation for the seventh and final session of the Long Parliament of the Reformation Cromwell took pains to ensure the attendance of the most loyal supporters of the King – if peers could not be at Westminster in February 1536 they were pressed to return proxies, if possible leaving the names blank. Opponents of the regime and potentially hostile ecclesiastics were encouraged to stay away, including ten abbots, for the main plank of government legislation was the act to dissolve the smaller monasteries (see pages 194–6). Courtiers at last had the prospect of rich pickings from monastic lands. Many ends were tidied up with regard to uses, Wales, the poor law and Calais; indeed economic and social measures bulk larger on the Statute Roll than the series of acts bringing about the Reformation settlement, and much time was spent framing and discussing private acts.

With the dissolution on Good Friday 1536 an epoch had ended. It is fair to say that the legislation of the previous three years, which had been largely planned by Cromwell and then piloted through the House of Commons by him, had placed a burden on him that no previous minister of the crown had borne. The complexity of measures such as the Act in Restraint of Appeals or the First Fruits and Tenths Act had been a triumph of close reasoning and detailed drafting. Cromwell had proved himself a great Parliamentarian in the process, amply fulfilling the promise he had shown as a private member in 1523. He had cemented the partnership of Parliament with the crown, while Wolsey had always urged Henry against summoning so troublesome an assembly. Through Cromwell's work the legislature had become the crown in Parliament. Rather fittingly Cromwell's work in the Commons ended with the conclusion of the Reformation Parliament, for when next Parliament was summoned he would be in the House of Lords.

The King had hoped that Sir Thomas More, who had in his final years as Chancellor persistently opposed his ecclesiastical policy, could be attainted over the treason of the Nun of Kent, yet Cromwell and other councillors had convinced him there could be no case to answer. But even in retirement, standing quite aloof from politics, More knew that the net was closing around him. Henry would have forgiven all if he had taken the oath to the succession, for to have received so important a token of allegiance would have been invaluable propaganda and shown the King's critics at home and in Europe that the supreme head of the Church was, after all, on the side of the angels. More's silence was as embarrassing as if he had spoken out against Henry. When he was called to Lambeth on 13 May to take the oath he maintained he could not do so 'without the jeopardy of my soul to perpetual damnation'. With great skill he pointed out the difference between the clause in the statute and the more extensive oath (as had been taken by members of both Houses) that was now offered for his subscription. Among laymen only he had been summoned to Lambeth and on his refusal to subscribe he was sent to the Tower after four days.

Cromwell fully expected that the rigours of imprisonment and careful reasoning would persuade him to change his mind, but More's native stubbornness, fortified by the support of family and friends, could not be turned. Time and again in the second half of 1534 he was approached, but refused to be trapped, giving no reasons for his stance, for they were, he said, 'secret in my conscience'. When Parliament met in November he was attainted on the King's instructions and the tone of the act conveys Henry's personal exasperation: More had 'unkindly and ingrately served our Sovereign Lord by divers and sundry ways'. He remained in the Tower out of mortal peril, but all his property was now forfeit to the crown. Cromwell hoped this would be the end of the matter – that he would stay imprisoned, if all persuasion failed, not forgotten, but ignored, and for six months he was. The Secretary was not vindictive. As a matter of principle he wanted to secure More's agreement to the royal supremacy, on which the King insisted, but he would by no means hound him to death. On 7 May 1535 he led a deputation to the Tower which comprised the Attorney-general, Christopher Hales, the Solicitor-general, Richard Riche, and two civil lawyers. Cromwell asked the prisoner if he had seen the Act of Supremacy (which he had), and then told him the King wanted his opinion concerning the title of supreme head. More replied that he had decided never again to argue about this. He had hoped the King would never have asked him such a question

considering that I ever from the beginning well and truly from time to time declared my mind unto his Highness; and since that time I had, I said, unto your mastership, Master Secretary, also, both by mouth and by writing. And now I have in good faith discharged my mind of all such matters and neither will dispute Kings' titles nor Popes', but the King's true, faithful subject I am and will be . . . and otherwise than this I never intend to meddle.

He knew as well as Cromwell that the Treason Act (as worded) did not punish silence. The Secretary tried hard to reason with him. The King, he said, could find More's evasiveness disturbing and 'would exact a full answer'. Apparently he did all he could to persuade More to take a reasonable course and hinted that Henry would gladly show mercy towards him if only he would relent. But More answered, 'I had fully determined with myself neither to study nor meddle with any matter of this world, but that my whole study should be upon the Passion of Christ and mine own passage out of this world.' (These words were to be included in the indictment against him.) The commissioners sent him to another room while they conferred. Summoned back, Cromwell told him that the fact that he was a perpetual prisoner did not mean he was not under the King's obedience, and More agreed. The Secretary then went on to point out that if obedience could bring forgiveness, obstinacy would make the King 'follow the course of his laws', and by his example he was encouraging others to be obstinate. More answered him:

I do nobody harm, I say none harm, I think none harm, but wish everybody good. And if this be not enough to keep a man alive, in good faith, I long not to live. And I am dying already and have, since I came here, been divers times in the case that I thought to die within one hour . . . And therefore my poor body is at the King's pleasure; would God my death might do him good.

Cromwell appears to have been much moved by these words and spoke 'full gently' assuring More that no advantage would be taken of what he had said. Privately he may have thought death in the Tower a release not only for More himself but for the King and his ministers, though the signs are that he still hoped More might change his mind.

Henry waited only four weeks before striking again. Cromwell returned to More's lodging in the Tower on 3 June in very different circumstances. Since the first interrogation news had reached England that Pope Paul III had created Bishop Fisher a cardinal and this provoked the King into demanding that both Fisher and More be brought to justice. The Secretary was on this occasion accompanied by three senior councillors – Audley, Suffolk and Wiltshire. The Lord Chancellor had an oath in his pocket and in all likelihood the deputation had been instructed by Henry either to persuade More to sign or to force him into making some treasonable statement. Cromwell was no longer 'gentle', but informed him that the King considered he 'had been occasion of much grudge and harm in the realm', and was demanding a straightforward answer on his supremacy. At last Cromwell realized that there was no hope; if More persisted in his silence he could not be saved. More said he was presented with an impossible choice – either to affirm the statute 'against my conscience to the loss of my soul, or precisely against it to the destruction of my body'. Cromwell was exasperated at this, and said he liked him 'much worse' than at their former meeting. Almost at once he began putting together what he knew on technical grounds would be a difficult case for the state trial. Sterner treatment meant taking away More's collection of books and it was during their removal that Richard Riche had his chance conversation with More about the supremacy, which Cromwell, when he perused the Solicitor-general's memorandum, seized upon, since More's words were rather more than an academic, hypothetical argument and appeared to transgress the borderline.

There were four counts in the indictment that Cromwell drew up. First, by his sentence during the interrogation on 7 May, More had denied the supremacy, and his claim that he was meddling no more in affairs of this world suggested a positive line of action. Secondly, he had engaged in correspondence with John Fisher, a traitor, since condemned. Thirdly, while maintaining his offence of silence at the interrogation on 3 June he had maliciously called the Act of Supremacy 'a two-edged sword', saying that a man might jeopardize either his soul or his body. Finally, there was the charge that on 12 June he had spoken treasonable words in his conversation with Riche (see page 85).

At his trial More defended himself with consummate skill and Cromwell heard the court in Westminster Hall uphold the defendant's submission that the first three counts could not be held to be offences under the statute. Everything now rested on the Riche conversation, which More denied. The man was, he said, a 'disreputable person' and what he was accused of saying could not be collaborated by the two men who were present packing up his books. Many difficulties concerning the validity of this count remain. Richard Riche has gone down in history as the man who perjured himself by transforming something More said to him off the record into a malicious statement. Certainly Riche's behaviour in Westminster Hall inspires little confidence, yet Cromwell did not regard the Solicitor-general as an unreliable witness, for he based the final count in the indictment on Riche's memorandum, written almost immediately after the conversation. Riche did not appreciate that this was providing a vital piece of evidence, even though he had been present with Cromwell at the first formal inter-rogation. There is some likelihood that in discussing with Riche the validity of Acts of Parliament More *did* slip up and move from the ground of hypothetical 'putting of cases' – so dear to Tudor lawyers – into a form of speech that technically questioned, even if it did not positively deny, the royal supremacy. He was found guilty of treason on this count and Cromwell was satisfied that the trial had been conducted according to the law.

When in February 1531 Convocation had been required to recognize Henry as 'Supreme lord of the Church', Archbishop Warham had said, 'He who is silent seems to consent.' Yet in More's case it was plain to all that silence on the royal supremacy counted as denial. In his heart More denied Henry's title and all it implied, and it was for this that he paid the penalty. In his second interrogation on 7 June Cromwell had drawn a parallel between More's activities as Lord Chancellor, requiring heretics to answer 'yea' or 'nay' to questions of papal supremacy, and King Henry's action in compelling his subjects to answer unequivocally on his own supremacy. When More had denied that this was a true parallel Cromwell had answered that the heretics 'were as well burned for the denying of that, as they be beheaded for denying of this'. More went to the block on 6 July, protesting his loyalty to the King no less than to his conscience. Cromwell questioned this, for under the law this was a contradiction in terms. Ironically, five years later, it was Cromwell's turn to die protesting no less fervently than More his loyalty to the King and his belief in the Catholic faith.

Anne Boleyn's general unpopularity could have been redeemed, and the King's affections retained, only by the arrival of a prince. Henry had taken very badly the fact that the heir for whose sake he had defied the Pope had been a mere girl. Some detected signs that, after waiting for Anne so long he rather soon was 'tired to satiety of this new Queen'. Cromwell must have been thankful that his rise to power had not been as a result of Boleyn patronage. About Christmas 1534, we are told, the King discussed with him and Cranmer the chances of ridding himself of Anne without having to return to Catherine. The imperial ambassador believed wild tales that Cromwell was intending to do away with both Catherine and Mary, so that he warned him he would hold the King and his minister responsible for any mishap that befell either mother or daughter. Sensing her insecurity Queen Anne became imperious and spiteful. When she dared rebuke her husband for enjoying liaisons with other women he told her to 'bear with it as one of her betters had done'. She did not have far to look to find compensations for Henry's neglect – at court there were several young men, nurtured in the idea of chivalry, who were eager to profess their undying love for her. Anne still clutched at the chance of bearing a son and in the autumn of 1535 began another pregnancy. While she remained quietly at Whitehall, Henry went on progress to the west country, accompanied by Cromwell, and while staying at Wolf Hall, the Seymour residence in Wiltshire, he fell in love with Jane, the daughter of the house, who modestly rejected his advances. Catherine's death at Kimbolton the following January was cause for special celebration at court and Anne, as well as Henry, wore 'yellow for mourning', though she took no part in the dances because of the child she was carrying. A fortnight later Henry had a serious fall while riding in the tiltyard at Greenwich and for some hours his life was in the balance.

Norfolk broke the news to his niece and, according to her, the shock of hearing about Henry's accident brought on a miscarriage, so that on the day of Catherine's burial Anne lost her baby, which 'had the appearance of a male', of fifteen weeks. She knew Henry would not give her another chance. When he visited her bedchamber he complained that God had deserted him and would never send him the prince for whom he hungered. Soon he was telling others that when he had married her he had been 'seduced by witchcraft and for this reason considered it null. It was evident, because God did not permit them to have any male issue and that he believed he might take another wife.' Cromwell could see what was coming long before he was asked to vacate his rooms in Greenwich Palace, which were to be assigned to

Edward Seymour (Jane's brother) and his wife, so that Henry could conveniently meet his lover, duly chaperoned. Yet it was Anne's conduct, not Henry's latest affair, that caused alarm, for enough gossip, hearsay and circumstantial evidence fitting the case reached Cromwell to enable him to piece together an unseemly chronicle of the Queen's relations with five paramours. On 24 April the King appointed a commission headed by Cromwell to discover sufficient evidence to bring Anne to trial. Indiscreet remarks by Mark Smeaton, a groom with a talent for the lute, had been overheard and on the rack he confessed to adultery with the Queen. Sir Francis Weston, Henry Norris and William Brereton, all senior officials of Henry's chamber, were found to be implicated. During the May day tournament at Greenwich Anne was arrested and sent to the Tower for adultery with these four courtiers and for alleged incest with Lord Rochford.

Apart from the racking of Smeaton there is nothing to suggest that undue pressure was put upon the accused men or witnesses. Cromwell who had charge of the interrogations knew he must act within the law. His letter to Gardiner, written on 14 May, reveals that the ladies of the Queen's privy chamber dared no longer keep their knowledge of her offences to themselves, but after discussions broached them to

some of his Grace's Council, that with their duty to his Majesty they could not conceal it from him, but with great fear, as the case enforced, declared what they heard unto his Highness. Whereupon in most secret sort certain persons of the Privy Chamber and others of her side were examined. . . . I write no particularities, the things be so abominable that I think the like was never heard. . . .

Cromwell also knew that Henry demanded verdicts of 'guilty' for all six. His own profligacy had convinced him that Anne must be guilty; she was a nymphomaniac, he raved, who had had sexual relations with a hundred men, including her own brother. The handsome men of the Privy Chamber had undoubtedly been playing with fire in paying court to the Queen, with their fulsome compliments to her, the giving and receiving of love tokens, the passionate songs and the carefree dances. Such was the stuff of chivalry, yet the goddess they worshipped had been the King's wife. She had responded to their several flirtations, when she should have shown she was above suspicion, and could but expect to be labelled 'the English Messalina'. If anything should happen to the King, Norris had told her, he would 'look to have her for himself'. How far he and the others overstepped the bounds of propriety could never be known, but Cromwell was satisfied that the charges in the indictment were true. His timing of the series of state trials was masterly, since Anne did not have to face her judges until the four commoners had already been convicted of adultery with her. As he wrote to Gardiner, the four 'be already condemned to death upon arraignment. . . . She and her brother shall be arraigned tomorrow and will indoubtedly go the same way.' In Westminster Hall Norfolk declared that his niece had been found guilty by her peers and pronounced sentence of death. By the King's command Cromwell attended the scaffold on Tower Green with Audley, Suffolk and Richmond on 19 May when Anne was executed.

Eleven days later Henry married Jane Seymour in the queen's chapel at Whitehall. Anne's father, the Earl of Wiltshire, was removed from the office of Lord Privy Seal, which he had held since the beginning of 1530, and the vacant post went to Cromwell, who was created a baron. It was a fitting recompense. Cromwell had been the instrument through which Anne became Queen and then the instrument for her dethronement. Now he consolidated his position by marrying his son Gregory to Queen Jane's sister, Elizabeth Seymour.

8
The Logic of Statecraft

His elevation to Lord Privy Seal demonstrated Cromwell's extra-ordinary power in the state. His peerage was not simply a recognition for past services, for, far from being put out to grass, he was expected to continue to serve as chief minister for years to come. He had no rival. Lord Treasurer Norfolk was in disgrace following Anne's fall and Lord Chancellor Audley was a close colleague with no ambitions to challenge his position. Bishop Gardiner, though partially restored to royal favour, was anchored in Paris and together with the moderate Archbishop Cranmer provided no threat. In little over three years Cromwell had achieved all that Henry had expected of him: he had framed the formula for effecting the breach with Rome and translated it into practical politics, which enabled the King to rid himself of Catherine and to strengthen his power in church and state; he had solved the problem of More, and he had stage-managed the fall of Anne Boleyn. Through his work Parliament had acquired a much more positive role in the government of the realm and he had mastered its ways. Already he was deeply immersed in bringing about the dis-solution of the monasteries, in bringing forward further administrative reforms and in maintaining public order – and he was full of schemes for introducing social and economic reforms. He found Archbishop Cranmer an ideal colleague and, having settled the constitution of the Church, he hoped they could together devote their attention to doctrinal questions and advance the cause of an English bible. There was no indication of flagging interest, no falling off in efficiency in anything that Cromwell undertook and the relationship between King and minister showed no sign of strain.

Soon after Anne Boleyn's execution, Princess Mary, now twenty, wrote to Cromwell from her banishment at Hunsdon, imploring him for the love of God to be her suitor to her father. 'Nobody durst speak for me so long as That Woman lived,' she wrote, but at last there was opportunity for reconciliation. Cromwell arranged for a delegation consisting of Norfolk, Sussex and Bishop Sampson to call on her. They reproved the Princess for her obstinacy in refusing to acknowledge her father as supreme head of the Church, yet handled her tactlessly. The girl persisted in her refusal and Norfolk told her that if she had been his own daughter he would have knocked 'her head against the wall until it was as soft as baked apple', for she had chosen to be a traitress in the manner of Thomas More. Mary now wrote to Henry craving forgiveness and asking for his blessing, for she would submit to him 'in all things next to God'. This was not at all what Henry wanted from her. He demanded total submission and her obstinacy showed how like her mother she was.

Seeing the King's rage Cromwell realized the extent of the danger – not just to Mary, but to the realm. A princess banished from court would remain a focus for the Catholic party and if she were degraded, as Henry threatened, all chances of securing a foreign marriage for her which might strengthen England's position would be forfeit. Cromwell sought Chapuys's help to bring home to Mary the great peril in which she lay and then wrote her a forceful letter to frighten her into obedience, for rational persuasion was hopeless.

If you do not leave all sinister counsels, I take leave of you for ever and desire you to write to me no more, for I will never think you other than the most ungrateful, unnatural and obstinate person living, both to God and your most dear and benign father.

She must yield to Henry, he told her, without apparent reservation. He enclosed the draft of a letter of submission set out in the most grovelling terms, which he insisted she must copy out. His vigorous counsel succeeded for two days later Mary told him she had followed his text 'word for word' and signed it. She thus acknowledged her 'merciful, passionate and most blessed' father to be supreme head of the Church, rejected papal authority and declared that her mother's marriage to Henry had been incestuous. Chapuys had advised her that she could make mental reservations, which he would convey to Rome, and Cromwell must have suspected as much. After some initial uncertainty Henry agreed to accept her submission as a sincere gesture and Mary was allowed to return to court, where he prized her now as 'his chiefest jewel'. By 5 July Cromwell could write with relief to Gardiner that 'my lady Mary is also a most obedient child to the King's Highness and is as conformable as any living faithful subject can be'. He had avoided a most awkward situation.

Ever since the summoning of the Reformation Parliament people had been expecting an onslaught on monastic privilege and wealth, and even before then Henry had raised with Cardinal Campeggio the morality of the state taking over the Church's possessions. So extensive an undertaking was in an entirely different category from heavily fining the entire body of the clergy or assigning to the King the dues formerly paid to Rome, yet if Henry VIII was indeed supreme head of the Church in England, all religious foundations lay at his disposal and their inmates had, with remarkably few exceptions, taken the oath of loyalty. The King, wrote Chapuys in February 1534, 'is very covetous of the goods of the Church, which he already considers his patrimony'. It was not a case of Cromwell persuading Henry he could make him the richest King in Christendom, but of the sovereign requiring his minister to devise a workable plan for exploiting what he already regarded as his own possessions, at a time when he was in great financial need.

In October 1534 Cromwell drafted a paper headed 'Things to be moved for the King's Highness for an increase and augmentation to be had and for maintenance of his most royal estate and for the defence of the realm, and necessary to be provided for taking away the excess, which is the great cause of the abuses in the Church'. This memorandum envisaged drastic savings from the revenues of bishoprics, cathedrals and collegiate foundations, which would be diverted to the crown; the new incumbent in every benefice was to hand over his first year's revenues in their entirety; all monastic foundations with less than ten inmates were to be dissolved and the income from the rest was to be taken over by the crown, which would apportion from it allowances for the brethren for their needs and sums for the abbots for the maintenance of the fabric and for hospitality. To implement so far-ranging a scheme would have posed very considerable administrative problems and also have encountered widespread opposition. The state of the country was too unsettled to risk penal confiscations from bishops, deans and archdeacons and to undermine the basic loyalty of parochial clergy by grasping so much from them.

It is entirely unlikely that Cromwell seriously intended to 'move His Highness' to endorse a programme on such a scale at that juncture. He had no means of quantifying the benefits that any or all of such proposals would bring to the royal coffers and this was the key point that interested his master. No one could make more than a guess about how much the Church owned. As a result commissioners were appointed early in 1535, under the First Fruits and Tenths Act, to survey and value all ecclesiastical benefices throughout England and Wales as well as the properties of all monasteries, convents and hospitals. Their detailed returns were entered in a massive domesday of church property, the *Valor Ecclesiasticus*, which is a monument to Cromwell's administrative skill; the original returns even comprised certain material for Ireland (though these were not edited for inclusion in the *Valor* itself). The wealth of the Church was found to reach the incredible sum of £800,000 a year in revenues. The information on benefices was needed for bringing payments of first fruits to the crown into effect, but what was no less significant was the mass of detail about every monastic foundation – how much of the wealth of each derived from rural estates, manorial charges, corn mills, tolls or from urban properties, from offerings at shrines and from other sources. On the basis of these figures King and minister could frame their plan for diverting monastic money to other purposes.

Cromwell's experience in disbanding the score of small houses as a preliminary to Wolsey's intended foundations from 1525 to 1528 convinced him that the most feasible scheme would be to deal first with the remaining lesser monasteries and priories (numbering between 250 and 300). The largest group were the houses of Austin Canons, followed by nunneries of the Benedictine rule. He already knew a good deal about the state of various establishments where the numbers of inmates were well below complement and he saw the virtue of transferring those with a real vocation for the monastic life to larger houses. Small units were, indeed, wasteful as regards the use of resources and he reckoned that the smaller the house the more lax was discipline. The scheme for dissolution that he proposed had the great merit of gradualness and, ever believing in moderation, he could regulate the rate of change according to circumstances.

It is easy to portray Cromwell, as R. B. Merriman has done, as the hammer of the monks: 'The sinister genius of the King's minister particularly fitted him for the task of destruction and his title of *malleus monachorum* is thoroughly well deserved,' he wrote. This argument overlooks the minister's plan to use monastic wealth in a constructive way, making proper employment of a national asset for the good of the commonwealth. Personally unsympathetic to the monastic ideal, he found the existence of so many religious houses an anachronism and the more he learned about them the less it seemed that they were fulfilling their founders' intentions. Too many men found comfortable sinecures in their enclosed communities, contributing very little to scholarship and even less to leavening the life of the neighbourhood. There were, of course, exceptions – holy men and women, consecrating their lives to worship, regularly saying the offices and using each day for spiritual exercises – yet he felt there must be a limit to the number of those under the strictest vows who, like the lilies of the field, toiled not and were supported by ancient benefactions and modern alms-giving. Monasteries pure and undefiled fitted uneasily into Cromwell's ideas of practical Christianity, and the puritanical streak in him made it hard for him to question the veracity of all the reports of loose-living that came to his ears. Yet essentially he saw the dissolution of the monasteries as a matter of financial policy, as relevant to the needs of Tudor England as later would be the establishment of a hearth tax, the introduction of death duties or policies of nationalization to statesmen of subsequent ages. The theme is developed in a later chapter (pages 224–5). His policy was harsh, but it was realistic.

On 21 January 1535 the King appointed him Vicar-general with the intention that he should hold a general visitation of all monastic and collegiate foundations. In carrying out these duties, which were a considerable burden on top of all his other offices, he chose as his henchmen two clerics who were doctors of civil law, Richard Layton and John London, and two laymen, the lawyers Thomas Legh and John ap Rice. Cromwell had selected them with care. Layton, like his master, had been in Wolsey's service, specializing in ecclesiastical law, and had later practised as an advocate in the Court of Arches, as had Thomas Legh; both were to become Masters in Chancery. The Welshman was a notary public who had been working in Cromwell's household for the past three years where he had worked on the cases of

Fisher and More. The fourth visitor, Dr London, was the odd one out. The Warden of New College, Oxford, he was much older than the others and much harsher. London's personal life later earned him – from a Cambridge man – the label 'that fat and filthy prebendary'. At the same time the Dominican, John Hilsey, and the Augustinian, George Brown, made joint visitations of the four orders of friars. The visitors were armed with a list of seventy-four questions for putting to the religious about every aspect of monastic life, with additional points for nunneries, and were soon sending their reports to the Vicar-general, who needed their *comperta*, diocese by diocese, as speedily as possible for presenting to Parliament.

Cromwell infected the visitors with his customary zeal for vigorous action and efficient paperwork. If monasteries realized their days were numbered, certain monks would not scruple to part with their plate and other treasures. Certainly Layton and his colleagues drove themselves hard in their itineraries, though one may doubt whether their enquiries were always searching; if they claimed to have covered on average ten houses a week there were obviously places for which they could not provide first-hand reports. Layton wrote that there was not a religious house in the north, but either he or Dr Legh 'have familiar acquaintance within ten or twelve miles of it. . . . There is matter sufficient to detect and open all coloured sanctity, all superstitious rules of pretensed religion and other abuses detestable of all sorts.' This was six months *before* they were to begin their northern circuit and shows how far they had prejudged the issue.

The contents as well as the tone of the *comperta* have long remained the subject of controversy, but comparing the details with those of earlier episcopal visitations it is likely that while some of the passages from Layton's pen are highly coloured, others are by no means distorted and not a few of his reports show the house in question to have been reasonably well conducted. Cromwell had perforce to 'edit' the returns to avoid giving the impression to Parliament that the larger houses (which were for the present to be spared) were no better than the smaller ones. He had very little time, since the *comperta* from the visitors in the north were not sent to London until the last day of February 1536, and the Bill was to be introduced in the Lords on 6 March. He needed a summary report that would justify the government's proposals. In the Upper House the lesser monasteries had no lobby and the few mitred abbots who were in their places, instead of seeing the measure as the beginning of a slippery slope, felt it politic not to oppose legislation that did not touch their own foundations.

The presentation of the visitors' findings caused a great stir. Years afterwards Hugh Latimer recalled the scene: 'When their enormities were first heard in the Parliament House, they were so great and abominable that there was nothing but "Down with them".' So much of it seemed to bear out the jibes of the pamphleteers, like Simon Fish, who asked, 'Who is she that will set her hands to work to get 3*d*. a day, when she can get at least 20*d*. a day to sleep an hour with a friar, monk or priest?' In a sermon at Paul's Cross Latimer called the abbots knaves, while Cranmer in more moderate language told his hearers that the King had no use for friars or monks unless they would preach the gospel. Cromwell had taken immense trouble with propaganda in and out of Parliament. Some members were undoubtedly hypnotized at the prospect of grants of monastic land (even before the Bill had passed into law the Secretary was being bombarded by requests for favours), yet others were hopeful that Cromwell could further his plans for new colleges. An anticlerical Commons had no intention of watering down the phrases of the preamble alluding to the 'manifest sin, vicious, carnal and abominable living' of monks and nuns, which had been made plain from the 'comperts of the late visitations, as by sundry credible informations'.

The Bill itself was but a mild, preliminary attack on monasticism, for only houses with incomes of less than £200 a year were to be granted to the King, and their inmates were given the option either of being transferred to larger foundations or of receiving pensions from the crown. Some 47 houses escaped suppression through royal licences, but this left a total of 244 foundations which were dissolved, with an average of not more than 6 inmates each. These possessions increased the King's annual revenue by about £32,000 a year, apart from the capital sum from plate, treasures, the lead from the roofs and the bellmetal, which was melted down. The Act came into force on 4 April 1536.

Cromwell has been vilified for undertaking the visitations with the aim of proving a damning case against the smaller monasteries. Whereas monastic visitations in the past had always been held with the intention of bringing maladministration to light, punishing those guilty of wrongdoing and inculcating in the tonsured higher standards of observance of their rule, it was felt that the great enquiry he directed was not an impartial series of proceedings but was from first to last prejudiced. As a practical man of affairs, however, Cromwell saw that the only way of achieving a dissolution without widespread opposition was to present a case based on the commissioners' findings, and if the facts produced were distorted or given wrong emphasis in the *comperta*, the Vicar-general cannot be made to bear the main blame. There *was* something of a smear campaign against the monasteries, yet it was grounded on up-to-date information of a most extensive kind. His method of presentation carried public opinion and for the most part the monks, nuns and friars concerned accepted the dissolution without question. Both King and minister regarded the Act of 1536 as a preliminary measure, which could be extended to the 235 larger houses where the chief wealth of the Church lay. It was said in the debate in the Lords that the small monasteries were 'the thorns, but the great abbots were the putrified old oaks and they must follow'.

To administer these properties and oversee the arrangements for making grants and leases a new Court of Augmentations was established, whose procedure was based on the administration of the Chamber of the Duchy of Lancaster. No existing financial department, as Cromwell well knew, was capable of the range of duties that would be involved, so he built afresh and brought into being an organization that was independent of the other, older departments. In the event the new Court proved equal to the immense task of overseeing the largest single accession of property that ever has come to the crown. It adopted a regional organization of receivers and auditors for administering the lands, buildings and rents so that there were fifteen groups for England and two for Wales. If the procedures of the Court of General Surveyors of crown lands had been followed, the possessions of a particular monastery, scattered over a number of counties, would have been kept as a unit, but Cromwell decided such an arrangement was inappropriate when dealing with such a mass of new properties. He chose as Chancellor of the Augmentations, Richard Riche, the Solicitor-general, who had been prominent at More's trial, and as Treasurer he selected Thomas Pope, a civil servant with the necessary legal and financial expertise; Pope had been attached to Cromwell before he became close to Audley. Each had great opportunities for feathering his nest and it is surprising that neither amassed more than a modest fortune. Cromwell would have been delighted had he known that in the fullness of time the first Chancellor would found a school (Felsted) and the first Treasurer a college (Trinity, Oxford).

For the rest of his life Cromwell took an intense interest in the Court of Augmentations, amounting at times to constant interference. In particular he was anxious to prevent widespread sales of ex-monastic property to courtiers, since it was much more provident for the crown to grant leases for terms of years. In the revolution in town and country that the dissolution brought, Cromwell took his own pickings (see page 226), but, considering his unexampled advantages, his acquisition of properties from religious houses of all kinds was modest compared with that of the Howards, the Russells, the Courtenays and the Paulets. He was not above reminding the Prior of St Faith's in September 1536 that his house had been saved from dissolution through his diligence and that accordingly some reward would be appropriate, nor did he scruple at the same time to ask the Prior of Coxford, whose foundation was threatened, to lend him £40 and then, 'I shall be ready to keep you out of danger.'

The dissolution was to leave its scars on the universities which would, in part, be healed over the next generation by new collegiate foundations; indeed the process had begun with Lady Margaret Beaufort's foundations in Cambridge. Cromwell took an intimate interest in university affairs and in 1535 had succeeded as high steward of Cambridge and then, on John Fisher's execution, became elected Chancellor. (His friend, Sir William Fitzwilliam, had become successor to Sir Thomas More as high steward of Oxford.) In October 1535 Henry appointed Cromwell as visitor of Cambridge University and he urged the masters and scholars to abandon the 'frivolous questions and obscure glosses' of the medieval schoolmen and devote themselves to studying the scriptures. Dr Legh wrote to him during his visitation at Cambridge that 'the students do say that you have done more good there for the profit of study and advancement of learning than ever any Chancellor did this heretofore'. There was a risk, Legh added, that some of the heads of colleges, 'for the most part addicted to sophisticated learning', might try to relax the strictness of his injunctions. Dr Layton wrote from Oxford about the welcome rout of the teaching of Duns Scotus, which had dominated the curriculum

for two centuries. 'We have set Dunce in Bocardo and have utterly
banished him from Oxford ... with all his blind glosses.' On the
visitors' return to New College they found the quadrangle 'full of the
leaves of Dunce, and the wind blowing them in every corner'. In both
universities civil lawyers supplanted canonists through Cromwell's
injunctions and the worst features of the system of disputations in the
study of divinity and philosophy were removed, while fresh attention
was paid to the teaching of Greek, Latin and Hebrew, very much in
the Erasmian tradition. To Cromwell's injunctions can be traced the
origin of the regius professorships, and through his special pleading both
Oxford and Cambridge were relieved of the payment of first fruits and
tenths. It was the dawn of a new era.

When Lincolnshire broke into revolt in October 1536 Cromwell
quickly identified the movement as a critical challenge to the New
Monarchy, whereas the King found it hard to take the movement
seriously until the more widespread rebellion gained ground rapidly in
the north country. Lincolnshire and Yorkshire were the two rural
areas to be most affected by the dissolution of the lesser monasteries.
Conservative in their attitudes, the inhabitants had tended to be
sympathetic to Queen Catherine and did not conceal their devotion to
the cause for which Fisher and More had died. Cromwell was for them
the source of all their ills. The people who rallied to the banner of the
Five Wounds of Christ proclaimed in the great tradition of English
rebels their utter loyalty to the sovereign whom they were bent on
rescuing from evil advisers. The Lincolnshire rebels demanded that
Cromwell, the evil genius of the King, should be banished; apart from
overturning the Church as it had been known, he was blamed for the
Statute of Uses, the Treasons Act and the fact that Princess Mary was
branded as illegitimate. Aske and his supporters in Doncaster aimed
less exclusively at the Secretary, yet he was still at the head of their list
of evil men: 'Lord Cromwell, the Lord Chancellor, and Sir Richard
Riche to have condign punishment as subverters of the good laws of
the realm and maintainers and inventors of heretics.'

With the first news of the rising, Cromwell's nephew Richard (the
son of Morgan Williams and Katherine Cromwell) was sent down to
Lincolnshire with some sixty workmen, who until then had been
employed on repairs to his uncle's house at Bermondsey, to swell the

army that Suffolk was gathering to oppose the rebels. Then came news that the cook of Dr Thomas Legh had been executed in Lincoln by the insurgents for being the employee of the hated visitor. Henry's answer to their petition, which was brought to them by Lancaster Herald, berated their presumption at thinking they had a right to choose his ministers: it was absurd that ignorant and inexperienced fellows of the 'most brute' shire in the whole kingdom should choose 'to find fault with your prince in the electing of his councillors and prelates'. With Yorkshire so firmly behind Robert Aske, Henry withdrew to Windsor Castle, which could stand a siege if need be, but Cromwell stayed on in London. Some historians have blamed him for timidity in not taking the field himself, but unlike Suffolk and other great landowners he had no tenantry of his own (though the workmen at Bermondsey were speedily pressed into service), his days of campaigning in Italy were a distant memory and it was essential for him to remain near the King to carry on the government.

After some hesitation Henry appointed Norfolk, co-victor of Flodden and probably the most experienced soldier that he had, to lead an army against the Yorkshiremen, though the Duke's discharge of his service earned him scant thanks. When he had been summoned from Kenninghall to Windsor for his instructions he had imagined he was being called upon to supplant Cromwell as chief minister; five months later, when peace had been restored, his hopes were again high, yet Cromwell again engineered his withdrawal to Norfolk under a cloud. Even the Duke's advice on the constitution of the Council in the North at York, to maintain public order in the disaffected counties, was rejected. Henry ended a bitter argument between Cromwell and Norfolk by telling the latter: 'We do accept in good part the declaration of your opinion for the Marches'; nevertheless he had chosen other means for remedying the situation. 'For surely we will not be bound of a necessity to be served there with lords, but we will be served with such men, what degree soever they be of, as we shall appoint to the same.' The snub hurt the Lord Treasurer to the quick. Bishop Tunstall of Durham became Lord President of the Council in the North and the old marcher wardenships were reassigned, to be held by able men. In York, as in Whitehall, the Lord Privy Seal had his way, for he had weathered the tempest that might have wrecked him and was as firmly as ever in the King's complete confidence. Norfolk had banked too much on the marriage of his daughter Mary to the Duke of Richmond, Henry's natural son, for while he lived the young man remained the most likely successor to the throne. But Richmond's sudden death showed the vanity of dynastic designs and Norfolk was in trouble for according his son-in-law a funeral that Henry thought inappropriate to his quasi-royal dignity.

Lord Darcy of Templehurst, a soldier of proven loyalty to the crown, had ineptly surrendered Pontefract to Aske and when Cromwell examined him as a captive at Audley's house the following April, before his execution, Darcy spoke his mind.

Cromwell, it is thou that art the very original and chief causer of all this rebellion and mischief and art likewise causer of the apprehension of us that be noble men, and dost daily earnestly travail to bring us to one end and to strike off our heads; and I trust that, or thou die, though thou wouldst procure all the noblemen's heads within the realm to be striken off, yet still there one head remain that shall strike off thy head.

It was a notable speech, one that only a condemned man would have dared to make, yet it summed up the hatred that Cromwell could arouse. Lord Darcy, like others from the particularist north where feudal ties were strong, saw him as an upstart who had subverted the constitution in church and state, and as a Londoner who thought there was nothing of England north of Uxbridge or west of Stockbridge. The fact that he had been ennobled as Baron Cromwell and appointed Lord Privy Seal made his offence the worse. Something of the views uttered by Darcy continued to be secretly harboured by other peers until the shrill outburst in the summer of 1540.

There is widespread evidence that the new ways were disliked in many places besides Lincolnshire and Yorkshire and that without Cromwell's vigilance a succession of little local difficulties could have escalated into a reactionary movement that would have disrupted government and split the fabric of society to a far greater extent than the Pilgrimage of Grace. Guiding a King and his subjects through a revolution was full of dangers, and at the purely doctrinal level the general disenchantment with change was made painfully clear by the ease with which the clock was put back in the acceptance of the Act of Six Articles in 1539. Some have detected in the methods used by

Cromwell to enforce the Reformation statutes sure signs of an organized spy system that, harnessed to the minister's wide powers, enabled him to impose a reign of terror. R. B. Merriman, for instance, credits Cromwell with the creation of a 'system of espionage, the most effective that England had ever seen', which amounted to an 'organised method of regulating treason'. Yet he goes on to say it was impossible to identify 'the government spies', thereby hinting that Cromwell master-minded operations so effectively that for security reasons anonymity was preserved and tell-tale evidence destroyed. Some contemporaries, especially in religious houses, certainly felt that the Lord Privy Seal had eyes and ears everywhere and that his visitors and their agents were interested in every scrap of gossip. When the Abbot of Peterborough found that a man wanted to enter Cromwell's service he asked him, 'What will ye do with him? Be one of his spies?' Perhaps on occasion a man *was* planted in a great household or a monastery where the head was suspected of hostility to the regime – as in the case of the Earl of Derby – yet the quasi-police reports in Cromwell's voluminous papers are almost certainly the offerings of public informers and not once is there cast-iron evidence that anyone was paid a reward. For all his efficiency in ordering the administrative machine, England was not a fully centralized state directed by a powerful bureaucracy, and there were no funds for establishing a network of spies and *agents provocateurs*.

The Treasons Act and the requirements of oath-taking were the lawyer's substitute for a system of surveillance, and propaganda in preambles to Acts of Parliament, from pulpits and in government-inspired tracts, was the politician's method of nipping disaffection in the bud and protecting society from its own disruptive instincts. The positive side of propaganda was Cromwell's recruitment of scholars and publicists to defend and explain royal policy, the negative side was censorship of the press. If the import of books printed in English on the continent and the products of presses at home were licensed, the printed word could be strictly controlled. Throughout his rule men and women were not secretly done away with, but faced trial at common law, conducted on established legal principles and procedures. Cromwell never knowingly operated outside the law. But the affair of the Nun of Kent, the London Carthusians and the tragedy of Fisher and More, the fall of Anne Boleyn, the wholesale executions of rebels that, under martial law, Norfolk ordered in the north, the end of the Abbots of Colchester, Glastonbury and Reading and the fate of the Poles and Courtenays have combined to give the epoch the character of a 'reign of terror'. Indeed, the fact that between 1532 and 1540 no fewer than 883 subjects were brought within the scope of the Treasons Act, of whom 308 were certainly found guilty and executed, while perhaps a further 21 similarly suffered, lends substance to such a view; as many as 63 individuals died for speaking against the royal supremacy in three years. The statistics cannot be argued away to suggest that Cromwell was in no way an innovator in ruthless methods, or to deny the savagery of the laws he had framed. They reflect, too, the ineffectiveness of his propaganda machine in persuading and cajoling men into accepting the new order. But merciless rigidity in enforcing the treason law had its effect for in the last thirty months of his rule there was a notable decline in cases of high treason and it seemed as if significant opposition to the Henrician regime had collapsed. Fear bred respect. This was the destructive side of Cromwell's work and it was those who saw him as the destroyer of dependence on Rome, of outworn orthodoxy and entrenched feudal interests who rejoiced when ultimately he fell foul of Henry's favour. The positive achievement of Cromwell, which detractors chose to ignore, does not excuse his methods, but it puts them in perspective.

Much has been written about Cromwell's Proclamations Act of 1539, once regarded as the instrument for giving the King's commands the force of a statute law, which erected an absolutism that itself could inaugurate and legitimize a 'reign of terror'. Royal edicts could, indeed, lead to despotism and possibly had done so in the past, yet this was precisely why Cromwell was uneasy about them. In any reign they were a most necessary means for the executive to issue instructions when Parliament was not in session and they depended for their force on the royal prerogative. Cromwell had sought the judges' opinions and was told that a proclamation issued under the King's authority was 'of as good effect as any law made by Parliament'. He was anxious to give the issue of proclamations a statutory basis and the tenor of the Act largely codified existing practice. In so doing, far from extending royal power it in fact limited it, by grounding proclamations on Parliamentary authority. Its main purpose however was to reform the machinery for their enforcement which, the preamble underlined, had been lax. A statutory tribunal was created with twenty-six judges, consisting in effect of Privy Councillors and chief office-holders, with a quorum of thirteen, provided not less than two of the great officers were present, before whom convictions for breaches of proclamations were to take place. It proved difficult to secure the passage of the Act, especially through the Lords, since it was feared that the powers of the crown could lead to a despotic imposition of taxes and invade the rights of property, so limitations on what the government had originally proposed were set. It is fair to see the Proclamations Act as the high point of Cromwell's policy of making the King in Parliament supreme as the legislature.

In his legislation Cromwell had created the concept of a truly nationalist monarch and the artists in Henry's service were able to sharpen the image in majestic portraits, statues and engravings that had an immediate impact on ordinary men compared with the arguments of political and philosophical treatises. Cromwell's seminal preamble to the Act in Restraint of Appeals was elaborated in a series of tracts, one of the most interesting being Lord Morley's, since he emphasized the novelty of Henry's kingship. He praised him as 'an ark of all princely goodness and honour' who was not only 'the noblest King that ever reigned over the English nation' – a phrase that speaks volumes – but was also '*pater patriae*, that is the father of our country; one by whose virtue, learning and noble courage, England is newborn, newly brought from thraldom to freedom'. This paternalism lay at the heart of much of Cromwell's social and economic legislation, which was undertaken as an end in itself and not as an instrument for ameliorating social conditions so that men would be the less ready to fall behind those opposing the regime. He was fervent in his wishes to prevent depopulation and to avert the decay of towns, to establish a poor law, to regulate the corn supply and the issue of coin. He was interested in the preservation of England's woodlands and in the drainage of fens (it was he who piloted through Parliament the 1532 Act for Commissioners of Sewers, setting up the organization for overseeing the nation's waterways and the related problems of drainage, that was to endure for three centuries). He was in close touch with Sir Richard Gresham, the chief city spokesman on currency questions, and, once convinced by him that a free exchange could encourage the export trade, he adopted this policy. Again, when Gresham proposed that London, like Antwerp, should have a *bourse*, Cromwell at once saw the significance of this for aiding London merchants and in 1539 he brought in a Bill to establish a Royal Exchange, though the measure failed in the Commons through insufficient time. It was Gresham's son, Sir Thomas, who succeeded in establishing the Royal Exchange in Queen Elizabeth's reign, but it was a chartered body and not, as Cromwell had in his time intended, an institution established by Parliamentary authority. Despite opposition in Parliament much was achieved, and if his plans were cut short by his fall from power the fruits of his comparatively short period of office contrast very markedly with the barren years of Wolsey's domestic policy. Cromwell preserved the ideal of a tripartite alliance of a godly prince, a learned clergy and an impartial magistracy that would order everything for the common good, so that Henry's subjects might indeed be 'brought from thraldom to freedom'.

In the fields of fresh legislation and in the administration of the law by the courts, Cromwell deserves a notable place as a legal reformer. His most obvious successes were the creation of the new Courts of Augmentations and Wards, General Surveyors and First Fruits and Tenths, for these not only improved the machinery of government, but provided swift and cheap justice for litigants. Allied to this was his work as Master of the Rolls to make the Court of Chancery more efficient, and there are sufficient indications to show that the conciliar Courts of Star Chamber and Requests developed their jurisdictions during his rule. He was able to achieve little with the church courts, for as vicegerent he had wanted to bring the whole of the Church of England under a single, unified jurisdiction, shorn of anomalies. There were, however, more urgent matters requiring his attention and Parliamentary time, as well as vested interests of ecclesiastical lawyers and the King's own attitude to contend with. Henry viewed his supremacy as comprising the powers of spiritual jurisdiction that had hitherto been exercised in England by the Pope and he would not have it abridged. Cromwell's plans for taking the bulk of testamentary cases away from the church courts were stillborn and, indeed, probate reform had to wait until 1857. His aim to reduce the privileges of sanctuary and of benefit of clergy, which had accounted for so much of the anticlerical outburst of the decade, met with similar opposition.

The law of real property had always dominated civil litigation and here Cromwell's Statute of Uses (1536) and Statute of Wills (1540), even in their modified forms, were to go far towards transforming the basic principles of land ownership. He even planned a comprehensive system of land registration, but it became watered down during the sessions with amendments made by the landed interest with the 1536 Statute of Enrolments, which required deeds recording bargains and sales of lands to be enrolled within six months either in one of the Central Courts at Westminster Hall or by the Clerk of the Peace in shire and borough. In his last months Cromwell was concerned to introduce further improvements to the land laws.

It has become abundantly clear through the detailed studies of Professor Elton that Cromwell's social and economic policies were the result of careful, systematic planning, in which the theories of men such as Thomas Starkey and Richard Morison were sifted, discussed, elaborated into feasible proposals and finally translated into practical measures to bring before Parliament. These covered a wide spectrum. Cromwell was regarded as the inheritor of the humanists' musings on the nature of the state, at whose hands general principles could be translated into statute law for the common weal. As Morison, a leading figure in his 'think tank', put it: 'I am a graft of your lordship's own setting; if I bring forth my fruits I know who may claim them.' The writers he encouraged were not merely using their pens to produce anticlerical tracts and pæans of praise for the royal supremacy, but were engaged in the practical business of Parliamentary draftsmanship.

Here it is worth examining the shape of Cromwell's poor law, which was so dear to his heart, for he regarded pauperism and vagrancy as scars on the face of the commonwealth, and his social conscience made it plain to him that relief and not punishment of the unemployed was the right course. Both Thomas Starkey and William Marshall had emphasized in their papers the need for a comprehensive poor law that included a system of public works for the able-bodied under the direction of 'overseers of poverty', and both men were well acquainted with the novel relief ordinance for Ypres in 1531. Cromwell's staff, led by Marshall, worked out detailed proposals for setting vagabonds to work on repairing roads and improving harbours, and the Bill that the Secretary brought before the Commons in March 1536 provided not only for the relief of the sick and aged poor by means of alms collected in each parish on a voluntary basis, but also for employing the able-bodied in a variety of ways for wages; these workers were also to receive medical attention and the undertaking was to be financed by direct taxation. The administrative machinery envisaged local overseers of the poor and a central 'Council to Avoid Vagabonds'. So anxious was Cromwell to have the measure on the statute book in its entirety that he persuaded the King to come down to the Commons to underline its importance. Henry told them he did not want them to pass the Bill simply because he said that they should, but 'to see if it be for a Common Weal to his subjects and have an eye thitherward'. He would return in four days to hear their views. Alas, the King's intervention failed. Clearly the financial provision, requiring levies akin to 'income tax', frightened the Commons, but Cromwell had ready a less controversial substitute Bill, which enshrined the principle of providing work for the able-bodied unemployed and the collection of a poor rate in each parish on a voluntary basis; a complementary clause discouraged indiscriminate alsmgiving from cutting at the roots of the new system. The Bill as passed was regarded as experimental and would lapse unless renewed before the end of the following Parliament. (In fact the measure expired in June 1536.) Cromwell never gave up hope of a comprehensive poor law and in his memoranda prepared for the 1539 session he wrote, 'a device in Parliament for the poor people of the realm'. The problem was not to be tackled until 1572, when legislation was passed in a much more limited direction on the lines he had demanded; even his name, 'overseers', was chosen for the local officials.

Measures such as these were the counterpart of the 'revolution in government' through which the Secretary transformed the medieval system, which had sufficed for the Cardinal, into an administrative machine suited to the modern national state. The details of his work have been subjected to close scrutiny in recent years, and research has emphasized that as Principal Secretary no area of government lay outside his purview. 'Household' government had depended on the King's personal actions, and Cromwell had to devise a system in which departments could function independently of the sovereign's own intervention. He left behind him a system of household officers as political heads of specialist departments, all of them Privy Councillors, who were the equivalent of cabinet ministers of a later age and who were fully supported by professional civil servants. Thus a thoroughly bureaucratic organization now replaced the personal control once exercised by kings. Antiquated methods of procedure were abandoned and paperwork supplanted orders by word of mouth. In the financial sphere specialist departments – such as the Court of Augmentations – were now created to administer the revenues of former monastic property, while the officials of the Chamber no longer accounted to the King himself, but became an integral part of the 'national' financial machinery. Gone for ever were the days when the King checked accounts himself and when an audit could be postponed indefinitely if he could not find the time for it. People now began to talk about 'the national revenue', instead of 'the King's finances', for in fact all the sovereign's private concerns had become 'nationalized'.

An essential part of these reforms was the remodelling of the royal household on the lines begun by Wolsey, but not resumed for another fourteen years. When he had first come to live at court Cromwell's eagle eye had found many things amiss and people began to talk about his plans for 'abridging the King's house'; yet his earliest schemes failed. Surmounting the crisis of the Pilgrimage of Grace had been costly and special measures for the defence of the country in the next two years added to Henry's liabilities, pointing to the need for economy at the centre, to be achieved in part by an onslaught on extravagance and waste, in part by administrative reforms that would curb numbers. At last, on Christmas Eve 1539, shortly before his marriage to Anne of Cleves, Henry inaugurated Cromwell's household ordinances, and the new system survived with little change until the days of the Prince Consort.

Henry was prepared to endorse reforms that would make for economies in the 'below stairs' departments, provided his own Chamber was given an establishment more appropriate to his idea of majesty and provided he could revive his personal bodyguard, the company of 'Spears' or Gentlemen Pensioners, founded on his accession but subsequently disbanded. He had been pressing for a revival of the Spears since early in 1537 and had thought in terms of one hundred men, though Cromwell managed to beat him down to fifty. The King had been envious of the bodyguard of Francis I, the famed *Becs de Corbin*, and wanted a similar corps of well-born young men with splendid physiques, like Wolsey's tall chaplains, who would be an ornament to his court with a full ceremonial role, and at the same time would form an élite of highly trained soldiers in time of war. In his orders re-establishing the Gentlemen Pensioners at Christmas 1539, the King declared that there were 'many young gentlemen of noble blood which have no exercise in the feats of arms in handling and reining the spear and other feats of war on horseback', but though the spear was to be their weapon in war, at court they would serve on foot with pole-axes to distinguish them from the ninety strong Yeomen of the Guard who were armed with halberds. Their duties were defined thoroughly and there were fines for absence and irresponsibility. Sir Anthony Browne, a gentleman of the Privy Chamber, was appointed the first Captain. There was a rush of applicants for the new posts and the first list of appointments is a roll-call of the families who would leave their mark on Tudor history – Carew and Zouche, Ashley and Wingfield, Herbert, Ferrers and the rest.

Since the Eltham Ordinance there had been fresh orders for the gentlemen of the Privy Chamber, who from 1533 had been required to attend in two groups of seven for a six weeks' tour of duty, yet even this arrangement had proved insufficient. Now Cromwell considered it as a whole and assigned the Privy Chamber sixteen gentlemen, two gentlemen ushers, four gentlemen ushers daily waiters, three grooms and two barbers. The outer chamber was now to be staffed by three cup bearers, three carvers and three sewers, four squires for the body – a reduction – and two surveyors. A yeoman and a groom sufficed for the King's robes and three officers and two pages for the beds, while there was now a single groom porter. As a reserve of servants, there were to be eight gentlemen ushers as quarter waiters, four sewers, four pages and fourteen grooms, all without livery and basic allowances at court. Taken together this represents a considerable increase in the establishment since 1526 and shows how successful Henry was in opposing Cromwell's plan of economies.

Twelve peers and senior officials were entitled, when at court, to feed at the King's board, from the Lord Chancellor downwards, but of those named in Cromwell's list only the Vice-chamberlain, Sir Anthony Wingfield, and the Captain and Lieutenant of the Gentlemen Pensioners were invariably present. The officials of other departments 'on the King's side' – Counting House, Chapel and Jewel House – and the King's doctors and minstrels were given clear instructions about where to take their meals, while similar arrangements were made for the Queen's Chamber and its sub-departments. Although Cromwell had acquiesced in the King's demands for staffing the Chamber he did succeed in controlling its expenditure by making it, and every other department of the household above and below stairs, subject to the counting house, or Board of Green Cloth, over which a new official, the Lord Great Master of the Household, was to preside. Until now the traditional separation of the King's and Queen's Chambers both from each other and, more significantly, from the household below stairs, had been maintained, hallowed by the complementary if not outright rival rule of the Lord Chamberlain and the Lord Steward. What was needed was a powerful administrative body that could regulate the entire court and Cromwell placed his faith in the Board of Green Cloth under the Great Master, on the lines of the '*grand maître*' of the French court. The time was propitious for a change, since George, Earl of Shrewsbury, Lord Steward since the opening of the reign, had just died and his post had been left unfilled, although Suffolk had been granted the reversion of it. Suffolk was a man of the right seniority and weight to impose his will on the court, and himself introduced the Bill in Parliament establishing the office of Lord Great Master and confirming his appointment to it.

At the new-style Board of Green Cloth with the Lord Great Master sat the treasurer and controller of the household, and at least one of these had to attend a meeting in the counting house at eight o'clock every morning with the cofferer, the two clerks of the Green Cloth and the two clerks controller. This arrangement ensured a thorough supervision of the domestic expenditure of every department of the palace, because all purchases had to be made through the cofferer who scrutinized the purveyors' accounts. The complicated financial checks and counterchecks now introduced were foolproof, collusion and fraudulent accounting became impossible, and if the paperwork increased, at least accounts were regularly balanced and audited, budgets estimated and a formidable campaign in business efficiency mounted. The Great Master and treasurer, with other commitments as Privy Councillors, could not expect to give much time to the affairs of the counting house, but the controller and particularly the cofferer were very much concerned with the intimate details of running a vast establishment. The clerks were required to go the rounds at mealtimes seeing that no interlopers were eating at the King's expense in the various household departments and that no meals were being sent to 'private chambers'. They checked all stores in every department and they alone authorized the payment of wages and allowances, even those of the Chamber officials.

To stop petty pilfering the perks of every office were laid down precisely and the knight harbinger was given undisputed authority to assign billets, which had always been a source of trouble, when the court was on progress. Most important of all, in a war on waste everyone's duties and the standard of their performance were set down, often within a timetable, to ensure that tasks were no longer skimped or unnecessarily prolonged and to achieve the maximum degree of supervision. Two clerks of the Green Cloth had to inspect the food in the larder provided for the King's table and witness its delivery to the master cook. Extra locks, which could be opened only by an official from the counting house, were put on the cellar and buttery doors. No household officer could leave court without the express permission of the Lord Great Master, treasurer or controller. Altogether the standard of service in the palace was elevated to a new level, and if the emphasis in Cromwell's Ordinance was on fines and discipline it is worth remembering how highly he valued professional service, whether it was in the spicery or the cellar. He envisaged every department being able to provide a satisfactory career structure; indeed, he wanted the head of each department not to take on any servant who seemed unlikely to qualify for promotion. The bureaucratic system swiftly took root. Any departure from the duties, numbers of staff or allowances provided in the Ordinance required specific authority. With the royal household, as with so much else, Cromwell's comprehensive reconstruction was built to endure.

9
The Road to Wittenberg

It was not until after the dissolution in 1536 of the Reformation Parliament, which had snapped the ties with Rome and erected a national Church, that detailed thought began to be given to the specific doctrines that the Church should profess, to the shape of its liturgy and to its distinctive ceremonies. In this debate theologians turned quite naturally to look at the experiments and experiences of the continental reformers, now in their twentieth year, and to see how far England should tread along the road to Wittenberg. Cromwell's appointment as vicegerent in spiritual affairs was a logical outcome of the Submission of the Clergy and underlined the Erastian nature of the Church. Henry, as pope in his own dominion, made Cromwell his legate extra-ordinary, entrusting him, a layman, with wide powers that overrode the authority wielded by the two archbishops. Nowhere was the vicegerent's power more apparent than in Convocation.

The Commons' 'Supplication Against the Ordinaries', in the drafting of which Cromwell had played so significant a part, had attacked the constitutional anomaly of convocations of the clergy, which 'do make daily divers laws and ordinances without your Royal assent or knowledge, or the assent or consent of any of your lay subjects'. Since Warham's submission the wings of Convocation had been clipped, but the reality of the changed balance of power was blurred until June 1536. Cromwell was himself fully occupied by Parliamentary business when the new session of Convocation opened, but he sent his proctor, Dr William Petre, who entered the upper house and claimed, by virtue of his master's powers derived from the crown, to preside in the assembly to the amazement of the bishops.

Later in the month Cromwell himself appeared and took his seat on a throne placed high above Archbishop Cranmer. He was to have no successor as vicegerent, but by the time of his fall the power of Convocation had been seriously weakened – effectively it had become a body for taxing the clergy and had ceased to play a dominant role in the shaping of ecclesiastical policy.

The first task of the new-style assembly, after formal recognition of Henry's marriage to Jane Seymour and the alterations to the line of succession, was to consider doctrinal questions. The lower house had already been ranging widely over 'new heresies' and it was important to settle the confusion in people's minds by issuing an official statement, since many clergy, no less than laity, were bewildered by the plethora of conflicting tenets. As a result a committee of the bishops, sitting most probably with the King or Cromwell, produced 'the Articles of Faith to establish Christian Quietness', more generally known as the Ten Articles, which were presented to Convocation on 11 July 1536 by Bishop Foxe of Hereford and received the royal imprimatur. These articles were the child of compromise, for the episcopate was fairly evenly divided between reformists such as Cranmer, and those who believed with Stokesley of London that orthodoxy must remain above suspicion of dalliance with Lutheranism. Five of the articles – those concerning the creed, the sacrament of the altar, baptism, penance and justification – could have been taken without much alteration from the Augsburg Confession, but the other five dealt with images, the saints, their invocation, ceremonies and purgatory in the traditional manner, as if Martin Luther had never been. This manifesto, designed to please everyone, in the event satisfied very few and if in some measure it healed the divisions it also succeeded in confusing still further all but those who could accept a truly middle way. Could it be otherwise with a basically eirenic document that such different men as Reginald Pole and Philip Melanchthon found satisfactory?

Within a few days of the acceptance of the Ten Articles Cromwell was charged by the King to forbid all preaching for three months, except by cathedral clergy or others in the presence of a bishop. This was to prevent ill-informed comment on the Articles throughout the realm before the text was available in print. Before those three months were up the vicegerent had himself issued a series of injunctions 'under the King's spiritual seal' without reference to Convocation. Here

Cromwell's concern for education at all levels showed through his religious zeal and the strict requirement of politics. The clergy were to preach four times a year, dwelling in their sermons on how the Bishop of Rome's usurped power, which had no grounding in God's law, was most justly abolished, 'and that the King's power is within his dominion the highest potentate or power under God', to whom all subjects owe obedience. Parents and schoolmasters, as well as the clergy, were to teach children 'even from their infancy their Pater Noster, the articles of our faith and the ten commandments in their mother tongue'. All clergy were to declare and explain the Ten Articles to their parishioners so that they knew which of them must be believed for salvation and which concerned ceremonies and the ordering of the Church. Priests had had a bad reputation long before the Supplication of the Ordinaries was framed, so Cromwell required them to look to their moral behaviour, avoiding taverns and alehouses and ceasing to play cards. They were to spend their leisure in reading holy scripture. Those of them with benefices worth £20 a year were to give to charity a fortieth of their income; clerics with a stipend of £100 were to provide funds for sending an exhibitioner to Oxford or Cambridge, or to a grammar school, while the wealthier were to found scholarships according to the scale of their means. Cromwell's own gloss on the article about images was that these were to be exhibited neither from superstition nor for lucre and priests were not to allure their flocks into going on pilgrimages to the shrines of saints, but rather to encourage them to promote the work of God in their neighbourhood and to undertake charitable works. He was passionately concerned that the Church should be both learned and caring.

The outbreak of the Pilgrimage of Grace a month after these injunctions had been issued and the attitude of mind that the examination of the rebels revealed meant that a much more sustained effort would have to be made to prepare and present a doctrinal statement. In February 1537 to produce an exposition of the Ten Articles Henry appointed a commission of all the bishops and twenty-five other clerics, including canonists and theologians, to sit under Cromwell's chairmanship. These commissioners met either at the House of Lords or at Lambeth Palace and at their first meeting Cromwell told them that the supreme head appreciated as well as anyone the nature of the controversies rending his Church and urged them to reach agreement on a tract that would expound the faith to everyone. Such was the origin of *The Bishops' Book*. Stokesley, Bishop of London, at once pointed out that four of the seven sacraments had been omitted from the Ten Articles – those of confirmation, holy orders, holy matrimony and extreme unction – but Bishop Foxe of Hereford, the vice-chairman of the commission, backed by Latimer, refused to be drawn. It was left to Cranmer to remind his fellows that the word 'sacrament' had been used indiscriminately by the early fathers of the Church and to appeal to them all to refrain from 'babbling and brawling about bare words'. Potential harmony was threatened by a tactical error of Cromwell's. On his way to the meeting he had chanced to come across the Scottish theologian, Alexander Alesius, who had been with the German Protestants and more recently had been forced by his outspoken views to leave a precarious lectureship at Cambridge. Regarding Alesius as an 'expert witness', Cromwell brought him along to the meeting, where it proved difficult to silence him, for he harangued them all, argued bitterly with Stokesley and even upset Foxe, who said they must keep their debate to 'the rule and judgement of Scripture', as the King had commanded them. As the morning wore on Cromwell had no option but to adjourn the assembly and refused to allow Alesius to come again, though he tactfully suggested he might write out the speech he said he had been unable to make.

It was Foxe who contributed the most thoughtful comment that day, which Cromwell, as the only layman present, probably felt came near to his own point of view: 'The lay people do now know the Holy Scripture better than many of us, and the Germans have made the text of the Bible so plain and easy by the Hebrew and Greek tongue, that now many things be better understood without any glosses at all, than by the commentaries of the doctors.' The word of God was paramount and what St Ambrose and St Thomas had to say about it was of no more than academic interest for the Lutherans now that they had Luther's excellent German text. Already, indeed, Convocation was taking in hand the problem of an authorized English version of the scriptures, but Cromwell was himself in close touch with Coverdale in the Low Countries, as we shall see. Confident of the probity of his vice-chairman and pressed hard by government affairs, Cromwell did not sit with the commissioners again.

Foxe was effectively the general editor of *The Bishops' Book* (or, to give it its correct title, *The Institution of a Christian Man*) and when through great diligence it was almost complete, in July 1537 he asked Cromwell whether it was to be published by royal authority and hoped that Sir Thomas Wriothesley might contribute a preface. Cromwell indicated that it should be Foxe himself who should undertake this task, though he probably had a hand in penning the very fulsome dedication, which stated that without the King's licence the compilers of the book had no *locus* in expounding doctrine, and went on to submit their work to Henry's 'most excellent wisdom and exact judgement . . . to be overseen and corrected if Your Grace shall find any word or sentence in it meet to be changed, qualified or further expounded'. Annexed to the preface was a statement that the King had had insufficient time to study the entire book, since he was 'otherwise occupied', but had 'taken as it were a taste' of it. The task of detailed criticism was shelved partly from worry about Queen Jane's forth-coming confinement and partly from inherent laziness, though at any rate he could claim that the treatise was not being issued under his personal imprimatur. When by the end of 1537 Henry found time and inclination to read the work carefully, he discovered much that he misliked and scribbled a host of comments and proposed changes, which worried Cranmer, not just because of their pedantry and occasional inconsistency, but rather because the King expressed stern criticism of the doctrine of justification by faith alone, which he discovered to be at the heart of the book. In his view, if this was an exposition of the Ten Articles, then the sooner those Articles were revised the better. Nothing made him more determined to check the drift towards Protestantism than his belated reading of the tenets of his own bishops; it hardened his innate conservatism and made him anxious to prevent Cranmer, Cromwell and the reformists from leading him any further along the road to Wittenberg.

The King proposed no fewer than 246 alterations to the text of *The Bishops' Book*, which he forwarded to Cranmer in January 1538. The Archbishop objected to eighty-two of these changes (many of them on stylistic grounds) and after much cogitation grudgingly assented to four other points, but the bulk of the King's alterations, as he told Cromwell, he accepted. For the rest, he excused himself to the vicegerent, 'I trust the King's Highness will pardon my pre-sumption that I have been so scrupulous and, as it were, a provoker of quarrels to His Grace's book. . . . I would have nothing therein that Momus could reprehend; and yet I refer all mine annotations again to His Grace's most exact judgement.' It seems that the King was not prepared to go over the ground again and accepted Cranmer's amended version provided that the work was issued as the *Bishops'* (not the King's) Book. Certainly in 1538 the Archbishop was not prepared to press forward as quickly as Latimer, and even Cromwell himself, wanted, though the latter appreciated that he must take his cue from the King. Although the four sacraments omitted from the Ten Articles were reinserted in *The Bishops' Book*, there was no reference to transubstantiation.

The work was at last ready to be published in May 1538, but was too late, alas, to appear in Edward Foxe's lifetime. Bishop Latimer wrote to Cromwell when the commissioners' labours were at an end, happy that

we shall not need to have any more such doings, for verily, for my part, I had liefer be a poor parson of poor Kington again than to continue thus Bishop of Worcester. . . . forsooth, it is a troublous thing to agree upon a doctrine in things of such controversy, with judgements of such diversity, every man (I trust) meaning well, and yet not all meaning one way.

Nor with publication achieved did the controversy abate, as Cromwell soon discovered to his dismay.

The fact that Henry had not himself issued *The Institution of a Christian Man* as *his* book encouraged both left and right to think that there would be opportunity, as well as room, for further changes. The reformist clergy, who looked to Hugh Latimer and to Shaxton, Bishop of Salisbury, took comfort in the waning of the monasteries and the pride of place that the new English bible had so quickly come to occupy in church life, which certainly stressed the scriptural basis of a truly reformed Church. Both these developments had been Cromwell's and so they placed their faith in his being able to pilot further measures through Council, Parliament and Convocation to ensure that Henry was really leading his people out of darkness into the marvellous light of Christ. They argued that the King could not expect to 'throw a man headlong from the top of a high tower and bid him stay where he was, half-way down'. By now, however, Cromwell had realized that the doctrine of the national Church must be a compromise.

A further complication was the eagerness of the continental reformers to instruct their English brethren. They were not prepared to regard Henry's reformation as a domestic affair and a series of embassies from Lutheran princes strove in London to correct the errors in Henrician doctrine wherever it differed from their own Augsburg Confession. Though an understanding proved out of the question and made the political alliance that Cromwell hoped for unattainable, these prolonged discussions alarmed Bishops Stokesley, Sampson and Clerk in particular, who sensed that orthodoxy as they knew it was in most serious danger. And from what he heard in Paris Stephen Gardiner was convinced that Cromwell's dallying with the German divines was betraying the Church.

The publication of the bible in English, in a fully authorized text, had long been an enterprise dear to Cromwell's heart as a 'man of the Gospel', and it would be a distortion of the facts to attribute this scriptural zeal to political motives. It had been a hard fight against episcopal obscurantism and royal opposition. Henry had at first regarded translations into the vernacular as a most dangerous innovation – the Lollards had claimed to need no priesthood because of their unauthorized access to 'the sweetness of God's Holy Word', so an English bible had an heretical pedigree to live down. The experience of Luther's German bible in spreading the heresy Henry had himself so forcibly denounced in his book reinforced his traditional fears, while William Tyndale's sojourn in Wittenberg made his scholarship suspect. By the time Cromwell had entered his service the King was regarding translations of the scriptures as more unnecessary than dangerous – those with neither Latin nor Greek could learn all they needed for salvation from sermons. To make available a volume in English for the general public would merely encourage the disputations and heresies that were rampant in the Netherlands. And how did a translation propose to present the crucial, mystical concept that was decently shrouded in a dead language – *Hoc est corpus meum?*

Eight years after Tunstall had made a holocaust in St Paul's churchyard of copies of Tyndale's English New Testament, printed in Worms and smuggled into England, Cromwell succeeded in persuading Convocation to petition the King for the suppression of treasonable books in the vulgar tongue and for the translation of the whole bible into English. At the instance of his friend Stephen Vaughan, Cromwell had previously nearly burnt his fingers over the possibility of Tyndale being granted a safe conduct for returning to England in 1531. The proposed bargain was that if Henry would allow his subjects access to the scriptures in English, Tyndale would pen no more polemics but leave the Netherlands to submit himself to the King's judgement. Henry had exploded at such impertinence and Cromwell had of necessity to adopt the King's opinion of the reformer as a man 'replete with venomous envy, rancour and malice', and warned Vaughan to dissociate himself from so dangerous a character. But when, through Henry Phillips's treachery, Tyndale was betrayed to the imperial authorities in May 1535 and arrested on the doorstep of the Merchant Adventurers' House in Antwerp, Cromwell was asked to intervene to save him. He asked his godson, Thomas Theobald, then in the Low Countries, to report on the situation and wrote to both the Archbishop of Palermo and the Margrave of Bergen-op-Zoom in Tyndale's favour. Alas, the exigencies of foreign relations made a more forceful plea impossible. After eighteen months' imprisonment the pioneer translator was condemned by the doctors of Louvain University and was burnt as an heretic in Brussels. His final words, it was said, were: 'Lord, open the King of England's eyes.' And in fact by then the rather similar translation by his old acquaintance Miles Coverdale was freely circulating in England.

In his days as an Augustinian friar, Coverdale had been befriended by Cromwell. A letter survives (May 1527) in which he alludes to 'the godly communications which your mastership had with me . . . in Master More's house'. Even at that date Cromwell was sympathizing with those who wanted an entire bible in the vernacular, not just the New Testament. Coverdale went on in his letter to tell Cromwell: 'Now I begin to taste of Holy Scripture, now, honour be to God, I can set to the most sweet smell of holy letters with the goodly savour of holy and ancient doctors', providing he had the books that he hoped Cromwell, as his patron, would purchase. Afterwards their ways parted, for Cromwell had no mind to support a renegade friar who lived in Antwerp and was reckoned by the company he kept to be an heretic. From his contacts with the English mercantile community in Antwerp, however, Cromwell knew that Coverdale had been busy at his translation in the intervening years.

The petition of Convocation in 1534 made all the difference to what until then could have been a risky affair and the inference is that Cromwell now encouraged the translator to have his great work printed abroad, probably in Antwerp, the following year. The text states that his translation was completed on 4 October 1535, though no name of the printer is given, simply because any work printed abroad would have fallen foul of the law. Early in 1536, through Cromwell's initiative, a Southwark printer made a new title page, embodying a woodcut designed by Hans Holbein in which King Henry holds the sword of justice in his right hand, while his left gives the book to his kneeling bishops. The other pictures on the page place the supreme head of the Church unmistakably in the line of Old Testament prophets and New Testament apostles. The title runs: 'The Bible, that is the Holy Scripture of the Old and New Testament, faithfully translated out of Dutch and Latin into English.' Here, too, was a dedication to the King: 'He only under God is the Chief Head of all the congregation of the Church', and the address to the reader emphasizes the translator's fervent loyalty no less than his utter orthodoxy, even though so much of his version of the New Testament was firmly based on Tyndale's 'suspect' work. The preliminary pages printed in Southwark were added to the gatherings printed off in Antwerp, or it may be Zurich. Here at last was an English Bible complete – from Genesis to the Book of Revelations – issued with the royal arms and the King in majesty on the title page. As an authoritative text it would soon be superseded, but it was the first available and the one that many churches acquired in obedience to Cromwell's injunction of April 1536 requiring a translation to be placed in every church by 1 August of the year following. Coverdale's bible sold out three folio editions and one quarto in a year. Cranmer wrote a complimentary letter to Cromwell, delighted that he had survived all the 'slanders, lies and reproaches' that the venture had earned him from the conservative bishops.

Coverdale could now safely return to England where he actively supervised the issue of his New Testament bound up with a Latin vulgate and was taken on by Richard Grafton, the London grocer, who had become a speculative printer. Grafton also brought out Matthew's Bible in 1537 – a composite work, part Coverdale, part Tyndale and the rest by Thomas Matthew, *alias* John Rogers, chaplain to the Merchants Adventurers in Antwerp. Cranmer told the vicegerent he liked this 'better than any translation' to date.

Though both Coverdale's and Matthew's Bibles were 'set forth' by the King's licence, neither was an authorized version in the recognized sense of the term. In commending Matthew's text Cranmer had said it should be sold and read by everyone until 'we the bishops shall set forth a better translation', which, he admitted to Cromwell, 'will not be till a day after Domesday'. In 1534 the Archbishop had parcelled out the books of the New Testament to his episcopal colleagues so that each might do his stint (we know that Gardiner completed both the Gospels of St Luke and St John by the middle of 1535 and that Stokesley made good progress with the Acts), but a corporate effort of this kind was bound to be uneven and, in the event, was abandoned in favour of a revision of Matthew's edition under Coverdale's direction, making use of Sebastian Munster's work on the Old Testament which had been based on a fresh approach to the original Hebrew. The 'Great Bible' that emerged earned its name, however, from the size of type used in the printing, for it was Cromwell's intention that it should be available for everyone who could read, in large print and handsomely bound in a single volume. To produce such a volume was quite beyond the resources of the English printing trade, so Cromwell instructed Stephen Gardiner early in 1538 to obtain a licence from Francis 1 to have the work printed in France under the supervision of Richard Grafton and Miles Coverdale. Unfortunately the licence did not afford sufficient protection from the Inquisitor-general, who ordered the entire impression to be impounded. By a stroke of fortune Grafton and Coverdale succeeded in rescuing not only most of the sheets that had been printed but also the type, and they made their way back to England with these and with the presses, accompanied by a few of the French printers. The work was finished in London in April 1539. The title page shows King Henry giving the word of God to Cromwell and Cranmer, who in turn distribute it to the clergy and laity. The next edition (1540) contained the Archbishop's preface, vetted by Cromwell, which made it abundantly clear that: 'This is the Bible appointed to the use of the churches.' It has ever since been called 'Cranmer's Bible'. When in the next reign Cranmer came to draw up the first English prayer book he used as a matter of course the text of the 1539 bible for the version of the

Psalms, and that text has remained with the Anglican Church for morning and evening prayer throughout the changes of 1552, 1559, 1662 and 1928.

Grafton and his associate Edward Whitechurch were the printers, yet it was Cromwell who provided much of the financial backing, for he invested £800 in the venture and looked for a modest return. When Grafton and Berthelet, the King's printer, asked that they might jointly be granted what amounted to copyright in the volume, Cromwell the same day shrewdly obtained a patent granting to himself the monopoly of all printings for a term of five years; Grafton at least knew that by associating himself with the vicegerent he was effectively becoming his agent and would be certain of a good commission. Yet Cromwell insisted on keeping the price down to ten shillings a volume, whereas Cranmer had thought thirteen shillings and four pence not unreasonable, and he insisted that good quality paper was used. In preparation for the issue of the Great Bible, when the arrangements for printing in Paris seemed to be running smoothly, Cromwell had on 5 September 1538 issued his injunctions ordering the bible – 'one book of the whole Bible of the largest volume in English' – to be placed in a convenient place in all churches by the following All Saints' day. The cost was to be shared equally between the incumbent and his parishioners. The clergy were to encourage everyone to read the book, which was 'the very lively word of God that every Christian person is bound to embrace, believe and follow', but they were to avoid disputations on the meaning of passages and, if in doubt, should refer obscure points to 'men of higher judgement in Scripture'. This was a revolution. It was hoped the volume and the manner of its presentation would 'encourage many slow readers and also stay the rash judgement of them that read'.

After Cromwell's fall his enemies played on Henry's fears that the Great Bible was very far from being an impartial translation and should be regarded as a specifically 'Protestant' text. Cranmer was now forced to ask the bishops in Convocation whether his bible could be retained 'without scandal' and as the majority ruled it could not, the text was sent to committees for careful examination. Before these had reported, Bishop Gardiner had persuaded the King to assent to legislation for restricting the study of the scriptures in English, and this Act of 1543, euphemistically called 'An Act for the Advancement of

True Religion', was warmly applauded by Henry, who himself told Parliament that the 'most precious jewel, the Word of God, is disputed, rhymed, sung and jangled in every alehouse and tavern' (it was, of course, in such places that bible readings to the illiterate generally took place). This counter-revolution did not, however, last for long. That at a later age the English people were to be called 'the people of the Book' was in large measure due to Thomas Cromwell's sustained efforts at promoting a bible in the vernacular and ensuring its availability in all churches.

The fate of the greater monasteries was sealed by the Pilgrimage of Grace. The property of the 304 smaller houses with incomes of under £200 a year had certainly whetted Henry's appetite for the untold wealth of the larger foundations. The more worldly abbots and priors knew very well that their houses were under sentence, so from 1537 there was a growing series of voluntary surrenders to the crown to achieve the best possible terms with Cromwell's visitors. Abbot Segar of Hailes, for instance, thanked God that he was living 'in an age of enlightenment', as he told Cromwell, for he did not himself believe in his abbey's relic of the precious blood of Christ and was quite content to seal a deed of surrender and retire with a sizable pension to the Yorkshire countryside. Ten abbots were to be consecrated bishops and most of the new suffragan bishops had come from monasteries or friaries; one, Robert Holgate, Prior of Sempringham, who was consecrated Bishop of Llandaff in 1537, was destined to become Henry's Archbishop of York. In the older cathedrals of monastic foundation practically all the reigning priors became the first deans, while their brothers were transferred into residentiary canons.

By and large the spoliation of monastic property provoked little opposition. Certain heads of houses with scruples about giving in were induced to retire, like Catton of St Alban's, and leave the act of surrender to an amenable successor. Cromwell had written in March 1538 to one abbot to assure him, on the King's instruction, 'that unless there had been overtures made by the said houses that have resigned, his Grace would never have received' their surrenders. The King, he said, did not intend to suppress any house 'except they shall either desire of themselves with one whole consent . . . or else misuse themselves contrary to their allegiance, in which case they shall deserve the loss of much more than their houses and possessions, that is the loss of their lives'. This was a very real threat, for few mitred abbots who had followed the events of the last eight years would be confident of defining exactly what 'misusing themselves contrary to their allegiance' meant. Broad hints such as this and the cajoling of Dr Legh and Dr Layton decided waverers in favour of reaching a sensible agreement.

Cromwell himself was granted not a few annuities, issued under conventual seals, which remained valid after surrenders had taken place, but those who tried to bribe him so that their houses might be spared made him unduly suspicious. In order to establish the King's title to these properties beyond all doubt, when Parliament met in May 1539 Lord Chancellor Audley brought in an Act to endorse the surrenders that had already taken place. He harped on the voluntary basis of the surrenders, which had been made 'under no manner of constraint, coercion or compulsion'. As a warning to those who had not yet made their overtures to the royal officers, Audley went on to say that 'other religious houses may happen in the future to be suppressed, dissolved, relinquished, forfeited, given up or otherwise come into the King's hands. Let him enjoy them!'

During 1538 the shrines of the English saints, where pilgrims had worshipped down the centuries, were destroyed. In the tomb of St Cuthbert in Durham Dr Legh found one particular jewel that was worth a king's ransom; in Canterbury the shrine of St Thomas à Becket produced twenty-six wagonloads of riches that went under guard to the Mint in the Tower of London, while the bones of the saint who had opposed Henry Plantagenet were burnt and scattered. From St Swithin's in Winchester, where the prior and all the brethren were 'very conformable', Wriothesley brought two thousand marks' worth of silver, the great cross called 'Jerusalem' and another enamelled.

Much of this wealth was used at once to finance the building of Nonsuch in Surrey, which Henry intended as a palace that would amaze the world and put Francis 1's Chambord Château in the shade. At last he had the money and the scope to build on a site unfettered by existing buildings (as had been the case with his improvements at Whitehall and Hampton Court), and so there arose a remarkable monument to royal ostentation. Cromwell was alarmed at the prodigal way in which James Needham, the surveyor-general of the works, was drawing up his plans, making use of foreign artists and sculptors to provide in a Surrey park the King's triumph of fantasy. 'What a great charge it is to the King,' wrote the minister, 'to continue his building in so many places at once. How proud and false the workmen be; and if the King would spare for one year, how profitable it would be to him.'

Cromwell had directed the dissolution with a zeal bordering on fanaticism. He had had no experience of the monastic ideal even at second hand, unlike the courtiers who had nieces at Wilton or Shaftesbury nunneries or younger brothers who had entered a religious order. A man of action, he found it impossible to appreciate the ordered life of an enclosed community, with the emphasis on the divine offices and meditation. There had been no great religious house near at hand during his childhood in Putney, teaching boys and dispensing charity, and by missing university life he had never mixed as a young man with saintly men of scholarship, whose lectures and sermons could be spellbinding. His experiences in Italy and the Netherlands in their different ways hardened him against monks, friars and nuns. Too readily he saw the worst specimens from the cowled and tonsured and later on he found it hard to believe that the *comperta* of the visitations could be exaggerated. For him the monasteries were at best comfortable places for those seeking an easy life and at worst they were sinks of iniquity. His reading of Bede's *History* and some of the monastic chronicles did nothing to make him change his mind. He saw the monks as papalists to a man, and if the clergy as a whole were a caste apart the religious orders constituted an extremist group, enjoying immunities and forming a body without responsibilities within the temporal Church. He found monasticism irrelevant to the age and an anomaly in a national church. His passion for reform and 'the renewal of the commonwealth' convinced him of the need for the secularization of monastic property, for far too large a proportion of the wealth of England was locked away unproductively. Their possessions were a national asset, which should be nationalized, and the monks should be compensated for their individual losses by state pensions. This harsh, yet realistic, view was tempered by the proposed redistribution of wealth, new educational foundations, the creation of new bishoprics and the building up of reserve funds, which were to be largely thwarted by Henry's greed.

Nothing can excuse Cromwell's callous scheming towards the end of 1539 over the downfall of the Abbots of Glastonbury, Reading and Colchester, who dared to put up so stiff a fight. In September he had noted in his 'Remembrances': 'Item: for proceeding against the abbots of Reading and Glaston in their countries.' To secure their abbeys Cromwell resolved to attaint them. It was not very difficult to find evidence that could be found to be incriminating. Old Richard Whiting of Glastonbury was shut up in the abbey tower while the visitors searched his lodgings and found a tract against Henry's divorce and a volume on Thomas à Becket. The plate and other treasures of Glastonbury, the richest abbey in the west country, had been hidden – nearly as rank an offence as the awkward possession of the two books. The next reference in Cromwell's memoranda names the persons to give evidence against Whiting, and continues: 'To see that the evidence be well sifted against the said Abbot and his complices. The Abbot of Glaston to be tried at Glaston and executed there.' Cromwell took for granted that guilt would be proved, since he was confident that Whiting had 'misused his allegiance' – though what the precise charges were at the trial in Wells is not known. Sir John Russell, who was present, reported that it was 'a most worshipful jury'. The same date as Whiting was hanged, drawn and quartered as a traitor on Glastonbury Tor, Hugh Cook of Reading was executed for denying the royal supremacy. At Colchester the Abbot paid the like penalty for being reputed to have said: 'I will not say the King shall never have my house, but it will be against my will and against my heart, for I know by my learning he cannot take it by right and law.' The fate of these three men was an example to the others who ruled the remaining great abbeys that held out, and very soon Gloucester, Canterbury, Westminster and the rest gave in to Cromwell's men.

When the last of the abbeys had ceased to exist the crown had acquired, in addition to the valuables and other movable goods, lands and premises worth £100,000 a year, and by selling or leasing much of these Henry could expect to reap £1,500,000. Almost all of the larger grants went to men connected with the court, so inevitably they became firmly committed to the reformation settlement. Sympathizers with the monks wept – and took their share of the booty. The Marquess of Exeter, in the early stages of the dissolution, remarked: 'They will all have to go back to the Church some day, but we may as well have them now.' Thus began the revolution in land ownership all over the country. Cromwell himself acquired the property of St Osyth's Monastery in Essex, the lands of Launde Abbey in Leicestershire and most of the extensive estates that had belonged in a score of counties to Lewes Priory, as well as the Grey Friars in Yarmouth. At his death these were to be valued at £24,000.

Throughout the campaign against the monasteries Cromwell had developed his own views on the best ways of employing the spoils. As with the score of small foundations that had been wound up to provide funds for Wolsey's projected colleges in 1525–9, Cromwell hoped that capital derived from the old order would be employed for educational purposes, which would at one level be an end in themselves, but also be 'to the great advancement of the common weal' by providing a training ground for future public servants. As a man with no formal education he had a vision of new scholastic foundations, properly endowed and affording opportunities to those at present denied them. He had for some years helped scholars at Oxford and Cambridge out of his own pocket with bursaries and book grants, and his first injunctions to the clergy in 1536 had dwelt on the importance of the better-beneficed supporting youths at schools and colleges. In the Bill that he introduced in 1539 for the disposal of ex-monastic property he spoke of the benefits that would accrue to the universities, as well as the foundation of eighteen new dioceses and various new collegiate churches, hospitals and almshouses. Yet in the event very little was done. Six – and only six – bishoprics were created, but the refoundation of Cardinal College (which Cromwell tended to regard with some degree of proprietorial interest) and the foundation of Trinity College, Cambridge, occurred as an afterthought by Henry, well after Cromwell had gone.

The final months of 1538 saw the destruction of the last of the Plantagenets. The activities of the *émigré*, Cardinal Reginald Pole, made his mother and brothers vulnerable. His vituperative tract, *De Unitate Ecclesiae*, against Henry had won him a summons to Rome, and Cromwell wrote threatening most dire penalties if he obeyed the Pope's summons instead of returning to England on his allegiance. But Pole continued his journey and in December 1536 was created cardinal and two months later was appointed a legate charged with the duty of encouraging English Catholics to rebel. His intrigues from Cambrai compromised the entire 'White Rose' party in England: 'The King, to be avenged of Reynold, will kill us all,' went the cry. The Cardinal's brothers, Lord Montague and Sir Geoffrey Pole, spoke their thoughts too rashly, predicting 'a jolly stirring' as the King's sore leg brought on a mortal illness. They also voiced their dislike of Cromwell: 'They were flatterers who followed the court and none served the King but knaves.'

Henry Courtenay, Marquess of Exeter, had not disguised his own opinion that he would not be sorry when the King should die. Through his mother he was a grandson of Edward IV and had a pertinent claim to the throne, so his tenants in the west country foretold that he would 'wear the garland' – the Rose of York – at last. Just as the Duke of Buckingham could never stomach Cardinal Wolsey, so Exeter could not abide Cromwell. Although Henry VIII had singled him out for advancement by creating him a marquess in 1525, Courtenay felt himself the heir to Buckingham's grandeur, embodying an older, more militant feudalism, and after the Pilgrimage of Grace he drifted into ineffectual plotting with the Poles. He had married Lord Mountjoy's daughter who, like Lady Margaret Pole, had been very close to Catherine of Aragon and remained a devout Romanist. The King needed little encouragement from Cromwell to trample on the White Rose, moving first against Sir Geoffrey Pole, then Lords Montague and Exeter, and finally cornering the old Countess of Salisbury, who were all to be snared in the trammels of the Treasons Act. Caught up in the Exeter conspiracy were two courtiers intimately known to Henry over the years: Sir Nicholas Carew and Sir Edward Neville. The former was Master of the Horse, the latter Master of the Buckhounds. Carew was friendly towards Princess Mary and had been heard singing political songs, featuring both King and Lord Privy Seal, in the gardens of Exeter's house at Horsley. (Ballads lampooning Cromwell were also current in Padua at this time and a correspondent of Cranmer's, knowing insufficient Italian to understand the ditties, in error sent copies to the minister on the assumption that all of them were anti-papal or anti-imperial, whereas 'other verses of a vile matter' touched Cromwell himself.) On 28 November 1538 Cromwell wrote to Sir Thomas Wyatt:

You have been advertised how the Lord Marquess of Exeter and the Lord Montague, with a sort of their adherents of mean estates and no estimation greatly, have been committed to the Tower ... for sundry great crimes of *lèse majesté* traiterously imagined and uttered as far as they durst against the King's royal person, his issue, his Council and the whole realm, so that it abhorreth any man to hear of it and the same their offences be not known by light of suspicion, but by certain proofs and confessions. . . .

Exeter was to be executed on 9 January following.

For political reasons Henry was prepared to reconsider his views about Lutheranism and swallow a further section of the treatise on the seven sacraments, which he had written at the height of Catholic orthodoxy. Ever since 1528 his fulsome defence of the sanctity of marriage, which formed an integral part of the tract, had been an acute embarrassment and for the past five years his pæan of praise for papal power, which formed the ground bass to it, he excused as a youthful piece of pamphleteering. Could he not have been mistaken also about Luther? In 1534 he had sent Robert Barnes on an informal mission to Wittenberg to discuss an accommodation with Philip Melanchthon and in the following year he had despatched Bishop Foxe of Hereford and Nicholas Heath to propose to the German princes that they might form an offensive and defensive alliance with him for the sake of the gospel. Foxe had, indeed, addressed the Diet of the Schmalkaldic League on Christmas eve and on Christmas day had signed the thirteen articles of faith proposed by the Lutherans and sent them to England for the King's consideration. Henry was perhaps flattered by the idea of becoming Defender and Protector of the League, which would have been a belated consolation prize for failing at the imperial election, but he soon found the earnest Lutherans to be deficient in tact when they tried to teach him his duty and the tenets he must profess. Cromwell had written feelingly: 'The King knowing himself to be the learnedest Prince in Europe, he thought it became not him to submit to them; but he expected they should submit to him.' However close Wittenberg and Whitehall might seem to outside observers, a great gulf remained. Both parties continued to flirt with each other for a further four years; neither expected to achieve a compromise, but each thought it could somehow browbeat the other into surrender.

The Ten Articles of 1537 had encouraged the Lutherans since, following the Wittenberg Confession, they had acknowledged that there were no more than three sacraments. Melanchthon, however, as a realist had seen them as no more than a half-way house – a '*confuissime compositi*', as he had termed them. Yet the international situation required Henry to continue the love affair with Protestant Germany, and the suit was encouraged by Cromwell for doctrinal no less than for political reasons. Early in 1538 the League at last agreed to send a deputation to England, headed by Francis Burckhardt, Vice-chancellor of Saxony, who was accompanied by the distinguished theologian, Frederick Myconius, and George Boyneburg, a lawyer. Martin Luther had sent a warm commendation to Edward Foxe, but, alas, by the time the delegates arrived Foxe had died. Cranmer undoubtedly hoped for some *rapport* with the continental reformers, but the bishops appointed with him to confer with them were Stokesley, Tunstall and Sampson, all three of them men of the right who were determined against reaching even the most general degree of understanding.

Throughout that hot summer with the plague rampant in London there was shadow boxing: the Evangelicals wanted to discuss the 'known abuses' in the Church (private masses, the restriction of the laity to the consecrated bread at communion, while only priests could share the cup, and a celibate priesthood); the orthodox Catholics were bent on debating the four omitted sacraments (holy matrimony, holy orders, confirmation and extreme unction). In desperation, as deadlock seemed certain, Cranmer wrote to Cromwell: 'They know certainly that the Germans will not agree with us, except it be in matrimony only; so that I perceive that the bishops seek only an occasion to break.' At one stage Cromwell thought that if Stokesley could be advised to absent himself from the colloquy there might be a chance of progress. Then, when it seemed useless to prolong discussions, he succeeded in persuading the Germans to stay on for a further month in the hope of an accommodation – yet the Augsburg Confession and *The Bishops' Book* were uneasy bedfellows. At last on 1 October the Lutherans departed. Henry had the good grace to present Burckhardt with a coach and three horses, while the Germans compared the supreme head with Achilles and considered Thomas Cromwell to be an English Moses. Frederick Myconius, the Superintendent of Gotha, reluctantly came to the conclusion that Cromwell had deliberately misled him about the King's evangelist zeal. He pithily summed up the attitude of the English sovereign; 'Harry only wants to sit as Antichrist in the temple as God, and that Harry should be Pope. The rich treasures, the rich incomes of the Church – these are the Gospel According to Harry.'

Somewhat surprisingly Burckhardt returned to England for another round of talks in April 1539, accompanied by Ludwig von Baumbach. On this, his last mission, Cromwell was much more pushing. 'These orators,' he wrote, 'shall be very formidable to the Bishop of Rome and to others of his adherents also, for doubtless if Your Majesty shall happen to join with them, the papists shall be half desperate.' Cromwell held various discussions at his house and there was a debate at St James's Palace at which certainly Norfolk, Suffolk, Audley and Tunstall were present. All hope of understanding at this late stage was dashed, however, by the news that the German Protestant princes had signed a truce with the Emperor with terms that forbade the admission of any new states to their League. Saxony, Hesse and the others were no longer potential allies; Robert Barnes had returned empty-handed from his mission to Denmark, and Cromwell's last hope lay in the Duchy of Cleves.

Within a month of the Lutherans leaving England in the autumn of 1538 occurred the *cause célèbre* of John Lambert's trial for heresy, in which the King took the keenest interest largely to demonstrate to the Catholic powers the strength of his own orthodoxy. Lambert had travelled far in his search for the truth since his days at Cambridge in the mid-1520s, when he had forgathered with Barnes, Latimer and Bilney in the parlour of the White Horse tavern to discuss the reform of the Church. Later on he had found a niche as chaplain in the English House in Antwerp, where he disseminated Anabaptist propaganda, before being turned over to Lord Chancellor More as an heretic. Archbishop Warham had saved him from burning (for he respected his patristic knowledge), but Lambert was not the man to lie low nor to conform. As a result of complaints from Norfolk and others he was summoned to appear at Lambeth Palace where he enjoyed arguing his position with Cranmer and Latimer. Imprisonment followed, but on release he continued his disputations in city churches. Dr Barnes, who as poacher turned gamekeeper had a commission to 'extirpate sacramentaries', showed to the Archbishop Lambert's own ten articles of faith, which denied the doctrine of the real presence, and once again Cranmer ordered him to appear before him, though this time Lambert refused to plead and foolishly insisted on appealing to the King for his judgement. Henry in fact leapt at the idea of conducting the heresy trial himself and the banqueting hall at White-hall was transformed into a court, with scaffolding erected to hold great numbers of spectators. To the right of the throne sat the bishops and doctors of law and opposite them the temporal peers, councillors and household officials. Henry had attired himself spectacularly in white. Cromwell, who was present, described to Sir Thomas Wyatt how his sovereign

for the reverence of the sacrament of the altar did sit openly in his hall and there presided at the disputation, process and judgement of a miserable heretic sacramentary. . . . It was wonderful to see how princely, with what excellent gravity and with what estimable majesty his Highness exercised there the very office of a Supreme Head of his Church of England,

and he would have liked all the potentates of Christendom, Catholic and Protestant, to have seen him in action.

After Bishop Sampson had opened the proceedings the King cross-questioned the prisoner, making great play of the fact that Lambert had an alias (Nicholson). 'What! Have you two names? I would not trust your having two names, although you were my brother.' Lambert maintained he could never forsake the truth from fear, or from the love of man, and denied to the King that the sacrament of the altar was the body of Christ. 'Mark well,' Henry pontificated, 'for now thou shall be condemned by Christ's own words, *Hoc est corpus meum.*' Once Henry had had enough of displaying his own grasp of theology, the bishops, including Gardiner who had by now returned from his embassy in France, kept up their questioning so that the trial lasted for five hours, until Lambert submitted to the King's will. Henry commented: 'If you do commit yourself into my judgement, you must die, for I will not be a patron unto heretics,' and commanded Cromwell to read the customary sentence of death by burning, which was executed four days later at Smithfield. Foxe the matyrologist writes that on the day of his death Cromwell ordered Lambert to be brought to his house and in an inner chamber asked the condemned man for his pardon before giving him his last breakfast. Had this been true it would have been most surprising had it not come to light eighteen months later when Cromwell was himself being charged with heresy.

On the day of Lambert's trial a royal proclamation imposed rigid censorship on all books in English, required foreign sacramentaries to leave England forthwith and forbade all persons, except learned divines, to debate the key doctrine of transubstantiation under pain of death. The orders went on to prohibit married priests from administering any of the sacraments of the Church and from holding any office. Parishioners were to observe all ceremonies that had not been specifically abrogated. There is no doubt that the whole tone of the proclamation was anathema to Cromwell, as it was to Archbishop Cranmer. In a letter to a friend Cromwell merely reported its issue, at the King's command, without risking any comment on its contents, and if Henry VIII was growing apart from both his Archbishop and his Viceregent, he can have framed the proclamation only with the help of such bishops as Gardiner and Sampson. Effectively the proclamation marked the beginning of a religious reaction, which was destined to bring about Cromwell's fall.

The summer of 1538 had been the high-water mark of Henry's reformation. The destruction of the shrines, the increasing pace of surrenders of the greater monasteries, the final preparations for the Great Bible, the planned move against Courtenay and the Poles, who were ardent papists as well as Plantagenets, and the renewal of negotiations with the German Lutherans all spelt the triumph of the reformist party in England. But before the end of the year, as we have seen, with the Lutherans leaving empty-handed and disconsolate followed by Lambert's conviction for heresy, the tide had begun to turn. In part the beginnings of reaction were due to the changed international situation. Habsburg and Valois had signed a ten-year truce, so there was a danger of their taking steps to implement the papal bull of 17 December excommunicating Henry and absolving his subjects from their allegiance; but if he could convince the Emperor and the King of France of his utter orthodoxy he would be reasonably immune from their crusading. In part the progress towards Protestantism was halted because King and Council realized that the average subject, basically conservative in religion, could no longer keep up with the pace of change in ceremony and doctrine and hankered almost as fervently as the rebels in the north for the traditional ways. That the tide turned so strongly and led to the Act of Six Articles is very largely due to the return to England of Stephen Gardiner from his long stint as ambassador in Paris and his alliance with Norfolk.

The Duke of Norfolk, who had expected to be the chief beneficiary from Wolsey's fall, had seen Cromwell rapidly overtake him. He had interpreted the erection of Cromwell's new Court of Augmentations as a threat to his own position as Lord Treasurer of England and he recognized that his rival, who still clung to his old offices of Chancellor of the Exchequer and Master of the Jewels, had a much wider appreciation of financial problems than he did. At Easter 1536 Chapuys had described Cromwell as being more powerful than Wolsey had ever been, so that Lord Chancellor Audley was his creature, yet three months later he was to succeed the Earl of Wiltshire as Lord Privy Seal and accept a barony, while Norfolk was necessarily discredited by his niece's fall. Here was a new threat, for Norfolk would find Cromwell meeting him on his own ground when Parliament should next meet and the days when he regarded himself as the most experienced and influential government spokesman in the Upper House were over (it was as if in the mid-Victorian era Mr Disraeli had been created Earl of Beaconsfield while the Earl of Derby was still prime minister). Norfolk and Cromwell would in April 1538 both be contending for power in the Lords.

In the aftermath of the Pilgrimage of Grace Norfolk had again removed himself from Henry's wrath (as he had after Anne Boleyn's execution), by withdrawing to his mansion at Kenninghall, where he was almost a king in his own domain. As Lord Treasurer there was certain administrative and judicial work for him at Westminster, but Cromwell endeavoured to keep him away from court and by the end of term he would be back in his county. There is a curious similarity to the behaviour and attitude of his father, who had been so jealous of Wolsey, in 1512: Howard 'being discountenanced by the King, he left the court' and Wolsey thought it would be good 'if he were ousted from his lodging there altogether'. The third Duke realized that a return to royal favour depended largely on Cromwell and so he schemed to become friendly with him. When a grandson was born in March 1538 he wrote asking him to stand godfather to him and also to be his executor; Cromwell saw through these overtures and was on his guard, for the Duchess of Norfolk had warned him: 'The Duke can speak [as] fair to his enemy as to his friend.'

His son, the poet Surrey, who was hot-tempered and self-willed as well as damnably proud, followed his father in regarding Cromwell the smithy's son as an upstart and called him 'that foul churl'. It was for dynastic reasons that Surrey loathed the Lord Privy Seal, since with Edward Seymour Cromwell embodied 'the new men', grasping for position and wealth, who were trying to displace the older nobility from their traditional place in the counsels of state and their customary role in the counties as head of an authoritarian, patriarchal society. That Cromwell and Seymour leaned too far towards Protestantism was for Surrey almost irrelevant, for the poet was not much interested in religion as such. Although very much a man in the liberal Renaissance tradition, his only straying into the paths of religion was the writing of verse paraphrases of certain of the psalms and of part of the Book of Ecclesiastes. It is one of the curiosities of the age that Sir Thomas Wyatt could count both Surrey and Cromwell as his friends.

Within weeks of his return to England Stephen Gardiner became the acknowledged leader of the conservative bishops who wanted to purge the English Church of all elements of Protestant doctrine and practice. He had succeeded Wolsey as Bishop of Winchester and saw himself filling the role of a clerical statesman in the late-medieval tradition as if the Henrician reformation had never happened. Though he was destined to become Queen Mary's Lord Chancellor, in 1538 he was ambitious enough to expect he could displace Cromwell, whom he had never forgiven for ousting him from the secretaryship four years before. More than any other churchman he disliked Cromwell's powers as vicegerent in spiritual affairs and objected most strongly to his holding the deanery of Wells and various prebends as a layman. Cromwell recognized the threat, for he had known Gardiner all too well since their service under the Cardinal. Time and experience of government had not altered his character and he retained the arrogance that had exasperated so many people when as a young man he had taught canon and civil law at Trinity Hall, Cambridge. Perhaps, as some claimed, Gardiner *did* have Tudor blood in his veins, for the tale is told that his mother was the illegitimate daughter of Jasper Tudor, Earl of Pembroke, the uncle of Henry VII. My lord of Winchester had always been a difficult colleague. Henry himself admitted as much in

1531: 'I have often squared with you Gardiner, but I love you none the worse, as the bishopric I give will convince you.' A quarter of a century later, on his deathbed, the King – questioned by Sir Anthony Denny about why Gardiner's name had been left out of the councillors named for the Regency – shrewdly summed him up: 'He would cumber you all and you could never rule him; he is so troublesome a nature.'

Making due allowance for the partisan views of the reformers, the sketch of Gardiner by his successor as Bishop of Winchester, Stephen Ponet, conveys something of the man with whom Cromwell and Cranmer had to deal: Gardiner, he wrote, was 'of a swart colour, with a hanging look, frowning brows, deep-set eyes, a nose hooked like a buzzard, great paws (like a devil) an outward monster with a vengeable wit'. Letters that passed between Gardiner and Cromwell were all the more vehement for having a personal edge; and at times each seems to have adopted a stance in order to rile the other. In 1536 when Gardiner was in France, Cromwell had occasion to chide him for being high-handed about the payment of a pension ordered by the King and presented a magnificent rebuff.

Truly my lord, though my talent be not so precious as yours, yet I trust with His help that gave me it to use it, so it shall do his office without gathering such suspicions upon friendship. I repeat that word again, friendship. . . . Your gifts received of God be great, and so much the more cause ye have to thank Him for them. Your other gifts received of the King be not small and therefore your service to His Majesty for the same is loyal and diligent.

Cromwell adds that all his advice has been given to Gardiner in a friendly way, though the Bishop takes great pains to accuse him of having 'neither friendship in me or honesty', and in a similar vein to that in his final letter to Wolsey (above page 159) brings the point home: 'that ye be much given to your own judgement, I durst make yourself the judge'. Later on Cromwell feared his rebuke had been too severe even for the thick-skinned Bishop and so he relented, saying what he had written had been penned 'somewhat quickly' and hoping they could let bygones be bygones, 'for I am for my part ever the same man I was before, that is your assured friend'. For his part Stephen Gardiner would never relent, never forgive the rebuff, never forget imagined injustice or remember friendship.

The Bishop had come to terms with Henry in 1535 by writing his tract on obedience, which had described the royal supremacy in terms that Cromwell undoubtedly approved. This was, indeed, written at the King's command in the month following the execution of Sir Thomas More. God, he wrote, had established kings who, 'as representatives of his image unto men, he would have to be reputed in the supreme and most high room and to excel among all other human creatures'. The Church of England he defined as 'that multitude of people which, united in Christian belief, has grown together in one body', and so by the doctrine of equivalence, church and state are different aspects of the same phenomenon. Authority, wrote Gardiner, is the prerogative of princes alone and to such power holy scripture sets no limit; it follows then that any suggestion that a subject's obedience to his sovereign can be limited is sheer wickedness. 'In England all are agreed that those whom England has born and bred shall have nothing whatever to do with Rome.' This was a powerful intellectual plea for Henry's supremacy, and yet in the fourteen years since he wrote his tract Gardiner failed to see that the conservative theological standpoint he now embodied conflicted with the legal and philosophical views he had expressed. Cromwell was no expert in civil law, but he saw that Gardiner was cutting off the branch that supported him.

There is a story related by John Foxe of a discussion at Hampton Court on the extent of royal power. Cromwell had suggested that anything the King willed should be regarded as law since this, he said, 'was to be a very King'. Gardiner (whom Foxe makes the narrator) was called in for his opinion by the Lord Privy Seal.

'Come on, my Lord of Winchester,' quoth he – for that conceit he had, whatsoever he talked with me, [though] he knew even as much as I, Greek or Latin and all. 'Answer the King here, but speak plainly and directly, and shrink not, man! Is not that that pleaseth a King a law? Have ye not there, in the civil laws *quod principi placuit*, and so forth? I have somewhat forgotten it now.' I stood still and considered in my mind to what conclusion this should tend. The King saw me musing and with earnest gentleness said, 'Answer him whether it be so or no.' I would not answer my Lord Cromwell, but delivered my speech to the King and told him I had read indeed of Kings that had their will always received for a law; but I told him, the form of his reign to make the law his will was more sure and quiet 'and by this form of government ye be established and it is agreeable with the nature of your people. If ye begin a new manner of policy, how it will frame no man can tell; and how this frameth ye can tell, and I would never advise Your Grace to leave a certain for an uncertain.' The King turned his back and left the matter after till the Lord Cromwell turned the cat in the pan afore company, when he was angry with me and charged me as though I had played his part.

When the new Parliament met, Lord Chancellor Audley told both Houses on 5 May that the King 'desires above all things that diversity in religious opinions should be banished from his dominions; and since this is a thing too arduous to be determined in the midst of so many various judgements, it seems good to him to ask a Committee of the the Upper House to examine opinions, and to report their decisions to the whole Parliament.' A committee was at once appointed, comprising Cromwell, Archbishops Cranmer and Lee and six bishops – Goodrich, Latimer, Salcott, Tunstall, Clerk and Aldrich; significantly Gardiner was not one. The committee was a balanced one, too well-balanced in fact to produce a speedy answer and possibly too evenly divided to achieve anything but a stalemate compromise over a long series of meetings.

The idea of appointing a committee of this kind, if not the actual membership, looks very much like a tactical move of Gardiner's. Cromwell did not attend a single one of the few meetings to be held, possibly because he saw through Gardiner's scheme, though at any rate he was far too preoccupied with Parliamentary business at the beginning of the session. On 16 May Norfolk announced in the Lords that because the committee had failed to agree on a formulary of faith, the King required the House to consider six matters of doctrine with the intention of passing legislation to enforce their conformity. When the Ten Articles had been framed in 1536–7 the bishops had enjoyed five months for their work, but now they had been deprived of their brief after eleven days. Indeed it seems probable that by 10 May Cranmer had already been told that his committee was to be wound up. Norfolk spoke in a complaining way of 'delays' and doubted whether the committee could ever have produced an agreed report. He put to the House in the King's name that they must all ascertain the truth about transubstantiation and also answer whether the laity should receive the consecrated wine at the eucharist as well as the bread; whether the vows of chastity should be observed; whether priests should marry; whether private masses and auricular confession were necessary by divine law. Norfolk could never have taken this stand without the King's direction. There is every reason to believe that the six questions being asked by proxy were questions that he as supreme head wanted answered in a particular way most speedily and translated into an Act of Parliament. Cromwell saw Norfolk's speech as the statement of a party programme, backed by the sovereign, that cut at the heart of his own progress towards Protestantism and, since it was being done behind his back, at his own political position.

Henry was himself present in the House of Lords on the first as well as the last day of the debate and was the only layman to take part. As grand inquisitor at Lambert's trial he had acquired a taste for public disputation on doctrinal questions, and, as the preamble to the resultant Act of Six Articles put it, he 'had most graciously vouchsafed in his own princely person to descend and come into his High Court of Parliament and Council, and there like a prince of most high prudence and no less learning and opened and declared many things of high learning and great knowledge'. Cranmer, we know, defended the marriage of priests (he was already secretly married), denied that confession was necessary and vigorously supported communion in both kinds. Shaxton of Salisbury and Latimer of Worcester were much more resistant. A lay peer who was present reported: 'Finally His Highness confused them all with God's learning.' In those debates, he noted, Archbishop Lee of York, Tunstall of Durham, Gardiner of Winchester, Stokesley of London and Sampson of Chichester 'have showed themselves honest and well learned men'. Those were the men Cromwell identified as opponents of his foreign and domestic policies and challengers to his authority in the state, because of their very different attitude to religion. 'We of the temporalty have been all of one opinion and my Lord Chancellor and my Lord Privy Seal as good as we can devise,' concluded the anonymous peer. Cromwell, seeing the basis of his power narrowing, did not attempt to take a positive line in public against the Six Articles: he would, as always, follow the King's lead and satisfy his conscience that, as vicegerent, he could do no other. The Bill, embodying the penalties of burning at the stake for any denial of the doctrine of transubstantiation and of death for maintaining views contrary to the other five articles, was formally termed 'An Act abolishing Diversity of Opinions' (soon to be dubbed 'the whip with six strings'). It passed the Lords on 10 June and went down to the Commons. It became law on 28 June.

When Parliament was prorogued Cromwell wrote to Latimer and Shaxton forcing them to resign from their sees; they were placed in the custody of the Bishops of Chichester and of Bath and Wells respectively. The French ambassador commented on the people's 'great joy at the King's declaration touching the sacrament, being much more inclined to the old religion than to the new opinions'. Archbishop Cranmer, who had finally ended his resistance by attending the House of Lords when the Bill was passed, felt insecure, but the King ordered Cromwell to go to him at Lambeth in the company of the Dukes of Norfolk and Suffolk to persuade him of his very great personal regard. The three stopped to dine with Cranmer, in turn praising him for his humility, and Suffolk contrasted this with Wolsey's arrogance. Mention of the Cardinal prompted Norfolk, spoiling for a fight, to make an uncomplimentary remark about Cromwell's years in Wolsey's service and it was with difficulty that the Archbishop contrived to pacify the two.

A day or two later Cromwell told Cranmer that the King had invited him to write down privately his objections to the Six Acts and he accordingly dictated a short treatise to his secretary, Ralph Morice. As a result of a commotion on the river Thames because of a bear baiting, during which the beast jumped into the wherry in which Morice was crossing from Lambeth to Westminster, Morice fell overboard, dropping the treatise he was carrying. It was rescued by the bearward who passed it to a priest, and he, having read a few paragraphs, pronounced it an heretical tract on the Articles. Morice came to claim the manuscript, whereupon the bearward said both he and his master deserved to be burnt. Unable to bribe the officious man Morice sought Cromwell's help and when the bearward arrived at Hampton Court next day to deliver his telling evidence to Gardiner, or Sir Anthony Browne, Cromwell intercepted him and forced him to surrender the treatise. Such was the mood of Londoners in the aftermath of the passing of the Act of Six Articles that a mere illiterate bearward was prepared to threaten the Archbishop of Canterbury.

Despite the machinations of Norfolk and Gardiner, Cromwell had succeeded in retrieving his position. He was still far too valuable a minister for Henry to be prepared to overthrow him and thus he retained the King's confidence. Without it he would have been lost. Accepting as a politique the passage of the Six Articles he recognized that he would be vulnerable if he deviated from that policy and he was too shrewd to play into his enemies' hands by giving the King cause for suspicion. By the summer of 1539 Cromwell was far more concerned about England's position in Europe than his own standing at court. He saw, too, that by rescuing England from the dangers of isolation and persuading Henry to contract another marriage he might well be able to strengthen his own hold on government and place himself out of range of Norfolk's volleys.

10

The Pillar Perished

In that age of matrimonial diplomacy Cromwell's search for an ally to stand by England, now that Charles v and Francis i had signed a ten-year truce, became caught up in his prospecting for another wife for Henry. Moreover, since Pope Paul iii had at last excommunicated Henry and declared him to be deposed, an ally could come only from a Protestant state. A potential alliance would therefore raise awkward doctrinal questions at home. With the passage of the Act of Six Articles in 1539 a policy of reaction was being officially pursued (even if Cromwell himself contrived to limit the operation of the law) and so he looked to a marriage treaty as offering opportunities to relax, if not overturn, that policy so that the 'true word of God' might be heard again in the land and in consequence enable him to re-establish his former supremacy with the King. The right bride for his master could neatly solve all the outstanding problems. It was on paper a brilliant plan, but because it involved Henry's affections it was necessarily a gamble. In the event Cromwell lost, and lost all.

He had already turned to the German princes in his desperation and after many false starts had settled on the Duchy of Cleves to provide both a political alliance and a queen. In 1537 John Hutton had written to him: 'The Duke of Cleves hath a daughter, but I hear no great praise either of her personage nor beauty.' More recently there had been other views about Anne's charms. According to German taste she was thought rather attractive and another verdict was that she excelled the seventeen-year-old Duchess of Milan, the widow of Francesco Sforza, whose portrait by Holbein had made

Henry determined to marry again, 'as the golden sun did the silvery moon'. Since Duchess Christina of Milan was now ruled out on political grounds, together with a group of nubile French princesses, Henry became much taken with the idea of marrying into the House of Cleves.

Anne's brother, young Duke William, had recently inherited the duchies of Cleves, Juliers and Berg and was engaged in a dispute with the Emperor about the territory of Guelderland. Like Henry he was anti-papal and Erastian in religion without being a Lutheran, and he had refused to join the League of German Princes. Because of the strategic position of his Rhenish principality he had great merit as an ally for England (Cleves formed a barrier between the Habsburg Netherlands and imperial Germany and it was also, like the Swiss cantons, a recruiting ground for mercenaries). Henry required his ambassador to find out everything he could about Duke William's attitudes to religion and the political struggle in Germany, entreating him 'earnestly to feel always the bottom of his stomach'. Clearly for the Duke an alliance with England had much to offer and to marry his sister to the King was a glittering prospect. Enticingly he told the envoy that her attractive appearance 'would get her a good husband', whether Henry remained interested or not, and he hinted that the Duke of Lorraine's son was still a contender for her hand. Christopher Mont wrote to Cromwell from Cleves: 'Every man praiseth the beauty of the same Lady [Anne] as well for the face as for the whole body, above all ladies excellent.'

In this difficult business of wooing by proxy Henry sent out Hans Holbein to paint the likenesses of both Anne and her younger sister, Amelia, for there was some difficulty about his being sent fairly recent portraits of them by Lucas Cranach. The King wanted the artist to see and capture on canvas as much of the two princesses as he could – much more, certainly, than was visible when they wore their 'monstrous hoods', which hid so much of their faces and figures – but his request shocked the Duchy Chancellor who commented, 'Why, would you see them naked?', before giving way. Nicholas Wootton who had accompanied Holbein on this delicate mission reported to Cromwell that the artist had 'taken the effigies of my lady Anne and the lady Amelia and had expressed their images very lively'; but Wootton underlined Anne's lack of accomplishments and education, implying what a dull girl the gentle-natured Princess was, spending so much of her time with her needle.

She can read and write her own tongue, but of French, Latin or other language she knows none, nor yet she cannot sing nor play any instrument, for they take it here in Germany for a rebuke and an occasion of lightness that great ladies should be learned or have any knowledge of music.

If Cromwell thought it fit to let Henry see Wootton's letter, the King was not put off by what he read. Holbein's flattering portrait was sufficient to make him reach a decision about Anne. Two years before when he was thinking seriously of a French bride he had suggested to Francis I that the five possible candidates might be taken to Calais for him to look them over and he had countered the French ambassador's comment, that holding such a parade was against chivalry and propriety, by saying, 'By God, the thing touches me too near. I wish to see them and know them some time before deciding.' Yet now, convinced by Cromwell of the urgent need for a political alliance, he threw caution to the winds and so the perliminaries were rushed through. The question of Anne's earlier pre-contract with Francis, Marquis de Pont à Mousson, the Duke of Lorraine's son, was regarded as satisfactorily answered and a marriage treaty was signed on 6 October 1539. By the middle of December King and minister waited impatiently for the weather to improve so that Anne could cross from Calais, where she had arrived on 11 December. The Lord Admiral, Southampton, was already in Calais to welcome Anne and prepare to escort her to England, but he found the King's instructions, 'to cheer my Lady and her train, so they may think the time is short', hard to carry out because of linguistic difficulties. Gregory Cromwell was with him and, through Dr Olisleger, helped to teach Anne the card game 'Sent' that Henry enjoyed – but it was fearfully heavy going. Southampton sent Henry a letter tactfully praising his bride-to-be, which he came to regret having written.

After Christmas better weather allowed them to cross to Deal and Anne proceeded to Canterbury, where Archbishop Cranmer welcomed her and presented the fifty sovereigns that Cromwell had provided. She was in Rochester by new year's eve, where Norfolk greeted her, and although Henry was not due to meet her until 3 January, he simply could not keep away and rode down to Rochester to see her for

himself and 'to nourish love'. His own father had ridden out un-
announced forty years back to inspect an unveiled Catherine of
Aragon, fearing that by Spanish trickery Prince Arthur might be
having a plain or even a deformed fiancée foisted on him, but Henry
VIII was much more concerned at confirming with his eyes the
second-hand opinions about the woman he was committed to marrying.
Stepping into her room in disguise he embraced her and was full of
embarrassment when the nervous Princess could not reply to him in
English. He retreated as soon as he could, forgetting in his haste to
present the gift of furs he had brought. He had been grievously misled
by Cromwell, by Master Holbein and the ambassadors. In the eyes of
this beholder there was no trace of beauty. Returning to Greenwich
in his barge he told Sir Anthony Browne, Master of the Horse, his
terrible disappointment: 'I see nothing in this woman as men report of
her and I marvel that wise men would make reports as they have done'.
That evening Cromwell asked him how he found the Lady Anne and
he snapped back 'Nothing so well as she is spoken of. If I had known
as much before as I know now, she should never have come into this
realm.' Was there no way of escape? Cromwell began to sense the
danger, for he had committed himself unreservedly to the Cleves
marriage and had even presented it as a striking diplomatic *coup*, yet in
the next few weeks it would become increasingly clear to him that
while his sovereign's and his own zeal for a national policy had never
been restricted by religious considerations, the King had not until this
moment been required to put his patriotism to the supreme test of
having to marry a woman he found incompatible with his decided
tastes.

Henry went through the formal meeting with Anne at Blackheath
as a painful duty and behaved with dignity before the assembled
company of peers, bishops, courtiers, ambassadors, London aldermen
and a contingent of merchants from the Hanseatic Steelyard. The
French ambassador, Marillac, reported that the Princess was 'not so
young as was at first thought, nor so handsome as people affirmed';
he noted that she possessed a determined countenance and found some
show of vivacity in her expression, yet this was 'insufficient to counter-
balance her want of beauty'. The King feared he was about to become
the laughing stock of Europe, for buying a pig in a poke. The clothes
worn by Anne and her German maids of honour did not help the

impression, for by English standards they seemed decidedly dowdy.

That night at Greenwich Cromwell had to endure a difficult audience with his master as he revealed his opinions about his future Queen and the most the King would say, when pressed to admit it, was that Anne had a regal manner. Clutching at straws, Henry raised the old question of Anne's pre-contract to the Duke of Lorraine's son which, if valid, might provide an effective ban to his marriage. The nuptials were postponed for two days, to Cromwell's concern, while further discussions took place with members from the delegation from Cleves. Although they had not brought with them the documents relating to the Lorraine betrothal, they drew up an instrument declaring that the Princess was legally free to marry Henry; and when Cromwell reported this outcome the King told him that he had been 'ill-handled', and that if he had not been scared of 'making a ruffle in the world', driving the Duke of Cleves into the Emperor's camp, he would have sent Anne and her entourage packing. There was no escape route, and he complained that the wedding was 'a great yoke to enter into'. On Twelfth Night, just before entering the queen's closet at Greenwich Palace for the ceremony, he made his reluctance fearfully plain to Cromwell: 'If it were not to satisfy the world and my realm, I would not do that I must do this day for none earthly thing.' The whole business was a ghastly mistake, perpetrated by the Lord Privy Seal, and Henry's description, 'ill-handled', brought reminders of his verdict on Wolsey when the legatine court broke up.

Though the royal couple shared the same great bed for a number of nights theirs was but a marriage in name, and outside the marriage bed they had hardly any interests in common. Cromwell fervently hoped that this Rhine maiden, whom everyone regarded as his own *protégée*, would miraculously discover some hidden resources of feminine wiles as she became less timid of the colossus by her side and rouse him to consummate their union. He unwisely asked the King after a day or so how he now found his bride and learnt that his distaste for her had, if anything, increased. He was sure that 'by her breasts and belly she should be no maid; which when I felt them struck me so to the heart that I had neither the will nor courage to the rest'. It was a disastrous honeymoon. In the Queen's apartments the ladies of her bedchamber secretly discussed among themselves the same problems that Henry talked over quite openly with the gentlemen of his bedchamber. Lady

Browne, wife of the Master of the Horse, had known at once that the King would never be able to love Anne since she saw in her 'such fashion and manner of bringing-up gross and far discrepant from the King's Highness's appetite'.

As the Queen's grasp of English improved, her ladies were able to question her discreetly. When she denied that she was pregnant, Lady Edgecumbe asked, 'How is it possible for your Grace to know that, and lie every night with the King?' They were assured she was still a virgin. Either from modesty or from failure to understand what they were driving at Anne said, 'Why, when he comes to bed he kisses me and taketh me by the hand and biddeth me, "Good-Night, sweetheart", and in the morning he kisses me and biddeth me, "Farewell, Darling". Is not this enough?' People blabbed at court and jumped to the conclusion that Henry would be rid of her as soon as he decently could. Henry discussed with his doctors the problem of a frigid wife who had no sexual appeal for him whatsoever, so that he could never be 'provoked to know her carnally'. Doctors Butts and Chamber assured him on their oaths that he was not impotent. All the faults for non-consummation were on the Queen's side because His Majesty 'had found her body disordered and indisposed to excite and provoke any lust in him'. Nothing changed as the days passed and by the spring Henry was telling those around him that he could never have any more children if he remained wedded to Anne, and declared – ominous phrase – 'that before God he thought she was not his lawful wife'. Cromwell could not help him to rid himself of his guilty feeling and the more the King's conscience nagged him the more sure he was that this was an invalid marriage, condemned to be fruitless and devoid of happiness. It was against the canon and the civil law, and as an expert in these affairs through his own sad past experiences he would have Cromwell and the others know that ways must be found to free him from Queen Anne. As Sir Anthony Browne well knew, the best brood mares in his stables came from Flanders, so if Henry dubbed Anne of Cleves 'the Flanders mare' it was done with devastating irony. In this mood it was not difficult for Henry to become extremely attracted to one of Anne's maids of honour, young Catherine Howard, who had been introduced to him by her uncle Norfolk at the Bishop of Winchester's house in Southwark.

Much had happened on the diplomatic front since Anne's arrival.

On new year's day 1540, while Henry was having his first unhappy meeting with Anne, Charles v and Francis i entered Paris together amid great expressions of cordiality, and for days there were banquets and jousts at the Louvre. Ever anxious to stir up trouble between his rival sovereigns Henry saw their prolonged meeting as an opportunity for sowing discord. Cromwell's fear was that the two Catholic Kings, having sunk their differences, might be planning to invade England to execute the papal bull of deposition and fulfil their pledge to extirpate Protestantism. Any chance of ruffling their relations therefore should be grasped, and for Henry such an exercise was worth the effort, even if his own security were not at stake. Sir Thomas Wyatt was speedily despatched to Paris to strengthen the efforts of Bishop Bonner, the accredited ambassador, in putting a wedge between the monarchs, though Bonner's own interventions had been so ham-fisted and rude-mannered that he was soon recalled, to be replaced by Norfolk.

Cromwell was, as always, relieved when the Duke was away from court and it suited his plans if Norfolk could remain in France for as long as possible, though in fact his mission was the King's own idea and Cromwell was only on the outer perimeter of the negotiations. Effectively there were two conflicting foreign policies, as there had been in the summer of 1528. Because Cromwell was by now completely identified with a German alliance he had no locus in the intricate dealings with the French, and at a crucial time of initiative in diplomatic affairs the negotiations were being controlled by his enemy Norfolk. The Duke swiftly healed the wound that Bonner had caused at the French court and was able to exploit the Emperor's touchiness about Henry showing scant regard for him, that had so recently led to Wyatt being snubbed in Paris. Norfolk's mission was an undoubted success and pointed to Henry finding a sure ally in Francis, as Valois and Habsburg went back on their truce to plunge themselves in another bout of continental warfare on the question of Milan.

The ground was being cut from under Cromwell's feet, since a fresh understanding with France would make the alliance with Cleves not merely irrelevant but a positive embarrassment: if Charles v, once he had suppressed the rebels in Ghent, went on to invade Guelderland, then Duke William of Cleves would demand Henry's assistance under the terms of his treaty obligations. Cromwell was hoping, even at the end of April, that the Cleves alliance would still justify itself, but he could not overlook the fact that his policy abroad and even more his position at home was vulnerable to the drift of events on the continent. The initiative was no longer in his own hands and he knew there was scant room for manoeuvre.

While Henry had in January been briefing Norfolk for his mission to France, Cromwell was once again treating with a delegation of German Lutherans, headed by Ludwig von Baumbach, Councillor of Philip of Hesse, and was discussing affairs once more with Francis Burckhardt, who had come over with Anne of Cleves's entourage. From the lessons of the previous year Cromwell had to put it to them bluntly that a firm political alliance must precede any undertaking on religion, yet they countered by saying that until there was doctrinal concord no alliance was possible. In 1538–9 Cromwell had been in the van of the negotiations for a closer relationship with the German Lutherans, but now these past conversations were an embarrassment to him and he wanted to terminate the fresh round of discussions speedily. Burkhardt found it hard to believe that he had changed his views, but he did not mince his words: as the world stood, he must profess the same belief as his sovereign, even if it cost him his life. They had further talks on 21 January and then the disappointed Germans found a boat home.

More promising were the negotiations for Princess Mary's betrothal to Duke Philip of Bavaria. Well before the marriage treaty for Henry to wed Anne of Cleves had been signed, the proposals for Mary to marry Duke William of Cleves had foundered, but Henry was still, with Cromwell's encouragement, looking to Germany for a husband for her, though he was fully prepared to extend the search beyond the Protestant camp. Towards the end of 1539 the name of Duke Philip of Bavaria had cropped up: he was a member of the house of Wittelsbach who had fought loyally for Charles v, being wounded at Laufen, but since then had been at odds with the Emperor. Charles had refused to compensate him for the serious financial losses incurred in his service and had blocked his attempt to marry Christina, Duchess of Milan. Perhaps it was this that gave Henry some fellow-feeling towards him. In religion Philip appeared an orthodox Catholic, yet he was certainly no militant papalist. Delighted at the rich prospect of marrying into the house of Tudor he had come to England in December 1539 to have an audience with Henry, pay his court to

Mary and negotiate with Cromwell. The minister had by now – as his firmness to the Lutheran envoys showed – seen the impossibility of establishing for the present any doctrinal *rapport* with the continental Protestants that would satisfy the King; so keeping to the basis of a political alliance he looked to Catholic Bavaria to balance Protestant Cleves. Though at first Philip jibbed at having to take Mary as a bastard, thus acknowledging that she had no place in the English succession, and though he was also uneasy about the possibility of having to take up arms against the Pope, he finally gave way and accepted that the Catholic nature of the Six Articles broadly corresponded with his own religious position. A marriage treaty was signed on 24 January 1540, which would not however come into force until the following Whitsun, by which time he was to have the document fully ratified by his Wittelsbach relatives. In the event nothing came of the affair and its significance lies in the fact that Cromwell under Henry's firm lead was moving so far away from dalliance with the Lutherans.

The ambassadors from Saxony had reported to the Diet of Schmalkalde that Cromwell was the effective king of England and it was he who was preventing the Act of Six Articles from being executed in all its horror, as Dr Robert Barnes had assured the Lutherans would be the case. The French ambassador Marillac, who was much more astute than the German envoys, knew that tremendous pressure was being exerted by the Norfolk–Gardiner faction (with which he was intimate) to dislodge the Lord Privy Seal. 'If he remains in his former credit and authority,' wrote the Frenchman on 10 April, 'it will only be because he is very assiduous in affairs . . . and does nothing without consulting the King.' During Lent Barnes played into the hands of the conservatives and made Cromwell truly vulnerable. Thinking himself immune from attack – with Anne of Cleves in Whitehall as his patron and Stephen Gardiner temporarily excluded from the Council – Robert Barnes decided to speak his mind 'for the sake of the Gospel'. He contrived to be selected by Cranmer to deliver the first of the series of Lenten sermons at Paul's Cross – the most influential pulpit in London – from which he intended to fly his particular theological kite. As soon as Bishop Gardiner discovered that Barnes was to preach he had his own name substituted and in his sermon made a most virulent attack on the ex-Augustinian friar who had drunk so freely of the waters of reformist doctrine. 'The devil is not yet gone, for men who no longer wear friars' habit offer heaven without works', so that a man 'might live in his pleasure and get heaven at the last'. The Bishop had a personal score to settle here, for it had been his criticism of the appointment of Barnes to an embassy that had provoked his removal from the Privy Council. Two Sundays later Barnes made his reply at Paul's Cross, with his own jibes at My Lord of Winchester. This was theological controversy at its most unseemly.

When Gardiner complained to the King, Henry, as mediator, summoned the two of them to court so they might 'reach concord in truth' – a role that, as supreme head of the Church, he took on as a pleasurable duty. Barnes, overawed by the scene in the Privy Chamber, submitted, but the King reproved him and led him across to the altar, which stood in the room, to genuflect before the reserved host and to say to the turbulent doctor, 'Submit not to me; I am a mortal man, but yonder is the maker of us all, the author of truth.' He ordered Barnes and Gardiner to discuss their differences in the presence of witnesses – after two days the former implored the Bishop to instruct him and gladly accepted the offer of a pension from him. This new-found amity was of short duration for Barnes found Gardiner's company too burdensome; whereupon the King required the doctor and two of his fellow Lutherans, Gerard and Jerome, to recant their heresies publicly. This they did, but almost at once withdrew their recantations and were sent to the Tower. Henry's close interest in the case and the Bishop of Winchester's victory were for Cromwell alarming developments. London was full of rumours about further arrests and about Cromwell's eagerness to counter-attack, yet he knew better than to risk intervening to save Barnes.

That Gardiner had the ear of the King in ecclesiastical appointments at this time is clear from the election of Nicholas Heath, the King's almoner and an unbending churchman, to the see of Rochester on 26 March, which Cromwell had kept vacant for seven months. The enthronement of Edmund Bonner in St Paul's Cathedral a week later was also something of a rally for the conservative bishops.

Norfolk's return from his embassy in France during the first half of March had already stiffened Gardiner's resolve to attack Cromwell's position by aiming at Barnes. While at the French court the Duke had discussed Cromwell with Francis i, who had for long regarded him as the stumbling block to good relations, and there are signs that he led Norfolk to believe that if the minister were removed the way would be open to a treaty of amity. Cromwell was suspicious of the Duke's show of friendliness towards him and was soon trying to get him away from court. Neither could forget their quarrel, which had been simmering for so long and had then boiled over, as we have seen, in Cranmer's presence in June 1539; after that incident there was scant chance of understanding between the two, and it is too mild a comment of Burnet's that they 'were never afterwards hearty friends'.

Cromwell heard there was a case of sweating sickness at Kenninghall and now used this as a pretext to have Norfolk exiled from court. The Duke saw through this plan and denied there was any risk of infection to the King or others, since he had not seen the man who was ill for a long time; he demanded to know what Henry's views were and made it plain that if he were to be denied access to the court he would still stay at his house in London and not remove himself to his county. Cromwell did not underestimate the risk to his position from the continued presence of both Norfolk and Gardiner about the King.

On 30 March, the day on which Barnes tore up his recantation, Cromwell tried desperately to achieve some degree of reconciliation with Stephen Gardiner, and he invited him to dinner. He must have known that the King had decided to reinstate the Bishop in the Privy Council. Gardiner was with him at Bermondsey for four hours and it was apparently an amicable dinner, for they 'opened their hearts' to one another and at the end of their conversation (we are told by Sir John Wallop), 'not only all displeasures be forgotten, but also in their hearts be now perfect, entire friends'. It may be that Cromwell brought himself to make some form of apology about his earlier support of Barnes, but it is more likely that the Bishop admitted that he had been harsh in pursuing him. At any rate a compromise was achieved. Apart from the fate of the ex-friar, Cromwell must have been satisfied that Gardiner, if not openly an ally, was not in a position to be an effective enemy. For his part the Bishop recognized that the attempt to undermine Cromwell's position through the Barnes affair had misfired. Before long he expected to be offered a better opportunity and he was prepared to wait for it. What he and Norfolk wanted was a cast-iron case against the Lord Privy Seal that would not merely lead to his removal from office but ensure his attainder. As men seeking power they were perhaps haunted by the memory of 1529–30, when for months the possibility of a pardoned Wolsey being restored to office seemed very real. Alexander Alesius heard the rumours and reported to his friends in alarm: 'In England Satan begins to rage and storm. . . . It is forbidden to bring in the books of Luther or Philip [Melanchthon].' Another in Protestant Germany understood that 330 preachers had been put in chains in London.

Just before Parliament assembled Cromwell arranged for two men on whom he was sure he could rely, Sadler and Wriothesley, to succeed him in the secretaryship, which he now laid down. In retrospect it was probably fair to rate the burden of routine work he had been bearing as Principal Secretary as enough for two ordinary administrators, yet what counted in 1540 was the fact that he could now command two firm votes in Council, where he had neglected to build up a personal following. The French ambassador, Marillac, who had been listening too exclusively to Norfolk's wishful thinking, judged that there would be great changes within a day or so, with Cromwell being forced to relinquish much more than the secretaryship. He expected Clerk, Bishop of Bath, to become Lord Privy Seal and Tunstall of Durham to be vicegerent; Cromwell and Cranmer, he said, 'do not know where they are'.

Cromwell had taken great care in preparing his speech for the opening of the Parliamentary session on 12 April. Parliament was his forum and he the most adept manager of its affairs. The reassembly at this moment was a heaven-sent opportunity for him to reassert himself; by securing an easy passage of the Subsidy Bill and the other measures on which the King's heart was fixed he could show him what an indispensable servant he remained. Any hopes of his enemies that the session might open (as in 1529) with a Bill denouncing him were quickly dashed. Immediately after Lord Chancellor Audley's short address on the theme of amity and concord Cromwell made his plea, in the King's name, for a *via media* in religion, a mean hallowed by scripture:

The King's Majesty, knowing that concord is the only sure and true bond of security in the commonwealth, knowing that if the head and all the members of the body corporate agree in one, there will be wanting nothing to the perfect health of the state, has therefore sought, prized, and desired concord beyond all other things. With no little distress, therefore, he learns that there are certain persons who make it their business to create strife and controversy; that in the midst of the good seed tares also are growing up to choke the harvest. The rashness and carnal licence of some, the inveterate corruption and obstinate superstition of others, have caused disputes which have done hurt to the souls of pious Christians. The names of Papist and heretic are bandied to and fro. The Holy Word of God, which His Highness, of his great clemency, has permitted to be read in the vulgar tongue, for the comfort and edification of his people – this treasure of all sacred things – is abused, and made a servant of error or idolatory; and such is the tumult of opinion, that his Highness ill knows how to bear it. His purpose is to shew no favour to extremes on either side. He professes the sincere faith of the Gospel, as becomes a Christian prince, declining neither to the right hand nor to the left, but setting before his eyes the pure Word of God, as his only mark and guide. On this Word his princely mind is fixed; on this Word he depends for his sole support; and with all his might his Majesty will labour that error shall be taken away, and true doctrines be taught to his people, modelled by the rule of the Gospel. Of forms, ceremonies, and traditions he will have the reasonable use distinguished from the foolish and idolatrous use. He will have all impiety, all superstition, abolished and put away. And, finally, he will have his subjects cease from their irreverent handling of God's book. Those who have offended against the faith and the laws shall suffer the punishment by the laws appointed; and his first and last prayer is for the prevailing of Christ – the prevailing of the Word of Christ – the prevailing of the truth.

Cromwell's hearers needed no telling that the unseemly wrangling at Paul's Cross had degraded theological debate, undermined authority and confused the laity and he took it for granted that sensible men would want the King to steer a middle course between the extremes of Gardiner and Barnes. Though in his capacity as vicegerent Cromwell doubtless emphasized the scriptural basis of religion rather more than Henry would have done, the ideal of a golden mean for the national Church expressed what was in the King's mind; five years later he would himself dwell on this theme. Two committees of divines were to be appointed, one to state the authoritative position on doctrine, the other that on ceremonies, and they were in effect to review the contents of *The Bishops' Book* of 1537, which lacked explicit royal authority and was not free from ambiguities, quite apart from the fact that the Six Articles had rendered part of it out of date. These two committees, Cromwell said, would not 'lack His Majesty's voice and his true and accurate judgement'. By their appointment he had skilfully succeeded in preventing both Houses of Parliament from embarking on far-ranging debates that would merely have intensified divisions. It is worth noticing however that in the doctrinal committee the conservatives, headed by Gardiner, outnumbered the reformists by three to one, for Cranmer was supported only by Barlow and Cox.

Having moved the religious question out of the political arena, Cromwell proceeded with the main business of the session – the confiscation of the possessions of the Knights of St John and the voting of four-fifteenths and two-tenths in lay subsidies. He seemed now as firmly in the saddle as ever and, clear confirmation of his stature as one in whom the King was well pleased, on the fifth day of the session he was created Earl of Essex and the following day was appointed to the high office of Lord Great Chamberlain. Power seemed as much out of Norfolk's grasp as ever and Francis I thought the new Earl 'was in as much credit with the King as ever he was, from which he was near being shaken by the Bishop of Winchester and others'. Ironically Cromwell was kept in London by Parliamentary business, working his usual long hours, while Norfolk and Gardiner were frequently with the King at Greenwich and saw to it that Catherine Howard was often in his company.

During the Whitsun recess Cromwell became aware there were fresh schemings afoot to topple him, and he now lashed out in all directions like a cornered animal. Lord Lisle, hitherto thought an ally, was brought home under arrest from Calais on the charge of alleged dealings with Cardinal Pole. Next it was the turn of Sampson, Bishop of Chichester, who was a henchman of Gardiner, and with him was arrested Nicholas Wilson, Dean of the chapel royal; they were taken while at service in Westminster Abbey and sent to the Tower. Marillac, writing on 1 June, understood that others on whom Cromwell had his eye, would follow them.

We may presume them to be those who lately shook Cromwell's credit and brought him nearly to his ruin. However that be, things are now at a pass when either Cromwell's party or the Bishop of Winchester's party must fall; and although they are both high in favour and authority with the King their master, fortune will most probably turn in favour of Cromwell.

For an envoy who usually followed Norfolk's opinions this is an interesting prediction; at that late date Cromwell *still* retained the

King's confidence. There were also rumours afoot that Robert Barnes was to be released from the Tower and Latimer from house arrest. Tunstall of Durham was certainly under heavy suspicion, but he vehemently denied that he had advised Bishop Sampson to make a stand for the ancient liberties of the Church. Cromwell introduced a Bill declaring as traitors three priests who had served Catherine of Aragon and refused the oath of supremacy, a fourth who had sided with Aske in the Pilgrimage of Grace, and a woman who would not acknowledge Edward to be the heir to the throne. All five were summarily executed without trial.

By now Henry had determined upon a divorce from Anne of Cleves and had turned, of course, to Cromwell to effect it: the man who had promoted the match, he argued, must find the means of untying the knot, as he had with Catherine of Aragon and Anne Boleyn; he would find no technical difficulties such as he had encountered with the Great Matter, and since the King had never consummated his fourth marriage the process should in his view be remarkably simple. But Cromwell saw the terrible logic of the situation, for once free to marry again Henry would choose as his bride the beautiful and orthodox Catherine Howard, the niece of Norfolk who would displace him. (It was as if Wolsey *had* been able to secure Henry's divorce from Catherine of Aragon only to put the relatives of Anne Boleyn, who were his sworn enemies, into power.) Much more than Howard dynastic ambitions and the prize of power were at stake, for young Catherine would be the saviour of conservative theology, just as Anne Boleyn had been the handmaiden of Protestantism.

Sir Thomas Wriothesley called at Cromwell's house in Bermondsey one evening early in June to find his master disconsolate, alone in the gallery. Cromwell asked him if there were any news from abroad and, when told there was none, said: 'There is something that troubles me. The King loves not the Queen, nor even has from the beginning insomuch as I think assuredly she is yet as good a maid for him as she was when she came to England.' Wriothesley lamented the King's trouble and then said to Cromwell: 'For God's sake, devise how His Grace may be relieved by one way or the other.' 'Yes,' answered Cromwell, 'but what, and how?' They both pondered the problem in silence until the Lord Privy Seal sighed: 'Well, well, it is a great matter,' and they parted. Next evening Wriothesley returned to the charge, imploring Cromwell to effect what Henry required, 'for if he remain in this grief and trouble, we shall all one day smart for it. If His Grace be quiet, we shall all have our parts with him.' Cromwell agreed, but could only repeat 'It is a great matter,' for he saw his policy in ruins, his vision of a Christian commonwealth fading and his power crumbling.

The parallel with Wolsey's fall is striking. In 1540, as in 1529, the chief minister of the crown discovered too late that his policies had embarrassed the King's matrimonial affairs and harmed England's foreign relations, that he was regarded in the country at large as a tyrant and was vehemently hated by his colleagues in Council for his monopoly of power. There the immediate parallel ends, for Cromwell was not to be put out to grass like the Cardinal after proceedings in the courts, but speedily attainted in Parliament and sent to Tyburn.

It all happened very quickly. On 10 June Cromwell was as usual at the House of Lords in the morning and after dinner attended the Council meeting in Westminster Palace where, without warning, Norfolk stood up to denounce him. 'My Lord of Essex, I arrest you of high treason.' The lieutenant of the Tower was at the door with a royal warrant and a posse of guards; there was to be no possibility of a personal appeal to the King, so he was utterly defenceless and knew the dread consequences. His enemies who had tried so often to ensnare him had triumphed, for this was not just another episode in political manoeuvring, but the final act. In his fury Cromwell threw his cap of maintenance on the floor and (as Marillac has it) said to the Duke and the others:

This, then, is my guerdon for the service that I have done. On your consciences I ask you, am I a traitor? I may have offended, but never with my will. Such faults as I have committed deserve grace and pardon; but if the King, my master, believes so ill of me, let him make quick work and not leave me to languish in prison.

Some in the room merely shouted 'traitor', others that he should be tried by his own treason law. Howard of Norfolk reproached him for his villainies and with relish tore off the St George he wore round his neck. Lord Admiral Fitzwilliam, once his friend, then snatched at the order of the garter. To their satisfaction the upstart had been degraded. He was bundled down a staircase that led to the water's edge, put in a barge and taken to the Tower.

As yet few outside the Council knew the grounds of his alleged treason, but tales were circulated that he had hoped to be a king himself one day and the implausible remark he was supposed to have made to Chapuys was passed on: 'I know the Emperor will go to Constantinople and will give me a Kingdom.' At court the gossip that had started on the continent two years back was dredged up, crediting Cromwell with plans to marry Princess Mary and have himself proclaimed heir to the throne. In his rage Henry now wrote to Wallopp in Paris to see if he could obtain any confirmation of that bizarre report. On the day of the arrest Henry sent a message to Marillac so that he should know the truth and not be misled by common rumours. As King he had been attempting 'by all possible means to lead back religion to the way of truth', yet Cromwell being 'attached to the German Lutherans, had always favoured the doctors who pretended such erroneous opinions and hindered those who preached the contrary . . .'. Warned by some of his principal servants that the minister was 'working against the intention of the King's Acts of Parliament, he had betrayed himself and said he hoped to suppress the old preachers and to have only the new'. His party would soon have been so strong that he could have forced the King to bow to the wishes of Lutherans and heretics, and to achieve this Cromwell was, said Henry, prepared to take up arms against him.

No man was more shocked at the *coup* than Archbishop Cranmer and with exemplary courage he wrote at once to Henry to intercede for his friend.

Who cannot be sorrowful and amazed that he should be a traitor against Your Majesty – he whose surety was only by Your Majesty – he who loved Your Majesty, (as I ever thought), no less than God – he who studied always to set forward whatsoever was Your Majesty's will and pleasure – he that cared for no man's displeasure to serve Your Majesty – he that was such a servant (in my judgement) in wisdom, diligence, faithfulness and experience as no prince in this realm ever had. . . . I loved him as my friend, for so I took him to be; but I chiefly loved him for the love which I thought I saw him bear ever towards Your Grace, singularly above all other.

If the Earl of Essex was a traitor, the Archbishop was sorry he ever loved or trusted him, though he rejoiced that the treason was discovered in time. Yet he wrote with a most heavy heart: 'For who shall Your Grace trust hereafter, if you might not trust him? Alas, I bewail and lament Your Grace's chance herein, I wot not whom Your Grace may trust.' Henry was unmoved, for he had been stunned by the accusations of treasonable heresy.

A week after his arrest a Bill of Attainder was brought in; the minister who had made the King in Parliament sovereign would be declared to be a traitor in that place and not be required to face a trial. To add to the irony, the Bill opened with a fulsome statement of that royal supremacy which Cromwell had erected, and then deplored the fact that a man of 'very base and low degree', promoted to be the King's most trusty counsellor, had proved a false traitor. The biting allusions to his lowly birth that recur in the document have the flavour of Howard malice. The charges of maladministration and abuse of his power were little more than generalities: 'Full of pride' he had dealt in 'weighty causes' without the King's knowledge and pretended to great power over him, saying *he was sure of him*, a thing which no subject, however high his status, should say of his sovereign.

In the list of charges there are only two items which, if true, would be sufficient for Cromwell's condemnation under his own Treasons Act of 1534. These were first the words allegedly spoken on 31 March 1539, declaring that the teaching of Robert Barnes and others accused of heresy was good and that 'if the King would turn from it, yet I would not turn; and if the King did turn I would fight in the field in mine own person'. Secondly there were the words allegedly spoken nine months later when, taunted about his humble origins, he said that 'if the Lords would handle him so, he would give them such a breakfast as never was made in England, and that the proudest should know'. Both sets of incriminating 'proofs' of treason were produced by his enemies, George Throckmorton and Sir Richard Riche, whose reliability as a witness was open to question. Henry believed the fabrications and could not in such a mood be persuaded to question their truth. No one therefore dared to raise any doubts. Moreover there was circumstantial evidence that fitted – Cromwell's abhorrence of executing the Six Articles in the full vigour that the Act prescribed, his unwearying search for an understanding with the Lutheran princes, the Cleves marriage itself, the reports that Robert Barnes had been before his arrest often in the Queen's company and, finally, the fact that Gerrard, like Barnes in the Tower for heresy, was reputed to be friendly with Cromwell, while Jerome, the third member of the trio, was vicar of Stepney, the Earl's London parish. He had told the Lutheran envoys that 'as the world stood he would believe even as his master the King believed', and yet in his quest for doctrinal truth he had found himself ahead of his master, who now rated him as dangerous an influence as John Lambert whom he had sent for burning at Smithfield.

When he had broken with Rome, Henry had launched on his theological voyage with no clear destination in view; he envisaged a national church it is true, but still forming an integral part of western Christendom and retaining its well-worn system of organization and hierarchy, even if shorn of cardinals. But doctrine, especially the fundamental question of the sacraments, had proved a stumbling block. The reformers, by contrast, knew precisely where they wanted to go in order to achieve a revival of the Christian life, while their conservative opponents, appalled at the loose talk of justification by faith alone and the priesthood of all believers, wanted a Catholic Church, without Pope and Cardinals. Herein lay the King's dilemma. Cromwell's last great speech in Parliament on the golden mean had represented the royal intention probably more succinctly than Henry himself could have expressed it, but Cromwell had now been shown to be diverging far to the left of centre. The King was satisfied that his minister's hobnobbing with Lutherans and befriending Anabaptists had exceeded the requirements of either diplomacy or Christian charity and he was now convinced that he shared their heretical creed. Gardiner had most skilfully manoeuvred Henry into the firm conviction that the Lord Privy Seal was like Lambert 'a Sacramentary', or Anabaptist, far more extreme than a Lutheran. For the King this was as great an enormity as Buckingham's treachery, Wolsey's perfidy, More's self-righteous denial of his authority or Anne Boleyn's outrageous sexual conduct, and Cromwell would have to pay the same penalty that they had done; indeed, it would have been most inexpedient to have relaxed the Six Articles to enable the heretical vicegerent to escape the consequences of the law.

Two letters that Cromwell wrote to Henry from the Tower have survived – the first touching the charges against him in the Bill of Attainder, the second regarding the King's marriage to Anne of Cleves. The pleas for mercy and forgiveness that he had helped Wolsey to draft at Esher were staid and limpid compared with what he now wrote as his own advocate from the Tower: 'written with the quaking hand and a most sorrowful heart of your most sorrowful subject and most humble servant and prisoner'. Should any point of treason be proved, then he deserved to be confounded, he said, by all the devils in hell. 'Sir, as to your Commonwealth, I have after my wit, power and knowledge travailed therein, having no respect to persons (Your Majesty only excepted) and my duty to the same.' But if he had offended he craved mercy. Many false accusations had been levelled against him, but, denied access to his papers, he could not rebut every one. 'Nevertheless, Sir, I have meddled in so many matters under Your Highness, that I am not able to answer them all.' Though he had not wittingly or wilfully offended the King by his actions, it was hard for him, active in so many areas of government, not to have been guilty of technical breaches of the law, for which he sought pardon. He touched on 'a matter of great secrecy' – his conversation with Henry about disliking his Queen, on which he would be required to answer in greater detail – but there is nothing in this letter of 12 June bearing strictly on his religious position. It was taken by Sir Ralph Sadler to Whitehall and the King had it read through to him three times. He 'seemed to be moved therein'.

Norfolk, Lord Chancellor Audley and Lord Admiral Fitzwilliam visited him together to extract detailed statements about the royal marriage and Cromwell's knowledge of its lack of consummation, which was needed for the annulment proceedings. As Henry so succinctly put it in the declaration about his marriage that he himself made to Convocation: 'I doubt not but the Lord of Essex will and can declare what I then said . . . not doubting but (since he is a person which knoweth himself condemned to die by Act of Parliament he will not damn his soul, but truly declare the truth . . .).' Cromwell was not providing the answers the King wanted to save his life. His second letter, written on 30 June, the day after the Bill of Attainder had been passed, set down detailed answers to the questions in good faith, so far as can be judged. He is ready to die, but although he realizes there is no hope of reprieve he still makes his special plea: 'Most gracious Prince, I cry for mercy, mercy, mercy.' This plea was not for a reprieve from the death sentence itself, but from the manner of its execution. He knew better than anyone that a condemned traitor would normally suffer the barbaric sentence of hanging, drawing and quartering, and it was this mutilation he wanted desperately to avoid. His plea was granted and instead of the common hangman he was allowed to face the executioner.

Henry would never have pardoned him, and Cromwell knew it. Although the King had been provided with all he needed for an annulment of his marriage – which was legally brought to an end on 12 July – he had lost all confidence in the minister who had proved, until the last six months, a far more effective and reliable partner than Wolsey had ever been. He could never forgive him because he had had to endure the humiliations of the Cleves marriage, could never again trust someone who was reputed to be an Anabaptist. He was tired of Cromwell, too, and bored with his endless memoranda. Henceforth no one man would hold so great a sway over policy.

Cromwell's speech to those who had come to witness his end at Tyburn on 28 July was printed and circulated by the government as 'A true Christian confession'. No doubt this was an edited version, for it is unlikely that Cromwell would himself have referred to his lowly origins, even under the shadow of death. But the theological content of the speech raises problems for which there are no simple answers. He asked his hearers 'to bear me record, I die in the Catholic Faith, not doubting in any article of my faith, no, nor doubting in any sacrament of the Church'. Was this a piece of propaganda inserted in the authorized text, or did Cromwell speak those words, and if so, did they come from the heart?

Writers who have concluded that Cromwell was a person to whom religion meant very little, or that for him the state was the god to be worshipped, are on weak ground. Throughout he had been intensely interested in religion. A man who had once learnt by heart the whole Latin New Testament of Erasmus, who looked with pride on the steps he had taken to make the bible freely available in English, who had been intimate with divines – not least with Cranmer – was a person fundamentally concerned with the Christian life. Since he became vicegerent in ecclesiastical affairs, it would have been rank hypocrisy had he paid no more than lip service to belief and worship. He was no *dévot*, it is true, and like most statesmen of the century many of his political ideas were grounded and shaped in theological terms. Yet he remained a fervent believer, a 'man of the Gospel', a figure who earned a deserved niche in John Foxe's hagiography. His religious development, so far as there are real clues to it, contains inconsistencies, but in the turmoil of doctrinal controversy that dominated Cromwell's decade the charge of inconsistency was no graver than it had been for St Paul, for Thomas Aquinas or for Martin Luther. The only sure way of holding to a consistent path lay in clinging blindly to the *status quo*, avoiding questioning, rejecting all chance of compromise.

That was not Cromwell's way, any more than it was Cranmer's. He found it hard to stomach Henry's retaining some of the same doctrines on which papal tyranny had been built, now that he had thrown off the yoke of Rome. Despite his evangelical leanings he had recently endeavoured to further the ideal of a middle way, as his speech to Parliament showed, counselling men to avoid unnecessary contentions. There is no incongruity between this central position that he had adopted and his statement about 'dying in the Catholic faith'. His creed expressed belief in that Holy Catholic Church that members of the Anglican Church he helped to found would continue to profess. He was aghast at the charge of heresy, branding him as another Lambert, and he fervently denied that there was any truth in the taint of 'sacramentary' with which Gardiner and others had so successfully besmirched his character. Indeed the very next sentence of the confession reads: 'Many have slandered me and reported that I have been a bearer of such as have maintained evil opinions, which is untrue.' As vicegerent in spiritual affairs of a King who was supreme head of the Church in England he was hurt to the quick. This was not merely untrue, it was a most monstrous lie. Since the chief justification for Cromwell's attainder lay in such slanders being true, the statement would scarcely have been included in his confession if it was a spurious document, or one altered to suit the government.

Edward Hall's *Chronicle* makes it plain that before the axe fell Cromwell spoke a long prayer. A moving prayer, purporting to be his last words, was printed by John Foxe some years afterwards, and who shall say whether or not it is by and large authentic? The hopes of the penitent in the hour of death seeking grace, firmness of faith and absolution as he prepares to meet his maker are framed in the language of one who knew his breviary as well as his bible. If there is nothing here that contravened 'Catholic' doctrine there is, equally, nothing that went against Lutheran teaching. A 'sacramentary' would, however, have found in the prayer much to offend him. He who had sent many to the scaffold for reasons of state, holy men like Fisher, More and the Abbot of Glastonbury as well as sinners like the paramours of Anne Boleyn, came at last to make his final petition: 'Grant me, merciful Saviour, that when death hath shut up the eyes of my body, yet the eyes of my soul may still behold and look upon Thee, and when death hath taken away the use of my tongue, yet my heart may cry and say unto Thee, Lord into Thy hands I commend my soul, Lord Jesus receive my spirit, Amen.'

That same day Henry left Hampton Court to ride to Oatlands, near Weybridge, to be married to Catherine Howard, who was in age, appearance and every other quality a complete contrast to his fourth wife. It was incongruous that when the secret of the marriage was known and Queen Catherine was in a position to make appointments to her own household, she included Prince Edward's aunt – a Seymour who had married Gregory Cromwell in 1537. Two days later, as an inevitable consequence of the scene at Tyburn, Barnes, Gerrard and Jerome were burnt at Smithfield as heretics.

Outwardly the victory of Gardiner and Norfolk seemed to be complete and they believed that the interest of orthodoxy and the position of the conservatives would be amply protected by Henry's passionate love for his new wife, 'a blushing rose without a thorn'. While the royal honeymoon proceeded Duke and Bishop contrived to distribute the offices that Cromwell had amassed over the years, endeavouring to take over much of the immense patronage he had exercised in Church and state. Yet long before Henry suspected Catherine of infidelities he had determined never again to allow a minister to encroach on his royal power. In 1540 he would become his own chief minister, as he had sworn he would do in 1529. After Wolsey's fall he had found that he needed Cromwell's service, but after Cromwell's disgrace no one of the same calibre offered himself. Indeed the problems were far less pressing now that Cromwell had made him master in his own house. Quite soon, as Henry watched Norfolk and Gardiner in action and measured them against the stature of Cromwell in his heyday, he came to regard Thomas Cromwell as 'the best servant he ever had', for he had paid far more attention to his interests than his old master, the Cardinal, had done. Seeing in the new men about him no hint of statesmanlike qualities and despising them for their plans to trap Archbishop Cranmer, the King came to conclude that Cromwell had been condemned 'on light pretexts'. His fall had made it easier to justify to the courts of Europe his parting from Anne of Cleves, but by the time Catherine Howard had gone to the executioner he had come to realize that Cromwell had been unnecessarily sacrificed.

In July 1540 there was much rejoicing at Cromwell's fall, for he was generally regarded as a tyrant and a destructive force. Few friends dared to speak up for his reputation openly and his constructive work went unrecognized until long afterwards. Yet one contemporary who knew his worth set down his feelings in the jewel of a sonnet. 'Gentle Master Wyatt', as Cromwell had so often written to him on public affairs during his service on diplomatic missions, in 1540 at last returned to his native Kent, where he was to enjoy barely two years of retirement before he died. On learning of Cromwell's execution Sir Thomas Wyatt composed this verse of surpassing beauty, which may serve as an epitaph for the statesman:

> The pillar perish'd is whereto I leant;
>> The strongest stay of mine unquiet mind:
>> The like of it, no man again can find,
>> From east to west still seeking though he went.
> To mine unhap; for hap away hath rent
>> Of all my joy the very bark and rind;
>> And I, alas! by chance am thus assign'd
>> Dearly to mourn, till death do it relent.
> But since that thus it is by destiny,
>> What can I more but have a woeful heart;
>> My pen in plaint, my voice in woeful cry,
> My mind in woe, my body full of smart,
>> And I myself, myself always to hate;
>> Till dreadful death do ease my doleful state.

Select Bibliography

I BIBLIOGRAPHIES

Levine, Mortimer, *Bibliographical Handbooks: Tudor England*, 1485–1603 (1968) cites a great many books and articles in periodicals relating to the age of Wolsey and Cromwell. It should, however, be supplemented by Read, Conyers, *Bibliography of British History: Tudor Period* (2nd edn, 1959).

2 RECORD SOURCES

More abstracts of the official correspondence of Henry VIII's reign have been published than for any other period, beginning with the eleven volumes of *State Papers of the Reign of Henry VIII* printed by the State Paper Commission (1830–52), which contains full transcripts of selected letters. *The Calendar of Letters and Papers, Foreign and Domestic, Henry VIII* (37 vols, 1864–1932) was an elaborate scheme for placing entries from the State Papers alongside abstracts from other selected classes of public records, materials in the British Museum's manuscript collections and transcripts from archives in foreign capitals and in the Vatican. Though the abstracts in this *Calendar* are a marvellous guide to the wealth of original material they cannot serve as a substitute for the documents. Supplementing the *Letters and Papers* are the separate series of Calendars of the Spanish, Imperial and Venetian ambassadors, culled from Vienna, Brussels, Simancas and Venice. The *Calendar of State Papers, Spain*, 1509–47, comprises fourteen volumes (1866–1947) and the *Calendar of State Papers, Venice* for the same period four volumes (1867–73). Selected documents with commentaries appear in *English Historical Documents* vol. v ed. C. H. Williams (1967) and in G. R. Elton, *The Tudor Constitution* (1964).

3 CONTEMPORARY CHRONICLES

Hall, Edward, *The Union of the Two Noble and Illustre Famelies York and Lancaster* (ed. H. Ellis, 1809; also ed. C. Whibley, 1934).

Holinshed, Raphael, *Chronicles* (ed. Ellis 1808).

Vergil, Polydore, *Anglica Historia* (ed. Denys Hay with trans., Camden Society 4th series, vol. 74, 1950).

Wriothesley, Charles, *A Chronicle of England*, 1485–1559 (ed. W. D. Hamilton, Camden Society, new series, vols 11, 12, 1875–7).

4 OTHER PRIMARY WORKS

Barclay, Alexander, *The Eclogues . . . from the original edition by John Cawood* (ed. Beatrice White, Early English Text Society, 1928).

Brown, Rawdon, *Four Years at the Court of King Henry VIII. Selections from the despatches written by the Venetian ambassador, Sebastian Giustinian*, 2 vols, 1854).

Cavendish, George, *The Life and Death of Cardinal Wolsey* (ed. Sylvester, R. S., Early English Text Society, 1959).

Collections of Ordinances and Regulations for the Government of the Royal Household (Society of Antiquaries, 1790).

Ellis, Henry (ed.), *Original Letters Illustrative of English History*, 3rd ser. (11 vols, 1824–46).

Fox, Richard, The Letters of (ed. Allen, P. S. and H. M., 1929).

Foxe, John, *Acts and Monuments* (ed. Pratt, 8 vols, 1874).

Giustinian, S. *See under* Brown, Rawdon.

Hughes, Paul L. and Larkin, James F. (ed.) *Tudor Royal Proclamations*, vol. 1 1485–1553 (New Haven, 1964).

Leadam, I. S. (ed.), *The Domesday of Inclosures* (Royal Hist. Soc., 2 vols, 1897).

Nott, G. F. (ed.), *Works of Henry Howard and Sir Thomas Wyatt* (2 vols, 1815).

Roper, William, *The Life of Sir Thomas More* (ed. Hitchcock, Early English Text Society, 1935).

Skelton, John, *Poetical Works* (ed. Alexander Dyce, 1843).

Strype, John, *Ecclesiastical Memorials* (3 vols, 1820–40).

5 SECONDARY WORKS

A lengthy list has been pruned to fifty titles –

Allen, J. W., *History of Political Thought in the Sixteenth Century* (1928).

Anglo, S., *Spectale Pageantry, and Early Tudor Policy* (1969).

Baskerville, G., *English Monks and the Suppression of the Monasteries* (1937).

Baumer, F. le van, *The Early Tudor Theory of Kingship* (New Haven, 1940).

Burnet, Gilbert, *History of the Reformation of the Church of England* (ed. Pocock, 7 vols, 1865).

Chambers, R. W., *Thomas More* (1935).

Chrimes, S. B., *Henry VII* (1972).

Dickens, A. G., *The English Reformation* (1964).

—, *Thomas Cromwell and the English Reformation* (1959).

Dodds, M. H. and Ruth, *The Pilgrimage of Grace,* 1536–7 *and the Exeter Conspiracy,* 1539 (2 vols, 1915).

Doernberg, E., *Henry VIII and Luther* (1961).

Elton, G. R., *Policy and Police: the Enforcement of the Reformation in the Age of Thomas Cromwell* (1972).

—, *Reform and Renewal: Thomas Cromwell and the Common Weal* (1973).

—, *The Tudor Revolution in Government* (1953).

Ferguson, C., *Naked to Mine Enemies: the Rise and Fall of Cardinal Wolsey* (1958).

Fiddes, R., *The Life of Cardinal Wolsey* (1724).

Fisher, H. A. L., *The Political History of England from the Accession of Henry VII to the Death of Henry VIII* (1912).

Friedmann, Paul, *Anne Boleyn; a Chapter of English History,* 1527–36 (2 vols, 1884).

Gordon, I. A., *John Skelton, Poet Laureate* (1944).

Hughes, Philip, *The Reformation in England, vol.* 1; *The King's Proceedings* (1954).

Jones, W. R. O., *The Tudor Commonwealth,* 1529–59 (1970).

Knowles, M. D., *The Religious Orders in England,* vol. 3 *The Tudor Age* (1959).

Law, E., *England's First Great War Minister* (1916).

Lehmberg, S. E., *The Reformation Parliament* (1970).

McConica, J. K., *English Humanists and Reformation Politics under Henry VIII and Edward VI* (1965).

Mackie, J. D., *The Early Tudors,* 1485–1558 (1952).

Mattingly, Garrett, *Catherine of Aragon* (1942).

—, *Renaissance Diplomacy* (1955).

Merriman, R. B., *The Life and Letters of Thomas Cromwell* (2 vols, 1902).

Mozley, J. F., *William Tyndale* (1937).

Muller, J. A., *Stephen Gardiner and the Tudor Reaction* (1926).

Newton, A. P. *See under* Seton-Watson, R. W.

Parker, T. M., *The English Reformation to* 1558 (1950).

Parmiter, G. de C., *The King's Great Matter* (1969).

Paul, J. E., *Catherine of Aragon and her Friends* (1966).

Pollard, A. F., *Henry VIII* (1905).

—, *Wolsey* (1929).

Powicke, F. M., *The Reformation in England* (1941).

Reynolds, E. E., *St John Fisher* (1955).

Ridley, Jasper, *Thomas Cranmer* (1962).

Richardson, W. C., *Tudor Chamber Administration*, 1485–1547 (1952).

Rupp, E. G., *Studies in the Making of the English Protestant Tradition* (1947).

Russell, Joycelyne G., *The Field of Cloth of Gold* (1969).

Scarisbrick, J. J., *Henry VIII* (1968).

Seton-Watson, R. W. (ed.), *Tudor Studies* (1924) containing in particular A. P. Newton's essay on 'Tudor Reforms in the Royal Household'.

Slavin, A. J., *Thomas Cromwell on Church and Commonwealth* (1969).

Smith, H. Maynard, *Henry VIII and the Reformation* (1948).

Wegg, Jervis, *Richard Pace* (1932).

Wernham, R. B., *Before the Armada: the Growth of English Foreign Policy*, 1485–1588 (1966).

Zeeveld, W. G., *Foundations of Tudor Policy* (Cambridge, Mass., 1948).

6 ARTICLES IN JOURNALS, ETC.

Bowker, Margaret, 'The Commons Supplication Against the Ordinaries in the Light of Some Archdiaconal Acta' in *Trans. Royal Hist. Soc.*, 5th ser., vol. 21 (1971).

Chambers, D. S., 'Cardinal Wolsey and the Papal Tiara' in *Bull. Inst. Hist. Res.*, vol. 35 (1967).

Cooper, J. P., 'The Supplication Against the Ordinaries Reconsidered' in *Eng. Hist. Rev.*, vol. 72 (1957).

Elton, G. R., 'The Commons Supplication of 1532: Parliamentary Manoevres in the Reign of Henry VIII' in *ibid.*, vol. 66 (1951).

—, 'The Evolution of a Reformation Statute' in *ibid.*, vol. 64 (1949).

—, 'Henry VIII's Act of Proclamations' in *ibid.*, vol. 75 (1960).

—, 'Thomas Cromwell's Decline and Fall' in *Cambs. Hist. Jl.*, vol. 10 (1951).

—, 'Parliamentary Drafts, 1529–40' in *Bull. Inst. Hist. Res.*, vol. 25 (1952).

—, 'Sir Thomas More and the Opposition to Henry VIII' in *ibid.*, vol. 41 (1967).

—, 'King or Minister? The man behind the Henrician Reformation' in *History*, vol. 39 (1954).

—, 'The Political Creed of Thomas Cromwell' in *Trans. Royal Hist. Soc.*, 5th ser., vol. 6 (1956).

—, 'Reform by Statute; Thomas Starkey's Dialogue and Thomas Cromwell's Policy' in *Proc. Brit. Acad.*, vol. 54 (1968).*

* These nine articles, together with other essays relevant to the study of Wolsey and of Cromwell have been reprinted in *Studies in Tudor and Stuart Politics and Government* (2 vols, 1974).

Harris, G. I. and Williams, P., 'A Revolution in Tudor History?' in *Past and Present*, vol. 25 (1963).

Hurstfield, J., 'Was there a Tudor Despotism after all?' in *Trans. Royal Hist. Soc.*, 5th ser., vol. 17 (1967).

Kelly, M., 'The Submission of the Clergy' in *ibid.*, vol. 15 (1965).

Lehmberg, S. E., 'Early Tudor Parliamentary Procedures' in *Eng. Hist. Rev.*, vol. 85 (1970).

Miller, Helen, 'London and Parliament in the reign of Henry VIII' in *Bull. Inst. Hist. Res.*, vol. 35 (1962).

Parker, T. M., 'Was Cromwell a Machiavellian?' in *Jl. Eccles. Hist.*, vol. 1 (1956).

Pollard, A. F., 'Thomas Cromwell's Parliamentary Lists' in *Bull. Inst. Hist. Res.*, vol. 11 (1931–2).

Scarisbrick, J. J., 'The Pardon of the Clergy, 1531' in *Cambs Hist. Jl.*, vol. 12 (1956).

Index

Adrian VI, Pope 45
Agnadello, battle of 13
Agostini, Agostino 63, 132, 136, 137
Aldrich, Robert, Bishop of Carlisle 237
Alesius, Alexander 214, 252
Alva, Duke of 14, 39
Amicable Loan, The 51, 101
Ammonio, Andrea 76
Angus, Archibald, Earl of 108
Anne of Brittany, Queen of France 17, 108
Anne of Cleves, Queen 241–7, 255
Anti-Clericalism: 96; anti-Roman feeling 102–4; Suffolk's anger 121; Wolsey's contribution to 141; supplication against the ordinaries 155, 165–7, 211; Act of Augmentations 194–6; Cromwell's 224–5
Arches, Court of 193; Dean of 120
Aske, Robert 198, 199, 200
Audley, Thomas, Lord Audley, Speaker and Lord Chancellor 164, 166–8, 178, 183, 188, 189, 223, 230, 233, 237, 252, 260
Augmentations, Court of 196–7, 207

Bainbridge, Christopher, Cardinal, Archbishop of York 19, 20, 54
Barcelona, Treaty of 120
Barclay, Alexander 71–2, 91
Barlow, Jerome 72
Barnes, Robert 74–5, 228, 230, 249, 250, 253, 255, 263
Barton, Elizabeth, The Nun of Kent 180, 181

Baumbach, Ludwig von 230, 248
Bayard, Chevalier de 5, 16
Beaufort, Margaret, Countess of Richmond and Derby 11, 19, 66, 197
Bell, John 110
du Bellay, French Ambassador 122, 125, 126
Bennet, William 120, 162, 163
Berthelet, Thomas, King's Printer 221
Bettes, James 54
Bible, the Great 220–2
Bishops' Book, The 214–16, 253
Blount, Elizabeth 65
Blyth, Geoffrey, Bishop of Coventry and Lichfield 103
Blythe, John, Bishop of Salisbury 7
Board of Green Cloth 209–10
Boleyn, Anne, Queen 107, 108, 109, 110; hatred of Wolsey 112, 113, 118, 158; turns Henry against Wolsey 123–4; sends a favour to Wolsey 132, 133; demands lawful marriage 174; created Marquess of Pembroke 176; secretly married 176; crowned 179; birth of Elizabeth 185–6; has miscarriage 186; arrested 187; executed 188
Boleyn, George, Lord Rochford 157, 162, 187
Boleyn, Sir Thomas, Lord Rochford, Earl of Wiltshire 92, 101, 112, 113, 122, 129, 132, 140, 156, 183, 188
Bologna, siege of 13
Bonner, Edmund, Bishop of London 247, 250
Boston, Lincs 144–5

Boyneburg, George 229

Brandon, Charles, Duke of Suffolk 16, 18, 19, 26, 27, 38, 95, 96, 109, 112, 121, 122, 126–7, 129, 183, 188, 230, 239

Brereton, William 187

Browne, Sir Anthony 208, 239, 244, 246

Browne, Lady 246

Bryan, Sir Francis 86, 117, 118

Buckingham, Duke of cf. Stafford

Burckhardt, Francis, Vice-Chancellor of Saxony 229, 230, 248

Butts, Sir William 132, 246

Cambrai, League of 13

Cambrai, Treaty of 120

Cambridge University 18, 74, 197, 213, 226; Trinity College 226; Trinity Hall 64

Campeggio, Lorenzo, Cardinal 29, 34, 46, 102, 108, 114, 115, 116, 117, 118, 119–25, 179

Canterbury Cathedral 39

Capua, Archbishop of 120

Carew, Sir Nicholas 86, 208, 227

Carne, Sir Edward 162, 163

Casale, Sir Gregory 114, 118

Catherine of Aragon, Queen 14, 15; Henry contemplates divorce of 17; friend of Buckingham 95; gives birth to still-born child 95; divorce 105–120; hatred of Wolsey 105; child-bearing 107; asked to enter a nunnery 116; produces papal dispensation 117; protests against divorce 119; Wolsey's concern for 135; reduced to dowager Princess of Wales 168; divorced 179; death 186

Cavendish, George, biographer of Wolsey, cf. The Life and Death of Cardinal Wolsey 59, 124, 138, 139, 140

Cawood Palace 57, 134

Chancery, Court of 80, 82, 129, 130, 204

Chapuys, Eustace, Imperial Ambassador 122, 125, 135, 136, 143, 151, 156, 160, 163, 164, 167–8, 180, 186, 190–1, 257

Charles v, Emperor 17, 18, 31–3, 35, 37, 39, 42, 44, 45, 47, 48, 50, 51, 110, 112, 162, 174, 207, 232, 241, 247, 248

Chieregeto, Francisco 53

Christina, Duchess of Milan 241–2, 248

Clansey, Dorothy and John 65

Clare, Lady 149

Claude, Queen of France 26, 27

Clement vii, Pope 32, 44, 45–7, 51, 102, 109, 110–20, 137, 162, 174

Clerk, John, Bishop of Bath and Wells 34, 44, 45, 46, 82, 112, 115, 120, 217, 237, 239, 252

Cognac, League of 51

Colchester, Abbot of 202, 225

Colet, John, Dean of St Paul's 6, 19, 22, 134

Colonna, Cardinal 46

Convocation 97, 100, 163–4, 211–12, 214, 217, 219

Cook, Hugh, Abbot of Reading 202, 225

Cook, Humphrey 56

Council, The King's 12, 14, 82, 134, 135, 136, 256–7

Courtenay, Henry, Marquess of Exeter and Earl of Devon 90, 112, 225–6, 227

Coverdale, Miles 218–20

Coxford, Prior of 197

Cranmer, Thomas, Archbishop of Canterbury 113, 143, 162, 175, 179, 186, 189, 195, 212, 214, 215–16, 219, 220, 229, 230–2, 237, 238, 239, 243, 252, 254, 257, 261

Creke, John 147

Cromwell, Elizabeth 188

Cromwell, Gregory 149, 188, 243

Cromwell, Katherine 142

Cromwell, Richard, alias Williams 142, 198

Cromwell, Thomas: birth and early years 142–3; Life: opposes French conquest 98; as a soldier 143–4; as merchant 144; enters Wolsey's service 146; enters Parliament 146; enters Gray's Inn 147–8; employed in Dissolution 148–9; financial practices 149; elected MP for Taunton 153;

seeks employment with the king 153–4; as Wolsey's solicitor 130; loyal support for Wolsey 132–3, 151–5; finds money for Wolsey 134; cautions Wolsey 135; enters King's service 155–6; the Tyndale Affair 161; becomes Chancellor of Exchequer 168; Principal Secretary 169; becomes Master of the Rolls 171; becomes Lord Privy Seal 171, 188–9; becomes Lord Great Chamberlain 171, 254; break with Rome 103, 175; Act in Restraint of Appeals 175–8; achieves divorce for Henry 179; More's execution 181; as Vicar-general 142, 193; trial of Anne Boleyn 186–8; reconciles King and Princess Mary 190–1; dissolution 191–8; at Cambridge 197–8; Lincolnshire and Yorkshire revolts 198–200; national security 200–2; legal reforms 204–6; revolution in government 206–10; translation of the Bible 217–22; arranges King's marriage with Anne of Cleves 241–5; parliamentary address 252–3; created Earl of Essex 254; created Lord Great Chamberlain 254; divorce of Anne of Cleves 255–6; arrest 256; death 261. Characteristics: appearance 180–1; attitude to clergy 224–5; health and pastimes 172–3; reactions to Wolsey's death 159; relations with Wolsey 154–5; religious views 143, 150, 259–262. Letters to: Bergen-op-Zoom 218; Crete 147; Gardiner 171, 187–8, 191, 235; Henry VIII 230, 259–60; Archbishop of Palermo 218; Wolsey 145, 148–9, 158–9; Wyatt 171, 227–8; From: Cranmer 219, 229; Hutton 241; Latimer 216; Princess Mary 190; Mont 242; Russell 157; Vaughan 155–156, 172; Wolsey 158–9; Wootton 242–3

Cromwell, Walter 142, 143

Dalby, Thomas, Archdeacon of Richmond 19
Darcy, Thomas, Lord 129, 200

Daundy, Edmund 6
Deane, Henry, Archbishop of Canterbury 8, 9
Denny, Sir Anthony 235
Derby, Earls of *cf.* Stanley
Dorset, Marquess of *cf.* Grey
Dudley, Edmund 11

Edgecumbe, Lady 246
Eltham Ordinance, The 89, 208
Empson, Richard 11
Erasmus, Desiderius 19, 22, 24, 28, 29, 42, 65, 66, 145, 261
Étaples, Treaty of 18
Exeter, 1st Marquess of *cf.* Courtenay

Ferdinand of Aragon 14, 17, 64
Field of Cloth of Gold, the 36–43
Fish, Simon 75, 195
Fisher, John, Cardinal, Bishop of Rochester 18, 38, 42, 110, 119, 179, 180, 183, 184
Fitzjames, Richard, Bishop of London 19, 103, 110
Fitzroy, Henry, 1st Duke of Richmond 65, 105, 188, 200
Fitzwilliam, Sir William, Earl of Southampton 83, 92, 134, 157, 197, 243, 256, 260
Flodden, battle of 15, 16
Foxe, Edward, Bishop of Hereford 114, 212, 214–15, 228–9
Foxe, John 143, 144, 145, 156, 167, 236, 262
Foxe, Richard, Bishop of Winchester 10, 12, 15, 17, 19, 23, 24, 32, 39, 54, 57, 65, 93
Francis I of France 21, 26, 27, 32–3, 47, 49, 50, 111, 120, 174, 232, 241, 243, 247
Francis, Marquis de Pont à Mousson 243

Gage, Sir John 152–3
Gardiner, Stephen, Bishop of Winchester 61, 65, 74–5, 83, 114, 117–18, 121, 125, 132, 134, 155–6, 160, 166–7, 169, 170, 171, 178, 187, 188, 189, 217, 220, 221, 231, 233, 234–7, 238, 239, 249–51, 253–4, 259, 262, 263

Garigliano, battle of 143
Gascoigne, Sir William 148
Gerrard, Thomas 250, 258, 263
Gigli, Silvester de, Bishop of Worcester
    19, 20, 21
Giustinian, Sebastian, Venetian Ambas-
    sador 22, 25, 32, 53, 54, 62, 80, 126
Goodrich, Thomas, Bishop of Ely 237
Grafton, Richard 219, 220, 221
Gray's Inn cf. London
Greenwich Palace cf. London
Gresham, Sir Richard 203–4
Gresham, Sir Thomas 204
Grey, Thomas, 1st Marquess of Dorset
    7, 38, 146
Grey, Thomas, 2nd Marquess of Dorset
    14
Guienne, invasion of 14
Guildford, Sir Henry 89
Guisnes Castle 37

Hadrian, Cardinal 29
Hainault 16
Hales, Christopher 125, 182
Hall, Edward, Chronicler 63, 81, 104,
    156, 262
Hampton Court 55–8, 102
Heath, Nicholas, King's almoner,
    Bishop of Rochester 228, 250
Henry VII 8, 9, 10, 11
Henry VIII: as prince 9; as king 11;
    early relationship with Wolsey 12;
    ambitions to renew 100 years war 13;
    joins Holy League 13; ambition to
    invade France 14; begins siege of
    Thérouanne 16; gives Tournai
    bishopric to Wolsey 16; contemplates
    divorcing Catherine 17; seeks to
    appoint Wolsey as Cardinal 21;
    sister's return from France 27; re-
    jection of Leo x's crusade 30;
    Maximilian's plan to adopt 32–3;
    Field of Cloth of Gold 37–43;
    declares war on France 49; devotion
    to Wolsey's accomplishments 53;
    ignorance of state affairs 54; envious
    of York Place 58; health 61–3;
    requires councillors 82; May Day
    Rising 84; over-familiarity of young
courtiers to 86; devotes more time to
    public affairs 87; reduces staff 89–90;
    despair of a son for the succession
    95; receives Hampton Court 102;
    schemes to divorce Catherine 105–20;
    threatens break with Rome 116–17;
    reluctant to dismiss Wolsey 124;
    takes over administration 124–6;
    gives Wolsey money 134; orders
    Wolsey's arrest 136–7; employs
    Cromwell 156–7; dissolves Wolsey's
    Colleges 158; resumes divorce pro-
    ceedings 162; Privilegium Angliae
    162–3; campaign against the Church
    163; marries Anne Boleyn 176;
    divorce achieved 179; More's execu-
    tion 181–5; wishes to leave Anne
    185–6; executes Anne Boleyn 186–8;
    marries Jane Seymour 188; reconcili-
    ation with Princess Mary 190–1;
    Dissolution 191–8; Lincolnshire and
    Yorkshire revolts 198–200; household
    reforms 207–10; Ten Articles, the
    212–14; Bishops' Book, the 215;
    builds Nonsuch 223; and Luther-
    anism 228–9; trial of Lambert 230–1;
    marries Anne of Cleves 241–7;
    Barnes/Gardiner dispute 250; divorce
    of Anne of Cleves 255–6; marries
    Catherine Howard 263; regrets
    Cromwell's execution 263–4
Hilsey, John 194
Holbein, Hans 150–1, 219, 241, 242,
    243
Holgate, Robert, Prior of Sempringham,
    Bishop of Llandaff, Archbishop of
    York 222
Holy League, The 13, 14, 15, 28
Howard, Catherine, Queen 246, 255,
    263
Howard, Sir Edward 85
Howard, Henry, Earl of Surrey 234
Howard, Mary, Duchess of Richmond
    200
Howard, Thomas, 2nd Duke of
    Norfolk 12, 16, 18, 19, 25, 26, 38,
    66–7, 85, 96
Howard, Thomas, 3rd Duke of
    Norfolk 25, 72, 85, 101, 104, 112,

122, 124, 125, 126-7, 129, 131, 132, 133, 136, 140, 153, 160, 165, 168, 170, 186, 188, 189, 190, 199-200, 202, 230, 233, 237-8, 239, 247, 250-1, 256, 260, 263

Hunne, Richard 96, 103

Hunsdon Manor Herts 63

Hursey, Sir John 100

Hutton, John 241

Institution of a Christian Man, The cf. The Bishops' Book

Islip, John, Abbot of Westminster 67

James IV of Scotland 15

Jerome, William, Vicar of Stepney 250, 258-9, 263

Julius II, Pope 13, 14, 17, 28, 108

Kingston, Sir William 87, 138-9

Knight, William, Bishop of Bath and Wells 81, 83, 112, 113

Lambert, John 230-2, 259

Lambeth Palace *cf.* London

Landriano, battle of 120

Lark, Mistress 64

Lark, Peter 65

Lascelles, Sir Roger 138

Lateran, Council of 8, 19, 29, 104

Latimer, Hugh, Bishop of Worcester 74, 165, 179, 195, 214, 216, 230, 237, 238, 239, 255

Layton, Richard, Dean of York 193-4, 197-8, 223

Lee, Edward, Archbishop of York 178, 237, 238

Legh, Sir Thomas 193, 197, 199, 223

Leicester Abbey 138

Leo X, Pope 15, 17, 20, 21, 29, 31, 34, 44, 102

Life and Death of Cardinal Wolsey, The 5, 6, 7, 10, 12, 56, 59, 72, 80, 109, 121, 127-8, 130, 132, 138, 139, 140, 152, 154, 156, 157

London, *in or near:* Austin Friars, House of, 75, 149-50, 173; Bath Place 80; Baynard's Castle 58; Bermondsey, Cromwell's House at 255; Bridewell 11, 58, 117; City of 97; Gray's Inn 147-8; Greenwich Palace 58, 254; Lambeth Palace 16, 19, 55, 59; London Stone, Walbrook 11; St Paul's Cathedral 18, 31; St Stephen's, Westminster 18; Tower of London, the 58, 250, 254-5, 256, 259-60; Westminster Abbey 9, 67; Westminster, City of 21-2; Whitehall Palace 55; York Place 22, 25, 54, 55, 58, 84, 127, 131

London, John 193-4

Longland, John, Bishop of Lincoln 94, 106-7

Longueville, Duc de 16, 17

Louis XII 13, 15, 16, 17, 18, 21, 26, 108

Lovell, Sir Thomas 10, 25

Lupset, Thomas 65

Lutheranism 213-14, 228-9

Machiavelli, Niccolo 145-6

Maiano, Giovanni da 56, 57

Margaret of Savoy 10, 43, 120

Margaret of Scotland 108

Marignano, battle of 21

Marillac, Charles de, French Ambassador 243, 244, 249, 252, 254, 256, 257

Marshall, William 205

Martyr, Peter 26

Mary, daughter of Henry VIII, later Mary I 30, 51, 55, 105, 189-91, 198, 248-9

Mary, sister of Henry VIII, Queen of France, Duchess of Suffolk 17, 18, 25-7, 55, 95

Matthew, Thomas, *alias* Rogers, John 219, 220

Maximilian I, Emperor 10, 15, 17, 31, 32

May Day Rising, The 81, 83-4

Mechlin, Treaty of 15

Medici, Giullo de, Cardinal *cf.* Clement VII, Pope

Melanchthon, Philip 228, 229

Modena, Renaldo di 19, 20

Mont, Christopher 242

More, Manor of the, Herts 54, 57

More, Sir Thomas 30, 54, 62, 80, 83, 98, 99, 100, 127, 128–9, 160–1, 168, 174, 179, 180, 181–5
More, Treaty of the 51
Morice, Ralph 239
Morison, Richard 205
Morley, Lord cf. Parker
Morton, John, Cardinal, Archbishop of Canterbury 8
Myconius, Frederick 229–30

Needham, James 223–4
Neville, Sir Edward 86, 227
Nonfan, Sir Richard 9
Norfolk, Dukes of cf. Howard, Thomas
Norris, Sir Henry 90, 122, 128, 157, 187
Northumberland, Earls of cf. Percy

Oliver, John 150
Oxford University: 19, 213, 226; Cardinal College 102, 226; Corpus Christi College 24; Magdalen College 6; New College, 194, 198; Trinity College 197

Pale, Richard, Dean of St Paul's 33, 34, 35, 38, 41, 44, 45, 83, 86
Palermo, Bishop of 172
Paris, Archbishop of 31
Parker, Henry, Lord Morley 146, 203
Parliament, Acts of: abolishing Diversity of Opinions 238–9; Annates (1534) 164–5, 179; Attainder (1529) 129; Attainder (1540) 258; Augmentations (1536) 194–6; Commissioners of Sewers (1532) 203; Cromwell's Poor Law 205–6; Dispensation (1534) 174; Enclosures (1515) 93; Enrolments, Statute of 205; First Fruits and Tenure 180, 192; praemunire (1529) 129; Proclamations (1539) 202–3; Restraint of Appeals 175–6; Royal Exchange Bill 204; Six Articles (1539) 200–1, 233, 238–41; Subsidy Bill 252; Succession (1534) 179–80; Supremacy 180; Treasons 180, 201–2, 258; True Religion 221–2; Uses, Statute of (1536) 205;

Wills, Statute of (1540) 205.
Miscellaneous: Reformation 151–81; Privy Council 83–129; forced loans 97–102; indicts Wolsey 125
Patent, William 6
Paul III, Pope 183, 241
Paulet, Sir Amyas 7, 81
Paulet, William 153
Peckham, Edmund 92
Penshurst, Kent 95
Percy, Sir Henry, 5th Earl of Northumberland 86, 95, 129, 137, 138
Peterborough, Abbot of 201
Petre, Sir William 211
Petrucci, Cardinal 45
Pexall, Abbot of Leicester 138
Philip, Duke of Bavaria 248–9
Pilgrimage of Grace, the 207, 213, 222
Plague, the 63
Plantagenet, Arthur, Lord Lisle 254
Pole, Sir Geoffrey 227
Pole, Henry, Lord Montague 227
Pole, Lady Margaret, Countess of Salisbury 18, 227
Pole, Reginald, Cardinal 143–5, 156, 167, 212, 226–7, 254
Pole, Richard de la 51
Pope, Sir Thomas 196
Poynings, Sir Edward 25
Pucci, Lorenzo, Cardinal 46, 114

Redmayn, Henry 54, 56
Reformation, the: origins in anti-Roman feeling 103–4; Wolsey's part in 141; Tyndale's views 161; Privilegium Angliae 162–3; Cromwell's part in 175; More's opposition to 185; Dissolution 191–8
Renée, daughter to Louis XII 17, 111
Requests, Court of 80, 204
Reynolds, William 7, 56
Rice, John ap 193
Riche, Sir Richard 182, 184–5, 196, 197, 198, 258
Richmond, Countess of cf. Beaufort, Lady Margaret
Ridley, Nicholas, later Bishop of London 120
Rochford, Lords cf. Boleyn

Rome, Church of: 13, 17; English attitude to 102–4; England's break with 175; Act in Restrain of Appeals 177. City of: sacked by Charles v's troops 110
Roper, William 100
Rouse, John 75
Roye, William 72
Russell, Sir John 128, 133, 156, 157
Russell, Richard 54
Ruthall, Thomas, Bishop of Durham 23, 25

Sadler, Sir Ralph 152, 153, 169, 252
St Albans, Abbey of, 49, 104, 157
St Paul's Cathedral cf. London
Salcott, *alias* Capon, John, Bishop of Salisbury 237
Salisbury, Countess of cf. Pole, Margaret
Sampson, Richard, Bishop of Chichester 16, 83, 190, 217, 229, 231, 238, 239, 254, 255
Sandys, Lord 92, 157
Schmalkaldic League 228–9, 249
Seymour, Sir Edward, later Duke of Somerset 187, 234
Seymour, Jane, Queen 186–8
Shaftesbury Nunnery 65
Shaxton, Nicholas, Bishop of Salisbury 216, 238, 239
Sheffield, Sir Robert 86
Shelley, Sir William, Chief Justice 131
Shrewsbury, Earl of cf. Talbot, George
Shurley, Sir John 92
Skelton, John 64, 66–72, 101
Smeaton, Mark 187
Smith, Ellis 56
Smith, William, Bishop of Lincoln 19
Somerset, Charles, Lord Herbert of Raglan, Earl of Worcester 14, 16, 86, 91
Southwell Palace 57, 134
Spurs, battle of the 16
Stafford, Edward, Duke of Buckingham 38, 72, 85, 86, 94, 95, 96
Standish, Henry, Bishop of St Asaph 120
Stanley, Edward, 3rd Earl of Derby 59, 201

Stanley, Thomas, 2nd Earl of Derby 38
Star Chamber 67, 81, 82, 130, 204
Starkey, Thomas 150, 173, 205
Stokesley, John, Bishop of London 103, 212, 214, 217, 220, 229, 238
Suffolk, Duke of cf. Brandon, Charles
Supplication against the Ordinaries 155, 165–7, 211
Surrey, Earl of, cf. Howard, Thomas

Talbot, George, Earl of Shrewsbury 14, 138, 209
Taylor, Dr John, Master of the Rolls 127
Ten Articles, the 212–16
Theobald, Thomas, Cromwell's godson 218
Thérouanne, siege of 16, 98, 146–7
Thornbury Castle, Glos. 95
Throckmorton, Sir George 178, 258
Tittenhanger, Beds 57
Toto, Antonio 57
Tournai, fall of 16; siege of 30
Tudor, Jasper, Earl of Pembroke 234
Tuke, Sir Brian 61, 63, 83
Tunstall, Cuthbert, Bishop of Durham 34, 35, 136, 199, 217, 229, 230, 237, 238, 252, 255
Tyndale, William 61, 72, 75, 161, 217, 218, 219

Valor Ecclesiasticus 192
Vaughan, Stephen 130, 152, 155, 161, 172, 218
Vergil, Polydore 20, 36, 66, 76–8, 85, 94, 106–7, 163
Vivaldi, Anthony 173

Wallop, Sir John 251
Walsingham, Norfolk, Shrine at 63
Wanstead, Royal Manor at 18
Warham, William, Archbishop of Canterbury 14, 19, 22, 23, 38, 75, 76, 96–7, 102, 103, 109, 110, 164, 165, 166, 167, 174, 185, 211, 230
Westminster Abbey cf. London
Weston, Sir Francis 187
Whitechurch, Edward 221

Whiting, Richard, Abbot of Glaston-
bury 202, 225
William, Duke of Cleves 242, 247
Williams, Morgan 142
Williams, Richard cf. Cromwell,
Richard
Williams, (Master) Patch 128
Wilson, Nicholas 254
Wiltshire, Earl of cf. Boleyn, Sir
Thomas
Windsor Castle 63, 199
Wingfield, Sir Anthony 208
Wingfield, Sir Richard 35
Wolman, Dr Richard 110
Wolsey, Joan, née Daundy 5, 6
Wolsey, Robert 5, 6
Wolsey, Thomas: Early years: birth 5;
enters Magdalen College 6; Fellow-
ship 6; ordination 7; bursarship 7;
Early preferments: 7, 8; canon of
Hereford 8; domestic chaplain at
Lambeth Palace 8; chaplain in
Calais 9; chaplain to Henry VIII 9;
diplomatic missions 10; Dean of
Lincoln 10; Royal Almoner 11;
Life in office: Doctor of Divinity 11;
appointed Councillor 12; appointed
Dean of York 15; appointed Chief
Minister 16; appointed Bishop elect
of Tournai 16; author of peace with
France 17–18; Precentor of St Paul's
Cathedral 18; Dean of St Stephen's,
Westminster 18; consecrated Bishop
of Lincoln 19; Archbishop of York
19; ambition to be a Cardinal 20;
appointed Cardinal 21; appointed
Lord Chancellor 22; intercedes for
Brandon 27; Arbiter of Europe 28;
treatment of papal legate 29–30;
rejection of Leo x's crusade 30;
creates the Peace of London 31; discouraged Henry's European ambitions 33–5; Field of Cloth of Gold
36–43; embassy to Francis I 39;
ambitions for papacy 43–7; embassy
to Charles V 48; fails to pacify
Francis and Charles 48; difficulty
financing the war 50; taking burden
from Henry 53; keeps much from

Henry and Council 54; as Lord
Chancellor 80–1; May Day Rising
83–4; Agrarian Reform 93; forced
loans from Parliament 97–102; presents Hampton Court to the King
102; Legate a latere 102–3; fails to
reform the Church 104; The King's
Great Matter 105–20; bypassed over
divorce 112–13; failure in legatine
court 120–2; indicted for praemunire
125; resigns as Lord Chancellor 127;
acknowledges praemunire 127; strip-
ped of property 131; banished to the
North 134; summons provincial convocation 136; accused of conspiracy
136–7; arrest 138; death 139; King
dissolves his colleges 158.
Characteristics: attitude to Parliament
96–7; expenditure and way of life
19, 55, 58–60, 131, 134; health 62–4;
lack of chastity 64–5; method of
government 79–80.
Letters to: Chapuys 135; Cromwell
133, 158–9; Foxe 12; Gardiner 118;
Henry VIII 110, 126, 128, 134;
Rome 20, 116, 119; Sampson 16, 17;
From: Brandon 27; Cromwell 145,
148–9, 158–9; Erasmus 29; Foxe 24;
Henry VIII 62; Margaret of Savoy
43; Tuke 63–4.
Opinions of: 22–5, 66–78, 85–6, 105–
106, 133, 146–9, 154–5.
Property: Esher 57; Hampton Court
36; Kingston-upon-Thames 57;
Limington Rectory 7; Lydd vicarage
8; More, Manor of the 54; St
Albans Abbey 49; Scotland Yard 54;
others 11, 57
Wootton, Nicholas, Dean of Canter-
bury and York 242–3
Worcester, Earl of cf. Somerset
Wriothesley, Sir Thomas 215, 223, 252,
255–6
Wyatt, Sir Thomas 171, 234, 247, 264
Wykys, Elizabeth, Cromwell's wife
144, 149
Wynter, Thomas 65

York House cf. London